D0425048

FROM *the* SOUL

FROM *the* SOUL

Stories of Great Black Parents
and the Lives They Gave Us

Phyllis Y. Harris

G. P. PUTNAM'S SONS
New York

G. P. Putnam's Sons
Publishers Since 1838
a member of
Penguin Putnam Inc.
375 Hudson Street
New York, NY 10014

Copyright © 2001 by Phyllis Y. Harris

Library of Congress Cataloging-in-Publication Data

Harris, Phyllis Y.
From the soul : stories of great Black parents and the
lives they gave us / Phyllis Y. Harris.
p.   cm.
ISBN 0-399-14706-3
1. African American parents—Anecdotes.
2. African American families—Anecdotes.
3. Conduct of life—Anecdotes.   4. African Americans—
Biography—Anecdotes.   I. Title.
E185.86.H37   2001   2001019323
306.85'08996073—dc21

Printed in the United States of America

10 9 8 7 6 5 4 3 2 1

This book is printed on acid-free paper. ∞

Book design by Amanda Dewey

Acknowledgments

Writing this book has been an intimate journey shared by many people who were exceedingly generous and kind. To Danya, Monica, Amani, Ganious, Phola, Ulysses, Joyce, Donna, Robert, and Eric, I offer you deep gratitude for trusting me and for sharing your precious memories, which flow through these pages. To each of your parents for their love, support, and sacrifice, all of which helped you to become who you are, thank you.

To Denise Silvestro, editor extraordinaire, photo consultant, and advisor, thank you for juggling so many roles and doing them all well. To Martha Bushko, thanks for your calm demeanor and ever-willing helpful nature; you are lovely. To the team at Putnam Berkley, thank you. Eileen Fallon, I am deeply appreciative of your tremendous insight and ability to see the bright side of things.

To countless other friends and family who were there to offer prayers, support, and laughter especially when the end didn't appear to be in sight, including Marie, Louise, Jane, Diane, Sandra, Jan, Violaine, Rune, Megs, and David, you are the best. Nancy, what would I have done without you? Susan Rabiner, *magnificent* agent, guide, and friend, thank you for pushing me beyond the initial thought, and to Al F. for supporting us both. Finally, to the one who made me free, thank you, Lord.

*To all the mothers and fathers
who deserve to be celebrated,
including my own.*

Contents

FROM *the* SOUL

Introduction

I first started thinking about the idea for this book several years ago. I was sitting in a basement room of an apartment building in a housing project, talking with a group of children during their after-school art class. In a moment of innocent conversation I asked one young boy a question I had asked in other forms as part of my work as a child advocate: If he could have lunch with anyone in the world, which one person would he choose? I intended to ask a few kids the same question, hoping to learn something about how kids choose role models. Would Michael Jordan be named most? Shaquille O'Neal? Would any choose some public service figure, maybe Colin Powell?

The first answer surprised me. "My mom," the boy answered, never even looking up from his painting. I asked the question of a girl in another knot of kids, and she responded, "My father." Other kids at this same table, without waiting to be asked, also began shouting their answers: "My grandfather!" "My uncle!" "My sister!"

A couple of days later, at a party mostly attended by blacks like myself, between the ages of thirty and fifty, all part of the growing black middle class, I described the basement incident. I expressed how surprised I was at how many children chose family members over celebrity role models. One of the other guests at the party then asked me, "Why does that surprise you? Is there anyone in this room who would be here today if it hadn't been for our parents?"

Over the next few weeks, I went back to that comment again and again and finally understood it. We in that room represented a special generation that strangely enough has a taint attached to it. Why? Because we are part of America's first large generation of privileged blacks. I began thinking about what our privilege had really been.

We were not privileged in terms of where we had grown up. There were people in that room who, despite clothes that called out success, were Southern rural through and through; still others, I knew, had grown up in modest circumstances in tucked-away black communities in the Midwest or Southwest. Some proudly wore the stamp of inner-city project backgrounds.

Nor were we privileged by our parents' socioeconomic backgrounds. Most of our parents were working-to-middle class; extremely few were upper class; and I would not be surprised to learn that many were only one or two generations away from having been dirt poor, because until recently it was hard to be black and be anything else.

What distinguished those of us in that room was that we were black Americans making it in America. We were mostly college educated, pursuing good careers, many successfully, some few supersuccessfully. But more than that, if this book has a message, it is that we shared the privilege of great black parenting. Without that, all the opportunity in the world would not have resulted in so many of us making it in America.

As I thought further, I next came to understand that many of us at that party were living the lives we were living because we were the products of not just one good black parent, or a couple who had made a good parenting team, but the product of extended family support, a tradition among blacks passed from generation to generation through the centuries of slavery and then through that period that the late Judge A. Leon Higginbotham, Jr. described as the hundred-year wasteland between emancipation and the Civil Rights revolution of this past century. Until our time came, all the parents of all those generations that preceded us, all those who had treasured and passed on the solid family values that are the foundation of black experience, had been deprived of the payoff of their labors that had so rewarded European immigrant groups—the chance to see their children doing better than they themselves had done.

But in the case of our own parents, it was now possible. All those generations of love and devotion could finally produce strong, loving, productive people, living successful lives by any standard.

So this book is meant to be a thank-you card—a recognition by a member of the first black generation that has had the opportunity to step onto the American ladder of opportunity—offered to those generations that could not make that climb themselves, but who selflessly preserved and passed on—with love and ever-enduring hope—the rock solid values that must underlie success in any endeavor.

This is a book black parents deserve to see in print. For far too long, they have been analyzed, chastised, and found wanting. Indeed, I do not believe it is an exaggeration to say that there is no more maligned institution in America than the black family. When I finally told some of the people who had been at that party that I had decided to undertake this book, it was as if I had announced I was running for president. People rallied around me, all charged up by the idea. One woman called out, "Go for it!" Another, "It's about time someone put an end to this ridiculous idea that blacks can't parent." Yet the most frequent comment was a plea: "Consider me. My parents were great."

Later on, I would show parts of the book to several white friends, and although I should not have prejudged their response—after all, prejudgment is what prejudice is all about—I was taken aback by the fact that these simple stories of growing up in the warmth of familial love were equally powerful to them. And yet, why not? Great parenting transcends racial and ethnic divisions, because the standards of all parenting are the same: Did it help the child grow into an adult with the ability and the desire to reach his or her own full potential? Is the child happy with the human being he or she has become? A line of the Nobel Peace laureate Elie Wiesel comes to mind: "Regardless of who we are, in the end, we are all gloriously human."

From the Soul: Stories of Great Black Parents and the Lives They Gave Us is a book about the power of love within black families. It is not focused on racism, suffering, anger, or hate. Nor is the emphasis on the struggle of African Americans as a people first for freedom, then for equal citizenship, then for acceptance as human beings. Nor is it about the rage and anger of many blacks who now consider themselves part of the privileged class and are guilty about it. And, most important, it is not a book about white racism, about the stubbornly surviving American caste system, or about the pervasiveness of race in American society. Those are all important issues, some already well treated, some never yet fully treated from the black perspective. But none of these is the focus of this book. Although some whites may find this hard to understand, most blacks I interviewed had the same experience I had growing up—we were not drilled on what it meant to be black in a white-controlled world. When we talked about living our lives, with all the joys and tensions that come with growing up, the words *black* and *white* rarely came into the conversation.

My hope is that this book will cut away at the long-held stereotype that blacks can't parent, in a way no sociological study could ever do.

The book consists of ten highly personal, emotionally honest, in some cases gut-wrenching, but in all cases, true stories that were written after extensive interviews and conversations with a variety of black men and women.

In putting together this book, I thought only about finding stories that other black families would resonate with, because they might hear echoes of themselves and their own experiences in these life accounts. And because they might enjoy confirmation of the reality that the single most important element in understanding the endurance of the black community is the role family love has played in keeping us strong.

The process of writing this book has been an education for me. I was taken by the fact that few of the people whose story I tell defined themselves as poor, even though some of their families endured economic hardships. I was amused and delighted by the fact that so many of those interviewed told me that their mothers were beautiful. Several commented on the fact that they lived much of their childhood oblivious of the white communities just a few blocks from them. Their world, as one participant put it, was a black world; he looks back on it, as the most warming, nurturing environment a child could ever want. Because he grew up in an all-black community in which every child was taught to greet by name every member of the community, and was in turn greeted by name, he cannot to this day get into an elevator and not say hello to another person who might join him, to acknowledge that other person's "humanity."

Other participants were surprised by the response of their own family members to their depiction of the family dynamic. "Black families are complicated," one of my interviewees told me as together we worked through the parts of the story that were simply too personal for public viewing, even in a book that strove to be honest. For instance, one father was finally persuaded to allow reference to an affair he had had, but his wronged wife would not hear of it. Still, the reality is that I was surprised at the willingness of so many people to allow their families to be portrayed honestly, warts and all, in a book that celebrates the role of family in forging an American black identity. An initial concern when I set out to do the book—that there would be a competition to be the best family in the book—never materialized.

The most difficult question for me centered on whom to include. I could easily have filled up a book of this size including only African-American high achievers—doctors, lawyers, academics, leaders of industry and commerce. I chose not to do so. While I do not pretend that those I have included are a statistically valid cross section of the greater African-American community, my hope is they are representative of most subsets of the greater community.

One last word: The stories that follow are not verbatim transcripts. Although I spent hours and hours with each interviewee, what you will be reading are edited and adapted versions of those transcripts. But they are faithful to the lives of these people. To ensure both my honesty and their own, I insisted that every participant be fully identified, that all substantive facts included be true—although some facts were left out—and that each supply family photographs. I knew that if these stories were as powerful on the page as they were to me, readers would want to see pictures of the family members.

I hope that at least some of my readers will read *From the Soul: Stories of Great Black Parents and the Lives They Gave Us* and say, "The book is incomplete. The author failed to include my family."

Daddy—Isaiah
Derius Bagwell

Me and Nana at my wedding

Nana—
Roxie Mae Dix Bagwell

Mama—Luvenia Ola
Justice Bagwell

A Time for All Things

The church was oppressively hot the day of my mother's funeral. Even though all the windows were open and we could see the wind gently pushing, pulling, and lifting leaves on the trees outside, the breeze apparently felt no obligation to cool those of us inside, even in our grief. So we were all forced to cool ourselves with those handheld paper fans usually found in Southern churches—you know, the kind shaped like a four leaf clover. On one side was either the loving face of Jesus or that of some black community leader and on the other an advertisement for the local funeral home.

I remember the collection of relatives who came to pay their final respects. They passed by my mama's open casket, their faces a mix of sadness, confusion, and fear. Fear, I guess, at seeing a woman who has died young, leaving a husband with five children to raise, a life that ended before its time.

Although it was perhaps the worst day of my life, I remember very little of the funeral service itself. My brother told me all about it much later. He said that my three sisters and I all wore white dresses and the service was a "going home ceremony" for my mother and little brother, who had died with my mother during childbirth. There was singing and shouting, and the preacher preached what people later called the sermon of his life. They said sweat was popping off of his forehead as if someone were pouring a dipper of water over it, and the women were shouting and fainting in the aisles from both the heat and the touch of the Holy Ghost who the preacher called to come to us all in this time of confusion and sorrow. My brother said that at the end of the sermon a chorus of Glory Hallelujah, Glory to God, and Thank You Jesus started as a low murmur from the front of the church and moved like a roaring wave all the way to the back as, one by one, our friends and relatives prayed to God to have mercy on our family's soul and comfort us in our grief. The service ended with the hymn "Precious Lord," which makes even the hardest-hearted person feel as though their heart has been touched by love itself. The whole time I sat in my father's lap with my head on his chest, a bit weary and half-asleep from the heat and the activity. We were in the front row of the church, which is where the family customarily sits, I guess, because to make it real for us, we needed to have a full view of the caskets as they sat beneath the cross. During that whole service I was in and out of consciousness, because I was tired, it was hot, we had been sitting for what seemed like an incredibly long time since the sun rose that morning, and, perhaps, because none of it seemed truly real. Especially because I was dreaming for part of it.

You know how it is when you fall asleep in the middle of someone singing to you, and the words of the music ring in your ears and start to fade and weave themselves into your dream. "Precious Lord, take me ho-o-o-m-m-m-e. Take my hand and lead me ho-o-o-m-m-m-e." The words were sweet and calming like balm on my sadness. I heard one voice in the chorus that sounded like the voice of an angel singing just to me as it carried me into my dream, the dream I had been having since Mama passed, a dream that brings the last time I saw her, smiling, happy, and alive, back to me with such force that it almost seems real.

It always begins the same way.

I grew up in the deep South, the segregated deep South. Even our rooster knew there were rules here for everything. He crowed in time with the sun's rising, everyday, rain or shine. Each morning, when I heard his crow, my little body would automatically roll over and stretch itself out, limb by limb, to make sure everything was in working order. On that last day with Mama, however, I didn't hear the rooster crow and woke up because the heat of the sun was hot on my face.

Usually the first rays of the day's sun sneaked into my window and wrote a line of warm light across the foot of my bed. But on that day that I would remember as Mama's last, the sun and its warmth poured into my room and covered my whole bed. I woke up with a start and rolled over to get away from the heat. Instead of stretching as usual, I jumped out of bed and dressed in a hurry, remembering with excitement that Mama had visitors coming and that I would get to spend the whole day with her and her friends.

I don't remember who those friends were now, I just remember the delight I felt at having my mother all to myself. Because there were so many of us kids, it was rare to have her undivided attention. But that day, it was to be just the two of us, Mama and me, no other brother or sister for the whole day, just me.

I remember too that Mama had a big belly. She and Dad called it being pregnant. I didn't really know what that meant—but I remember that she let me feel her tummy and she put my ear to it. She said if I listened carefully I could hear the baby's heartbeat. And even though I didn't really hear its heartbeat all the time, I liked to pretend that I did because of how she placed her hands very gently on my head to hold it still as I listened, and it made me feel warm inside to be held that close to her, my face against her body.

She also smelled good, like my favorite foods and the scent the wind carries when it blows across a field of wildflowers. And while I was listening to her tummy, her own scent floated into my nostrils, and the combination of her touching my head and her special smells made me feel safe and warm and always at home.

The whole day passed in a blur, because I was happy to walk beside her, sit next to her when we ate lunch, and listen to her voice as she talked and laughed with her friends. But what stays in my mind most vividly is the way the day ended. There we were standing together on the porch of our home, my mother and me, watching her friends leave. As they got into their car and drove away, she waved, and because I always wanted to be like my mother, I imitated her and waved too. We both stood there waving and waving until the car was out of sight.

Once they were gone, she sat down with a thump into the white rocking chair just behind her. I guess because she was so tired from carrying that big belly around all day. I mimicked her sigh, as if I too had carried around a big belly and the weight of hospitality through a long, hot day, and flopped down next to her. The sun that had awakened me with such force earlier in the day by now sat low in the sky, blessing us with only a fraction of its former brilliance. Mama sat there for a moment in the white rocking chair, breathing deeply, and I watched her, trying to breathe deeply too. Without uttering a word, she made to stand up, inching forward in the chair and pushing off the seat to rise with some difficulty. "You've had a big day, little lady, it's time for you to get ready for bed," she said.

Slipping my hand into hers, she led me into the house. As the screen door closed behind us, I heard the rooster crow.

The next day, she died. Again, the rooster didn't crow. It was a cloudy day, and I had a hard time waking up. When I finally got dressed and went into the kitchen for breakfast, I found that there was no breakfast. My brothers and sisters were sitting at the table, I thought waiting for me, until my brother said that Mama wasn't feeling good and my father would make breakfast. As a family we had every meal together, everyday, without fail. So it was very unusual for us to get up and find nothing on the table and the stove cold.

The rest of that morning passed in kind of a haze because, as children, we weren't really told anything. We were all talking amongst ourselves, wondering what was going on with Mama, and my father finally came to tell us that she needed to rest.

Sometime in the middle of that same day, my father collected us—myself and my four siblings, a brother and three sisters—and said we all had to go to Nana's. Nana was my grandmother, and she lived next door to us with my Aunt Margaret—my father's sister and our favorite aunt because she made us laugh like no one else did—in a house my father had built. We all lived on a huge lot that included about five acres of property. There was our house, and next to us was Aunt Margaret, with property to eventually build a separate house for Nana. Next door to Aunt Margaret was another family, and down the line were my daddy's three other sisters and their husbands. My father had worked very hard to buy the land we lived on. He was a master carpenter and a preacher and took both of those jobs very seriously. He and other people at the church built our house, Aunt Margaret's house, Nana's house, the church—they built everything.

Each house was built in perfect line with the next. As kids, we talked about going "down the line" whenever we went visiting Aunt Margaret or Nana, or our other aunts. Each house was separated from the one house alongside it by enough space so that it felt private. My father said part of the land in that area collected water instead of running off like it was suppose to, so there was bad drainage, and with every heavy rain—and it rained a lot in the South—sections of the lot turned to mud. To prevent flooding, each house was separated from the next by a ditch that Daddy and some men from his church had dug to allow for the rainwater to run off. Each ditch had a single wooden plank thrown across it to make a bridge for us. The plank across the ditch that separated Nana and Aunt Margaret's house from ours was so narrow that only one person at a time could walk across it. When more than two of us had to cross, we called it "walking the plank." Walking the plank could be tricky; sometimes one of us lost our balance and fell into the mud. The others stood laughing, and later Mama would have words about how in the world we could get our clothes so dirty so fast. But the plank was really the only way to get to their house, except for a long winding path that was rather isolated and took a while to walk, and my father didn't like for us to take it.

On the day of Mama's passing, Aunt Margaret fetched us to bring us to Nana's house, and we walked across that plank. We walked behind her single file like little chicks following a mother hen, one behind the other. I felt sick to my stomach, which is the only way I can describe the sinking feeling inside. No one said anything to us, only that we had to go next door and wait until my father came to get us. And waiting that day was the hardest thing I had ever done in my life.

Although we all loved going to Nana's house because she spent most of her time in the kitchen making something good to eat, today was different. We all tried to pretend that everything would be okay, but even the air was thick with the impression of something terribly wrong. We all felt it; no one looked at anyone, but we all gave Nana our undivided attention. And she just made us food, which was her way of showing us how much she loved us. Nana and Aunt Margaret were both the most pleasing fat women I had ever known in my life. They made anyone feel safe and protected, and it almost worked that day. Nana kept telling us to eat and that everything would be okay, but each time we heard a door close we all jumped up to see if it was Daddy, and it never was. Finally, Nana captured our attention with her famous sweet potato pie, which weakened the resolve of the most determined. It was creamy, buttery, and spicy and made you forget almost anything else except enjoying its rich goodness.

In the past, when Mama brought us to Nana's and Aunt Margaret's for visits, we were not allowed to play in the "real living room" or to sit on the sofa whose pillows were encased in protective plastic covers that were taken off only when company came. As part of our chores, which were always pretty light, we had to spend one afternoon a month keeping Nana company while she cleaned the real living room. Sometimes we helped her with minor details of the cleaning like sweeping the hearth or polishing a table that couldn't break, anything so that we could get points when Nana told Mama how good we had been. The real living room was a room that we lived our lives around but never a room we used for ourselves.

But that afternoon of Mama's passing, it was different. After what seemed like a very long time, but actually wasn't, my father finally came to get us. We had just finished the last bite of our pie when he called us into the living room. We knew something was really wrong because we were told to sit on the sofa in there.

We huddled together and my father told us that Mama had passed on, she had gone to be with God. Something had happened when she was having our baby brother. They didn't know why, only that nothing could be done to save her or him.

When my father stopped talking, my brother, who was nine years old, got up and walked out of the room. My father, who was no longer able to speak, looked at the four of us remaining. My sisters and I looked back at him and at each other, not knowing what to say or really understanding what was happening.

Then he did the only thing I believe he knew how to do at that point. Gathering our faces gently in his hands, looking into our eyes, he kissed each of us on the forehead. When my turn came, he picked me up and held me as well, maybe because I was the youngest, or maybe just because. Placing me on his hip, he carried me to the front door of the house to look for my brother. Through the screen door, we saw him standing on the corner of the front porch, leaning against the support post, shaking. Loud wails were coming from him. I watched my father look at my brother, and an expression came across his face that I had never seen before; his eyes looked like those of our dog, Bobby, after he had been in a fight and was wounded. Still carrying me, he went out onto the porch, reached for my brother, and pulled him into his free arm as we cried and wailed together.

Everything faded as I heard my father calling me. I opened my eyes. By now he had placed me on the seat beside him and he was softly shaking me awake. "Are you okay?" he asked, as he looked down at me, his eyes sad. I was watching him watch me; then I caught a glimpse of the cross behind him, and the caskets that sat beneath it. The people had begun milling around and were preparing to leave the church. Suddenly remembering where I was, I whispered, "Yes, I'm okay."

My mother was buried late that morning, almost noon on the fifth day after she passed. It was her favorite time of day.

We all went directly from the cemetery to Nana's house. It seemed as if everyone from the community, even some of the white people who had worked with my mom and at times worshiped God with us at our church, stopped by Nana's house that afternoon. Through it all, my father stood at the door, greeting people as they came into the house. My sisters and brother and I were standing with him, watching cars fill the yard. People got out of their cars and walked to the house, dishes of food in their hands.

By late afternoon, it was very hot inside the house and even hotter outside in the sun. The screen door was open all the time, letting in people and flies. Everyone said how sorry they were and looked at us with eyes that were filled with a mixture of pity and awe. Some even said it was impossible to believe that something like this could happen to the preacher and his family. After receiving their prayers and words of comfort, my father asked my brother and me to show each person where to go to get some refreshments. We took them all to the living room where they could sit or stand and talk and sip Nana's sweet lemony ice-cold tea while the food was being put out.

Nana, who was most at home in the kitchen, staunchly remained there putting everything together with Aunt Margaret and two or three other women buzzing in and out like little round honey bees. It was where Nana had always conducted business. She made almost everything we ate. From the strawberry and raspberry jams, canned tomatoes and peaches, to using all the stuff you can get from the hog. She raised her own ducks, chicken, geese, and pigs. She was always making some kind of food in the kitchen, and there was extra for anyone who stopped by on any given day.

Nana and Mama didn't always agree about what and how much she fed us, but everyone agreed that when Nana was in the kitchen, everything would be okay. She would make today okay too, I knew it. I watched in amazement as she arranged all of the food that everyone brought into a feast fit for the family of a king and his children. Collard greens with thick lean chunks of cured ham, yams, fried chicken, barbecue and coleslaw, baked chicken, fried catfish, stewed green beans, potato salad, coconut cake, chocolate cake, sweet potato pies, corn bread, and more. All the things that we loved to stuff ourselves with.

I watched as she worked her magic and tried not to get in the way. When she started dishing the collard greens into a serving dish, without thinking I said, "Nana, Mama will love those collards," and Nana looked at me and burst into tears. "Honey," she said, as she choked back sobs, "it's gonna be okay." Setting the pot down, she hugged me. "Nana's gonna make it all okay, just you wait." Drying my eyes, she offered me a spoonful of collards as she scraped the rest out of the pot. It's strange how a kid's mind works. At that moment with Nana, fixing food in the kitchen, food I knew my mama would never taste, I had the first glimpse of what it would be like to live my life without her.

Even though Nana was in the kitchen, she had the door open so she could hear everything that was being said in the living room. Relatives I had only seen at summer family picnics and others who had been a normal part of our lives were gathered together in small groups all over the living room, with some spilling into the dining room. From where I was standing, I could only see Mama's sister talking to a group of people I didn't really know. I was busy decorating a plate for Nana, who had by now become completely interested in what was going on in this little group. At one point, she stopped what she was doing to watch them more closely, and after a few minutes she went straight away to my father, who was across the room by the window talking to the bishop who often found his way to our table on a Sunday afternoon. I watched Nana pull Daddy aside and tell him something. My father nodded and looked around the room for us kids. He found my sisters and brother, and when Nana came back to the kitchen they all followed her single file, reminding me of that day we had walked single file across the ditch.

Daddy said we should go out into the backyard to play with some of the other kids who had come with their folks. It was cooler in the backyard and we needed some air. He said we had enough of being inside for one day. "You can eat something before you go out," he said. "And if you want more, you can come in at anytime to get it." With food in our mouths and hands, we walked down the steps into the backyard, my brother leading the way, as Nana and Daddy stood at the door watching us go out. My head was filled with the aroma of delicious food, a hum of voices that was flowing through the living and dining room, and the picture in my mind of the sofa that provided support for us the day my mom passed, its pillows still neat and clean but out of their protective plastic covers. But as I was being lead out of the house, I had a sense that something important was happening.

While we were playing in the backyard, the relatives, we were to learn later from Aunt Margaret, were all discussing how to divide us children up amongst themselves. And that was the conversation Nana did not want us to overhear.

The conversation was started by my mama's sister, who could not have any children of her own. "We have to help out because no man alive can raise five children by himself," she said. Nods of approval came from the attentive group she had gathered in the corner, mostly relatives from Mama's side of the family. The other relatives listened to her as she talked about how necessary it was that everyone jump in to help and that perhaps the best thing to do would be for each person to take one child.

While this discussion was going on, Aunt Margaret told us later, my father was not entirely clear about what was happening. He was busy with the guests, whom he indulged by listening to their heartfelt condolences for him as he refilled their glasses, while making sure that Nana and Aunt Margaret weren't working too hard in the kitchen.

Later he would tell us that he noticed how the conversation became quiet whenever he got anywhere near Mama's relatives. They would cast furtive glances in his direction as he walked by. Although they all loved him, he told us, they were also very worried about what would happen to us if he were left alone to raise us. So as they talked about "the children" and which one each wanted to take, Daddy was not included in their discussion. And he somehow managed not to intrude himself.

Later that day, when it was almost dinnertime, having come in from playing in the backyard, my brother and I were in the kitchen sitting with Nana. I didn't know where my sisters were. Of the people who were still there, eating and talking, most were either relatives or very close friends of our family. My brother and I sat around the table watching Nana pile food high on plates she was fixing for people to take home with them because there was so much food left over.

As part of our reward for playing so nicely outside, she gave us huge slices of her luscious sweet potato pie with glasses of cold milk laced with nutmeg. As I took the first bite I couldn't help but wonder about my sisters who were missing out on this very special treat. The pie was slightly warm, and I remember it tasting so smooth and delicious and spicy. That's how children sometimes arm themselves against fear. As long as the familiar treats remained, the worst had not happened, life had not really changed that much.

As we dug into the pie without hesitation, Nana finally stopped her plate fixing and sat down to join us. As she put her own plate on the table and sat down in the chair, she looked at me and my brother, watching us as we ate her pie. Without any kind of motion or indication that we join her, she just started praying, *"Lord Jesus, thank you for this day. It's a sad one for my grandchildren, for my son, and for me. We feel the weight of a very great loss of a mother, a wife, a daughter-in-law, and we pray that Your mercy will get us all through this time of doubt. We just don't always understand Your ways, but we thank You for this day and Your grace and mercy for all of us. Amen."* We both stopped eating to wait for her to finish. When she was done, she looked at us, picked up her fork, and said, "This looks and smells like the best pie I ever made," and she smiled at us and started to eat.

So there we were after Mama's funeral, gathered at Nana's house, with friends and relatives whom we knew and loved, with our destiny being decided in a living room that our lives had been lived around but never in. All this time my father, although very attentive to the guests, seemed more quiet than I ever remembered. After making sure everything was okay, he finally sat down and just listened to the rhythm of the noise in the room, observing everyone, taking it all in, saying very little.

Finally, someone—I can't remember who it was—decided to announce the fact that the children would be divided up amongst my mother's relatives. After the words were out, my father, who had been sitting in a chair in the corner, stood up and in his wonderfully quiet and authoritative way said, "Nobody will be taking the children away from me. The children will stay together with me and I will raise them." He didn't raise his voice, nor did he make a scene. That was all he said. And that, I would learn, was my father's way—to act through the greatest of times as if everything, regardless of how dire the circumstances, would work out okay in the end. No matter how difficult things got, he never complained about anything. Keep control of your head, he always said, for he believed if you think fine, you will act fine, and then you are fine. That no matter what life threw at you, you went on, and in time you somehow found the resources to overcome your troubles. Or at least survive them. And you did it simply by refusing to let life get the better of you.

The room became completely quiet in the wake of my father's declaration, and my relatives had the very good sense not to look at my father but instead found reasons to search their bags or pockets for handkerchiefs or to reach down to pick up forks that had not even dropped off their plates. One even stopped chewing in midstream only to begin coughing violently when he unexpectedly inhaled the mouthful of food. Everyone was stunned by my father's announcement. In those days especially, no one believed a man who had just lost his wife would want to raise five children on his own. And nobody believed my father was able to raise us. But he did. Because he loved us, and because he loved my mother.

A few days after the announcement, he sat with all of us at the kitchen table. He told us that Nana and Aunt Margaret would help us with the "girl stuff," like our hair and clothing and other things that women knew about. Nana would move in with us or would spend more time at our house. He also said, "We're in this together, and we have to help each other out." We saw this played out daily in our lives, but especially on days when one of us forgot to do our chores. Daddy would usually come home at dinnertime. Nana cooked every night, and it would be time to eat the moment Daddy came into the house. We were always hungry and ready to eat. But Daddy would notice whenever we didn't do what we were suppose to do, and he would wait until we all sat down at the table to ask who hadn't done such and such chore. We all blamed the other one, and he would give us a talk about being in this together. We were supposed to help each other. None of us could take a bite of food until that chore was done, and we all pitched in to help get it done before the food got cold.

I thought about death a lot after Mama died, especially when Granddaddy on Mama's side and one of my sisters died soon after Mama. My sister died of complications from an infection and Granddaddy from old age. I just kept wondering if Daddy would die soon too. I guess that a lot of the lessons I had to learn about life happened really early, during this time, and came out of these circumstances of death mingled with life and the need to go on even though there were times when none of us was sure exactly how to do so.

But somehow, with a lot of help from my father, help always expressed with a gentle firmness, we went on and prospered. Coming of age in the segregated South added its own dimension to the challenge of growing up black in America. And although my father was constantly teaching us that people were people and we were responsible for treating them the way we wanted to be treated, the realities of a segregated society often intruded on the life my father had made for us. There were constant tests to our faith in ourselves, in each other, and in our father's vision. My father talked about and believed in equality and not hating people for who they were or for the things they did out of fear or ignorance. I realized years later that he shared the vision of Martin Luther King, Jr. No man, no matter how great, draws his greatness out of thin air; he must find it in his roots. And my Daddy's roots, in the Southern black religious experience, were one and the same with Dr. King's roots. Though not a guarantee of greatness, or even of a good life lived, those roots were a commanding invitation to both.

Daddy's roots gave him the stamina to continue being an example for us. As time passed and just as our hearts began to heal from Mama's passing, something quite unexpected happened to fracture the delicate calm that my father had so carefully erected around us.

We had a dog named Bobby. He was a big, shaggy, happy dog. Although he was specifically my brothers' dog, we all loved him, fed him, and played with him. Back then, we didn't know anything about breeds, but now that I think about it, I believe he was a sheep dog mix. He was a very friendly dog and would bark and wag his tail at everyone. His bark, even though he was a big dog, was short, snappy, and playful.

Bobby slept in front of my brother's bedroom door and always licked our hands when we fed him, even before he tasted his food. When he first joined our family, my father wouldn't allow him to sleep in the house, so my brother would sneak outside after everyone went to bed. He would sit with him in the dark because he didn't want Bobby to be lonely or afraid, even though my brother was a bit afraid of the dark himself. When we were gathered together after dinner, catching up on the adventures that happened in each of our small lives that day, Bobby would lay his head on my brother's feet and just stay there. From time to time Bobby would sneak a peek, raising one hairy eyelid to see if anyone noticed him. My brother would reward him by playing with his ears and rubbing his head, which caused Bobby to bark in playful appreciation.

One cool summer afternoon, a white man my father didn't know came to visit. Because of Daddy's position as minister of the local black church, he was often consulted about things that were about to happen that would somehow affect the black community. So the day this white stranger drove into our yard in a red pickup truck, Bobby, who was constantly defending his territory and always barked at people who came into our yard, started barking and barking. The man got out of his red pickup with a rifle in his hands and shot Bobby in midbark, right in front of us. I remember everything happened in slow motion. We were crying, screaming, and yelling; we were angry and sad all at the same time. We were screaming for my father to do something, and my father, who we never saw do anything violent, just stood there completely still, looking at this white man who had come into his yard and killed his children's dog.

After what seemed like a very long time, my father knelt down and picked up Bobby, who was by then whimpering and bleeding all over the place. Daddy carried him around to the back of the house. My sisters followed Daddy, screaming and crying, while Bobby died in his arms. And during the shouting, screaming, and crying, my brother, who stayed in the front yard, picked up a rock. He weighed it in his hand, his face raw with emotion, as he watched that man get into his pickup truck and pull away, seemingly oblivious to the damage my brother wanted to cause him. When the truck was just a red dot in the distance, my brother threw that rock with all of the anger, hurt, and despair behind it.

I was just seven years old, and I didn't understand what had happened and why. I stood there in the hot sun crying and watching my brother, watching that truck as it got smaller and smaller. And when neither of us could see that truck any longer we turned around to go to Bobby. Just behind us was my father with blood all over the front of his clothes. He was watching my brother with a look on his face just like when Mama died and he saw my brother crying on the porch. My brother walked over to him with his head up and my father just looked at him. Finally Daddy grabbed him by the shoulders, shook him, and without saying anything, pulled him into his arms. I ran to my father and wrapped my arms around him and held on tightly.

After some time for healing had passed, we were at last able to talk about what had happened. We wanted my father to do something, we wanted vengeance, but in the Jim Crow South, he couldn't pick up a rifle and shoot the man's dog or punish him in a way that would honor our need for justice or give us any kind of satisfaction. He couldn't even demand an apology or any sort of restitution. So Daddy tried to explain to us that people do a lot of things out of fear and it doesn't make them bad people. This man, he said, feared for his safety, which is why he shot and killed our dog—because he was afraid for his life. I don't believe he just said that to us because there was nothing else he could say. I believe he said that because it was at least a part of the truth and because deep in his heart he wanted so much to believe it was all of it. He wanted us to see people who did stupid things as scared people, not people who felt free to change our lives in an instant, on a whim, with no regard for the consequences, no fear of retaliation from those offended because they were black. No fear of judicial sanction from the white society.

I did not always understand how, having lived his whole life in the segregated South, my father could be so forgiving. He had a way of putting the best spin on things and he always did, even when people's actions left little room for doubt about their true motives. He made allowances for people and was able to forgive them, to understand their fear and what they thought they were losing. He didn't impart rage to us because he didn't have it. He told us if we hate that man, our hating him would rob us of more of our life than it would damage that man. "Let it go," he said. "Don't keep it inside to build up and make you bitter. Let it go."

There are people who think religion is used to keep people in their place, respectful of authority and disinclined to challenge the rules set down by others. But my father was grounded in Christianity in the best way. He was able to make peace with what was going on in his time and pass that on to us.

In the black community where we grew up, my father was always called Reverend Bagwell, but in the larger white community where we did our shopping and went to school, all white people called him by his first name. Because it happened often when I was with him, and because I noticed everything and was perpetually curious thanks to him, I finally asked why this was so. He regarded me for what seemed like a very long time before he answered.

My father was tall, thin, with an oval-shaped face, smooth nut-brown skin, with eyes shaped like almonds. His eyes sparkled whenever he talked to us about anything. He had very big hands that were warm and strong. His touch was tender even though he was a part-time carpenter. He laughed easily and did not suffer fools gladly. He was also a very serious man and felt in his bones the need to teach us that freedom and learning are two companions linked forever and that anyone can oppress us outwardly but never inside. And so, when I asked my question, he said to me, "Calling a man by his first name is a way that some people have of trying to show that they are your superiors." Some people, he explained, need to know there's someone lower than they are, so at least they are not on the bottom. And he said that you, yourself are the one who determines who you are and that you shouldn't let anyone else determine that for you, no matter what they call you and how they see you, because "no one can ride your back unless it's bent."

My father died when I was fifteen, but he taught me so much about living. The principles he taught me have stayed with me all my life. Now that I am older and have become a mother myself, I believe he made it up as he went along, those years without Mama, but we never knew that he did. He gave all of us the necessary tools to make a life for ourselves in a world that can be hard at times. He taught us to live lives that we would not regret living. He focused on the things that were important and allowed us to explore anything that attracted our attention.

Although society classified us as poor, my father taught us to be content with what we had and see it as a bridge to the next level. He gave us a thirst for knowledge and learning that has stayed with me most of my life and that drove me to become the one thing I always wanted to be, a doctor. My curiosity and interests were born in the hours of our absolutely favorite family activity—reading. My father, who after high school spent his whole life educating himself and teaching us that education and self-reliance were the keys to freedom, guided our appetites and curious interests so that we could dream about becoming anything we wanted. Becoming a doctor was the first and only thing I wanted to do since I was a little girl, perhaps because so many people I loved died young, when I wanted and needed them the most. And maybe because my father said if you can believe it, it will happen. So I became a physician.

I often think about my father and what he would do as I go about the daily business of living and seeing patients. I never saw him get tired or complain about the pressure or make excuses for not doing what he had promised. His word was his bond, and I hear him saying that in my head nearly every day. Hardly a day passes when I don't think about him or something that he or Nana taught me—especially when a patient or a situation pushes and challenges me in ways that I find difficult to handle. I'm forced to dig deep inside myself and find that message I know he put there.

In retrospect, my father was way ahead of his time and much larger than the place he lived in the Jim Crow South. He was a man for all times and all places, a universalist, and his wisdom made his children citizens of the world.

e/r *Monica Sweeney, M.D., is the medical director of the Bedford Stuyvesant Family Health Center, where she works to provide medical care to low-income families, particularly teens at risk for HIV and early pregnancy. Although she loves working with her patients, her goal is to diminish their need to see her. She is happily married and has three children.*

Mama—Daisy Blackwell

Me and My father,
William Blackwell

Eric Blackwell—
second grade, age 7

It Ain't Nobody's Business
What You Do

I came into this world as damaged goods, with a tiny body, a really big head, and asthma. The doctor sat my mother down, took her hand, and began speaking to her like an undertaker talking to the bereaved. My big head, he explained, was because I had water on the brain. I might manage to hang around a couple of years, but I would never be a normal, healthy kid.

My mother always says it was the cocksure way they told her I wouldn't survive—like they knew the will of God—that saved me. Because that's when she just set her mind to proving them wrong. And I believe her, because on my mother's side, a flint-hard resolve not to be pushed around was a family trait.

First to come to my rescue was my great-grandmother Ida, who had already had the experience of burying her own daughter—my grand-mother, my mother's mom—long before her time. She pulled Mom away from the distractions of the doctors and said, "Touch him, Bebe. You got to go to that hospital and feel your baby! That boy will know your touch. Stop letting those doctors and nurses handle him so much and start feeling and feeding him yourself! He will know you and you'll see, he'll get better. You just wait."

If you know my mother, you know she never needed a lot of encouragement to go up against tough odds. Whenever I asked my mother to tell me the story of my birth—and I must have made her do it a couple of dozen times—I always waited for that one moment in the story when, no matter what she was doing at the time—ironing, making dinner, cleaning the floor for the fifteenth time—she'd stop and look me right in the eye with that defiant look of hers I knew so well. Her jet-black eyes locked onto mine, and she'd say, "The more those doctors kept saying you weren't gonna make it, the more I kept telling myself, 'Wait a minute, this is my child they're killing off.'"

I loved the way she said it, the anger at those doctors still in her voice after all those years. And then she'd tell me there was something about my face, at once helpless yet determined, that made her sure I was going to make it. She was not going to give in. She had birthed me, and she was going to stick with me.

I came home from the hospital a small, sick, but nevertheless intact baby boy. My father was allowed to name me. He called me Eric, after his own father.

Once at home, my mom started the ritual of bathing me in warm alcohol baths and tucking me tight under the covers to keep me from catching anything else. Over time, I grew bigger and got stronger. Miraculous cure? Well, I survived. My asthma was a problem, and big as I grew, my head remained the biggest part of my body. I eventually would become known as Big Head Eric, a name that would follow me throughout my childhood. But hey, I made it home and I'm still here and kicking.

For the first six years of my life, I now realize, my mom did most of the sticking with me largely alone, without much help from my father. It was not that my father was not around. He got up in the morning with all of us, went to work every day, and came home at the same time each night. In fact, I used to call out to my mother "Daddy's coming!" long before he knocked on the door, because before you ever saw my father you heard him. It was his whistle. It's hard to think of a moment when he wasn't doing one of three things: singing, whistling, or sleeping. By then my mother wasn't saying too many nice things about my father. The few good stories she had to tell were always about his magical voice, which had seduced her when she first met him in a Harlem nightclub. She always used to say he could "sang" with the best of the crooners, that he had "the voice of an angel." But by the time I came along she could no longer deny that he had developed a devilish habit to go with his angelic voice. He had a drinking problem.

If there are good and bad drunks, my father was the good kind. He was not a violent drunk. I was never afraid of him when he was drinking. In fact, he was the kind of drunk who didn't look drunk. He loved to sing, even when he was just conversing with you. Life was a musical comedy to him. He'd come in singing, "Ain't nobody's business what you do," which drove my mother crazy. Still, she once told me that it was because of my father's voice that she was finally sure that I was going to confound those damn doctors and make it.

Although from the beginning she insisted on treating me like a perfectly normal child, in one way I scared her. I was a very quiet baby. No matter how much she cooed to me, I never cooed back. I never giggled or laughed—things a baby is supposed to do. Until one day, when the telephone rang and my mother asked my father to stay with me while she took the call in another room. As soon as she left the room, I started crying fiercely. According to my mother, she could hear my father trying to talk me out of crying and trying to tempt me to take another spoonful of the baby food she had left for him to feed me. But my screams got fiercer and fiercer. And then she heard it quiet down—she heard my cries grow weaker and weaker and then the sound of his voice, barely audible.

When she came back in, she saw that he had picked me up in his arms and was very gently stroking my head and singing to me, very, very softly. And then it happened: I made a gurgling laugh in response to his singing, and then another and another. According to family legend, it was the first time that I ever laughed. Mom said she moved closer to see my face and saw that my eyes were locked onto my father's face, intent on the mysterious sounds coming out of his throat. Over time, as my body got stronger, my mom said that I started to pay more attention to noises and sound. She said that whenever my father came home and started whistling or singing, if she was feeding or bathing me, I would stay still, listening to his voice, comforted by it. When I started playing in the street, if my father was nearby, I would know it because before I saw him I heard him and his beautiful voice.

Because both my parents had full-time jobs, I was left most days with a baby-sitter, Ms. Edy. Mom had known her for quite some time, and she was the lady that most of my mom's friends hired to take care of their children. She lived nearby in the same neighborhood, which made it easy for my mom to come and get me. My mother was usually the first mother to arrive to pick up her child from Ms. Edy's, and she was never, and I mean never, late. She was a clock; ticktock, everything on time. I was usually out front before any of the other kids because I knew Mom would be there waiting for me. But one day something happened. She was not there. I looked into every face that rounded that corner of Ms. Edy's street, expecting to see hers, but she wasn't there. As I watched most of the other children leave, my head started to ache and I got scared.

Ms. Edy took my hand and had me stand next to her as we saw the last of the children leave with their moms, each of them saying their good-byes to her, until finally I was the last kid left, and my mother still hadn't come. Ms. Edy looked at me and her eyes said what I already knew, that she was concerned, that it was very unusual for my mother to be the last one to arrive. So she said, "Don't worry honey, I'm sure your mama's on her way and will be here soon. So why don't we go in the house and have a big old piece of cake. Why, she can even have a piece herself when she gets here. Come on, let's go in."

I looked up the street once more, but still no sign of her. I loved Ms. Edy's applesauce spice cake, but I'd rather be going home with my mom. Feeling the tears starting to sting my eyes, I turned to go into the house with Ms. Edy, and it was then that I heard it—whistling. Ms. Edy and I both turned to look at the same time, and coming around the corner was a tall black man, wearing a dark suit and a hat. Ms. Edy said, "Well I'll be, Eric. It's your daddy coming to get you."

I dropped her hand and took off running toward him. As I reached my father, he bent down to catch me and I jumped on him. He caught me and tossed me into the air saying, "Son, how you doing? How you doing?" Like nothing had happened. A big smile framed his face as he kept on whistling and throwing me up in the air. Finally putting me down, he said, "If I had known the kind of welcome I'd get, I would have come sooner," and the bad thoughts I had been thinking about my mother not being there for me disappeared in the joy of that moment with my father. Hand in hand we waved good-bye to Ms. Edy and started for home, my father whistling and singing every step of the way.

I still carry around inside my head the sound of his whistling echoing up from the streets to our window, drifting up the stairway, getting louder and louder until he reached our door. Pushing the door open he'd say "Thank-k-k God I'm home," and just collapse into the nearest chair or bed or whatever was convenient. And I'm telling you, he'd take in a long breath, close his eyes, and he was gone, still in his clothes. Good night and good-bye.

According to my mother, no one was out the door in fewer steps when she had something she wanted him to do. But I loved my dad because he was my dad. That was a good enough reason for me. Oh, for sure he was cool and had a lot of personality. He always dressed nice and knew what to say to everybody no matter what the occasion. I never had a problem walking down the street with my dad; even when he sang, I was never embarrassed. But most important was that when we were together, he was totally with me, listening to me and answering my questions. I was proud of him because he was there when he could be. A lot of the kids where I lived didn't have a dad, and the way he was there with me made me feel special. I wanted to be like him.

Being the youngest in the family, I was the last to figure out that my father was on the way to becoming a serious drunk. Over time, the rest of the family—my two brothers, two sisters, and two cousins who lived with us because their mother, my father's sister, had died young—had all gotten used to Dad's drinking and my asthma attacks. However, my mother, I guess being a mother, never got used to either.

One Friday evening, I had an asthma attack. Not one of my worst attacks, but my mother began frantically sitting me up, making sure I was able to get as much air as possible. She was touching my forehead and looking into my eyes, listening to me sucking for a breath and telling me to stay calm.

Just then my dad came into the house. She didn't even wait for him to take off his coat, but said in a stern voice, "Willie, we need to take Eric right to the hospital! He just had an attack and feels like he has a temperature!"

By then she seemed scared, and I got scared and began to cry. With his overcoat half off, revealing his favorite suit and tie, hat poised in his hand, my dad looked like he was ready to go anywhere except to a hospital. Dropping his coat on the floor, he came into the room and sat next to me on the bed. He took my face into his hands, and, rubbing my cheeks gently with his thumbs, he looked into my eyes searching for I don't know what. Putting his ear to my nose for a few seconds, he said, "Breathe, son," and I did, blowing spit on his face as I sent breath out through my nose and mouth. He stood up, gave my face a reassuring squeeze, kissed me on the forehead, and said to my mother, "He's all right. Just give him a few minutes to settle down."

"All right?" my mother snapped at him.

"You're always worried about nothing, Bebe. What you doing to the boy, taking him to the hospital every time he breathes the wrong way?"

My mother gave him one of her stares. "Oh Bebe," he said, "calm down. That boy don't need a doctor. He's not sick. He don't want to go to no hospital, do you Eric? He just wants to see those pretty nurses with those big legs! Don't you Eric?"

And then he just threw his head back and laughed. When he saw that my mom was not laughing with him, he stopped and said to her, "It's okay, don't worry. Eric will be fine." To me he said, "I'm right here. It's okay."

While my dad was rubbing my tummy and talking to me, my mother sat next to me and felt my forehead, ears, and bottom all over again and listened to my breathing.

"You see," my dad said to her, "Eric's fine, just look at him. He's fine." With that he gave my tummy a squeeze and then headed for the door singing, "That's my boy, that's my boy." He paused at the door, winked at me, and sang loudly, "That's my boy, right Eric?" and he made a funny face at me, making me laugh too.

My mom had her mouth open to say something, but she wasn't quick enough. She shook her head, turned to me, and said, "I'm afraid that man is your father." "That's my daddy," I said, not catching her irony. She let out a humph, putting her hand on my face, touching my head and my cheeks, holding my wrist. I don't know how long she sat there with me, but the next thing I remember was waking up the next morning in my bed, in my favorite pajamas. I know my mom changed me and tucked me in. That's how she was, always making sure that I was okay.

When I let my memory go back as far as it can, it's bath time that I remember the most. My nightly baths were always a pretty serious affair with Mom because she had to squeeze them in between all the other things she had to do before she got to go to bed. No time to play in the water and make a mess in the bathroom, for sure. Then one day my mother came to tell me that she had had a change of shift at work and that from now on my dad would be in charge of my nightly bath.

My father, I soon learned, had a completely different idea of what baths were for. As long as I was in the water and had at least one lathering and rinse off, that was my bath. The rest of the time was reserved for having fun. My father didn't even care when I tracked a trail of water from the bathtub to the toilet because I often forgot to take a pee before getting into the tub.

One night we were in the bathroom waiting for the tub to fill up and Dad was taking a pee. I watched as he made a perfect yellow arc into the toilet and I said, "Wow wee, am I gonna be able to do that some day?" "Sure you are, son," he said. "In fact, you will be able to do more than that," and he started to tell me about the bladder, and how I could tell by the color of my pee and how it came out when something was wrong. "If your urine comes out too yellow, it means you aren't drinking enough water. If it comes out in spurts, splat, splat, splat, splat, that also means you're not healthy. It should come out in a strong steady stream like this," and he demonstrated. I followed suit and practiced making arcs into the toilet but missed, and it landed on the floor to the left of the toilet, pee collecting in a little yellow puddle on the black-and-white tile, running into a crack. I looked at my dad, whose eyebrows were raised in mock surprise, and we both started laughing. We laughed so hard and loud that we didn't hear my mother until she knocked on the door and called out, "What's going on in there?"

My father called back, "Is that you, Bebe? What you doing home so early?"

"We got off early tonight," she said. "What are you two doing in there? And why haven't you put Eric to bed yet?"

"Ain't nothing going on in here, except we're taking a bath, woman," my father called back.

"Why is this door locked?" she asked, jiggling the handle.

"That door ain't locked, it's just stuck," my father said, looking at me, winking, and smiling.

"I don't care what you two do as long as you don't make a mess in there."

Trying hard not to laugh out loud, holding me steady as I was jumping up and down, my dad bluffed her. "Come on in here Bebe if you don't believe us."

There was only quiet from the other side of the door. Finally, she said, "Just make sure you wash that tub out when you're done. You know what kind of bathtub ring two men can leave," and we heard her footsteps echoing down the hallway.

My father exhaled and said, "Phew, that was close. Can you believe she almost came in here interrupting us grown men while we're taking a bath?" With me echoing his stage sigh, my father stepped into the bathtub with me, sloshing water and soap bubbles everywhere. I remember that he was smiling.

Gradually, despite my father's drinking problem, he became a bigger part of my daily life, especially when I was almost six years old. It was a hot summer afternoon, and we were walking home from the subway, down Willoughby Street, coming back from a visit to my father's sister's house in the Bronx. We were several blocks from home. It had been a long day, which I had spent running in the streets with my cousins, playing stickball and wading through the puddles of water from the open fire hydrants that cooled us on the hottest days of the summer. I was crazy tired as we left the subway and started the walk home. Although we didn't have far to go, I was falling asleep on my feet, and I just didn't feel like walking. Tired of being dragged down the street, I just shucked off my father's hand and in a whiney voice said, "I'm tired and I don't want to walk no more." He stopped, bent down on one knee, and said, "Come on son, get on my back." As I climbed on he said, "We're almost home, it won't be long now," and he rose up and strode on down the street with me on his back, humming a tune. I never expected him to just pick me up and carry me the rest of the way. I thought I'd have to put up a bigger fuss. My mother would not have heard of it, and I would never have even dared complain about being tired of walking, let alone ask her to carry me home. Even if I had a real good reason and could talk her into carrying me, I'd have to go through a big hassle first. But I was coming to realize that my father was really a different person. Easy like. He didn't let things get to him, took most things in stride, and helped if he could. He never said I was being selfish for wanting him to carry me, nor did he make me prove I really needed help. He just said, "Okay, get on my back." His aim was to please, make life easier for me when it got too much, and that is what he did on that day.

It was different with my mother. She was all business. She took her job of parenting seriously. She made sure we were well fed, minded our manners, and were diligent in our studies. By all accounts she was a good mother, but she had no time or patience for fooling around.

She was not like other mothers I knew. I can't remember sitting at the table having milk and cookies with her. Or snuggling up to her on the couch. Or watching a TV show with her. I used to envy my friends whose mothers knew how to just hang.

When I think of my mother, the first thing I see is her face. Her skin was the color of caramel and softer than anything I had ever touched. Her eyes were shiny jet black and shaped like ovals. She smelled clean and fresh all the time, a scent that comforted me whenever I was near her.

But if you ask me what feature I remember most, I'd have to say her mouth, her incredible moving mouth, talking to us, at us, about what to do, in a stern I-will-whoop-your-butt kind of voice that says, "Don't you even think of arguing with me."

But I knew my mother loved me. All I had to do was let out a scream when my older brother was picking on me and she'd be there in a second, protecting me. Sometimes I'd even use my asthma to get her attention, and that always worked. But as soon as the crisis was over, she was back at whatever it was she was doing. And she was always doing something.

She also expressed her love for us with her cooking. Boy, that woman could cook some food. She was raised in the South by Great-Grandma Ida, and, as she told us many times, fixing a fine meal brought back memories of her childhood, of the meals Great-Grandma Ida used to make. She was determined to do no less for us. We had two meats on Sunday, fish on Friday, and what she called "continental cuisine," like spaghetti, on Wednesday. But, of all the days of the week, Sunday was the best day to come by our house and be invited to sit down for a meal. Did I ever love breakfast on Sundays. It was worth waiting for. My mother made the best cheese eggs and sausage, with grits and hot biscuits that she baked from scratch. The cheese was oozing and bubbling in those eggs, and I would put spoonfuls on top of her perfectly flaky golden-brown biscuits. A few hours after breakfast we were back to the table for an early dinner. Collard greens, roast beef, macaroni and cheese, chicken with giblet gravy, rice and sweet potatoes, and homemade apple pie. They were feasts fit for royalty, and we had no problems putting it away.

It wasn't just cooking and working that kept my mother busy. Our house was always being cleaned, scrubbed, and something always needed polishing. You know how people would say, "It's such a nice day, let's go out and enjoy it"? Well, my mom would snap at me, "This ain't gonna be the last sunny day. Get in there and clean your room." I cleaned. She cleaned. We cleaned when there was no dirt, when the tiles on the kitchen floor were still shiny from the last cleaning. Oh, one more thing she got from her Southern upbringing: The windows were always open—day, night, winter, spring, summer, and fall—"to let in fresh air and sunlight."

My mother used to say we were a farm family who just happened to be living in the city, and we were to carry ourselves with pride and never bring shame on the family. She warned us that if we ever did anything that even sounded like it was outside of how we should behave, she would find out about it and there'd be hell to pay. And we knew she meant it.

The problem was, I was already bringing shame on the family. And I didn't know how to deal with it.

Once I began to play in the streets, my big head haunted me. First one kid then another began calling me "Big Head Eric." Skinny body, big head, that was me. It was brutal. We'd be playing basketball and someone would say, "Don't pass it to Big Head." Another time, the guy whose ball it was had to go home. "Don't sweat it," some guy said. "We'll use Eric's head." I laughed along with them, but it hurt. Even when I scored and won the game, I couldn't get credit for what I did. It was like my accomplishments couldn't change who they thought I was. When someone asked, "Hey, who was it scored the winning basket?" I would hear, "Oh yeah, it was that big head boy, that Eric." Whatever I managed to do, it was just a freak play, a freak shot from the freak kid. I tried to defend myself, jump into the exchange, but it was a pretty sad joke. Kids can be really cruel, and it didn't take long for me to realize that I couldn't defend myself or make enough excuses for every kid who called me Big Head. Nor did it take me long to figure out that I couldn't out rank everybody in the street when they started on me about my head. There was nothing I could say that would top anything they had to say about my head. But I also knew they had no other thing they could say about me. I wasn't a bum, they couldn't call my sister a "ho," my parents worked, and I wore pretty decent clothes. So the only thing they could rank on was my head. I was never the type to cry, and could crack as bad as anybody, so I became a great joker. And because I had a smart mouth and had an answer for everything, the role of the joker somehow fit. And that's how I survived.

Even though I managed to survive playing in the streets with a big head, I didn't think I would ever have a normal life in any way, especially romantically or sexually. I was sure I was always going to be a scorned person. Pathetic. I stupidly told my older brother about it, and he started calling me the Quasimodo of Fort Greene. When I asked him who Quasimodo was, he told me he was a guy who was as ugly as me.

Whenever my mother used to warn us not to bring shame on the family, I looked at my brother to see if he would tell her my big head was already doing that.

My granddaddy James, my mother's father, was the first person to give me any idea that having a big head didn't have to be all bad. In the black tradition of sending the kids south for the summer to get some fresh air, I spent most summers with my granddaddy, until I was too old to be packed up and sent off.

My granddaddy James, you have to understand, was one of the strangest people I ever met. He spent most of the day in a rocking chair on the porch of my great-grandmother's house, the house he had moved to after his wife, my grandmother, died, so that Great-Grandma Ida and he could raise my mother. He was usually very quiet, staying to himself most of the time.

One day, in the middle of talking about something altogether different, he looked at me and said, "Me and you, Eric, we both have big heads." I looked up at him really carefully. He was right. He had a big head, just like me. My crazy but lovable granddaddy James. He said, "Big head, big wit, little head, not a bit." Made sense to a kid with a big head.

But still, I wanted desperately to be normal, and I didn't want my mother to know I was bringing shame on the family with my big head. Especially because by then I was already getting into big trouble in school.

On report card day we had a routine. All of us kids had to stand up at the dinner table, one by one, and read through our report card for the whole family to hear. I'll never forget one report card day when I was halfway through the fifth grade. When my turn came, the whole table got quiet. My mother just said, "Eric," and I stood up, cleared my throat, and said, "Ah, hmm, ah okay, Mom, can I read this later?" And she said, "Is there something wrong?" I said, "Well there's a note here along with my report card." "What does it say?" she asked. And I said, "Well, ahh, hmmm." "What does it say Eric?"

Without much choice, I read it, mumbled it really, but she didn't miss a word of it. The note said, "Eric's disruptive behavior has made his grades and work suffer terribly this term. He is rude, wild, and totally uncontrollable and causes chaos in the classroom, causing other students to get into trouble."

The whole table was dead quiet for a split second until my brothers started laughing—first giggling, then throwing their heads back and laughing really loud. Finally one of my brothers stopped laughing just long enough to say, "Oh man Eric, you are bad." I thought for a moment I was off the hook because within a few seconds everyone at the table was laughing, even Mom and Dad. Then Mom said through her laughter, "Go ahead, read the rest of your card, read your grades. What did you get?" "Okay," I said. "Here goes. In geography, I got a D minus. In English, a D minus. In math, well, they gave me an F. In science, they gave me another F." At this point everyone at the table was trying desperately hard not to look at me, and snickers of laughter were spilling out of mouths covered by hands. Before I could read any further, Mom said, "Excuse me son, just wait a minute, wait just one minute! You mean to tell me after all that talking I did to your teachers and that principal, telling them what a smart child you were, you have the nerve to come in this house and read me grades that anyone at this table could make without going to school every day?"

She grabbed for the report card. "Let me see that." It was covered in red marks, D minuses, and Fs. I had ten red marks on my report card. "You're still bringing home these red marks, and Fs and Ds. I thought you were gonna try to get these red marks off."

By now everybody had stopped laughing. "Boy," she said while everyone else looked down, "I told your father he needs to whoop you. You are completely losing any chance you have to go to college. Here you are nearly at the end of the fifth grade and you're flunking everything."

"Well not exactly everything," I said.

"What did you say?" she asked. "You sit down and just listen to me. I'm sitting here listening to you read your report card, and there is not even a C minus on it. Can't you even get a C minus in the fifth grade? What are you doing in school?"

I think the expression is to stand mute. I stood mute. In my mind I was thinking, *A C minus, I just have to get rid of the red marks.* My thing was counting the red marks. I'm still afraid of red marks. I spent my whole life trying to get rid of the red marks. It wasn't about A, B, Cs for me, it was about getting rid of the red marks.

I didn't know how to respond to my mother, but my silence didn't stop her. "What are you gonna be, huh? A bum in the street? Is that what you want for yourself? Answer me, Eric."

I stood meekly with my head down, wishing I could just melt and slide into the floor. One by one, my brothers, sisters, and even my dad quietly slunk away while my mother worked herself up, her attention completely focused on me.

"I'm gonna whoop your behind straight up and down every time I have to come to that school and every time you get a report card that has less than a C on it. And don't look at me for pity. If you don't do it the way I prescribe it, if you're not doing right in school, then you got it coming. You're not a stupid boy. I'm gonna help you with your homework every day, and if you're still failing, that means you're carrying on, you're showing off, and you're gonna get it."

On and on she continued. "You will stay in and do your homework, stop hanging out in the street with your so-called friends, and pass your courses with at least a C. Do you understand?"

I mumbled something.

"I can't hear you," she said and repeated herself. "I said, do you understand what I just said?"

"Yes ma'am, I do."

And for the rest of the school year, like clockwork, she came every week to talk to the teachers and principal. She once said that her shoes knew the way to my school.

If her shoes knew the way to school, it was her mind that was figuring every angle. One day she came to school loaded down with bottles of perfume. My oldest brother worked for a fragrance manufacturer, where they made knock-off perfumes. So, as a gift to all of my teachers, my mom brought them bottles of perfumes. They loved it and came to school smelling sweet. Although I don't know if they would have outright flunked me, I do think my case was given special consideration after those countless discussions and bottles of perfume that my mom delivered.

But if I was going to shape up, I had another little problem to deal with. For a brief time I was hanging with a gang.

One way or another, I had to lose my shitty identity, to dump Big Head Eric and swap it for something that made me feel good. That's where the streets came in. You see, in the streets whoever has an interest like yours usually gets your attention. No matter what they are teaching you. That's the thing about "the streets": It speaks to you, in a language you can understand. Speaks to you through people. You could be in a certain place at a certain time and certain things are happening, and if those things meet your fancy, then you're into that. If you're a hustler, you will come across a con artist on the streets, and you're going to take to him and learn the tricks of that trade. If you're a selfish person and someone introduces you to drugs, your personality comes out in your drug use. One thing about the streets, you belong to something. Even if you're just a wanderer, at least you're belonging to a group of nomads who know you and have taken you in and given you a piece of what they have, a semblance of a place to belong. On the streets, anybody can be somebody, as long as being somebody—no matter who that somebody is—is more important than being nobody. And to kids, it usually is.

I have two older brothers and two older sisters. They are opposites of each other. I have a very educated older brother who probably benefited a lot from all those high hopes of the '60s. He got a really great corporate situation. My older sister is like him. Successful in what she does. Then I have another brother who was claimed by the streets. I wouldn't say the streets kidnapped him as much as I would say he found a lot of support in the streets. As did my younger sister. They survived, but they paid a price. You see, in the inner city, "the streets" is a character with a lot of appeal. In our house, we all learned from the streets for at least some part of our time. If you're going to survive, your family has to offer something better, more appealing to you.

The gang stuff ended when my mother found one of my schoolbooks with gang curse words and names written in the back of it. I had gone out to play after school and came in for dinner. She was standing at the door waiting for me, holding my book. As I came in, I knew I was in trouble. She didn't even let me put my basketball down. "What's this?" she asked. "What are you doing with this? Did you write these words in the back of your book?"

My mind worked fast. "Some kid wrote that," I said. "I let him borrow my book and when he gave it back to me, those words were in the back of it."

"I better not find out you wrote this, because if I do, you know what's coming."

I said, "It's not mine, okay?"

And giving me one of her "don't you try it" looks, she handed me my book and told me to go to my room.

I knew my mother would keep her promise. My mother was no joke. She was stern. I mean a black-woman-who-was-whooping-your-ass stern. She had no problem beating that booty. And when she did, you knew it was beat. No sitting down, no lying down without feeling pain. She grew up taking no mess, you know what I mean? And she didn't take no mess from her children. And when she saw those gang curses in my book, I knew she would keep watching me to see if I was telling the truth. And that was enough for me to start getting my butt in gear.

But maybe what saved me from the streets was that combination of my mother's strictness and something my father brought to my raising. Somewhere along the way, my mother had brought him in. I wish I could have heard the conversation when this decision was made, because by the time my father was taking a more hands-on role with me, my mother had already lost a lot of respect for him. But all I heard was a lot of mumbling, with my name thrown in every now and then. "Eric mumble mumble, Eric, buzz, buzz." They talked late into the night. I wondered what I had done wrong and dreaded the next morning.

My father got me out of bed real early and asked me if I wanted to play basketball with him. We had never even thrown a ball around before but I said sure. To my surprise he played a mean game of hoops, and soon the other boys started to come around to watch. My dad invited them to join us. Soon, nearly every Saturday morning he played basketball or baseball with me in the projects. My dad, who was already known as the fancy dresser who whistled and sang, became known to my friends as a cool-dude father who played a good game of pickup.

Soon, my father and I had a weekend thing going. Every Saturday we played ball in the morning, and in the afternoon we went to the movies. I saw the whole blacksploitation era with him. I loved those movies because I got to see black people save themselves. They saved their friends from evil, their communities.

There were times when my father would let me pick the movies, even though some of them I shouldn't have been watching. But whoever picked the movie, I knew that the moment the lights went down and the movie started rolling, he would slide down in his seat and fall asleep. At times he slept straight through the film. I always wondered how he could sleep so deep in the middle of a movie. Maybe I didn't want to know why. But like clockwork he fell asleep the moment the movie started until it ended, when he woke up fresh and ready to go.

It didn't matter that he slept straight through. The fact was he just wanted to sleep and be at the movies and be with me, and I wanted to be at the movies and be with him. My dad had style and he was very charismatic, and I wanted to be like him. On the street no one disrespected him. Everyone called him Mr. Blackwell. Even to this day they do. It made me like our name. When we came home from the movies, and other times I walked in the street with him, he always said to people, "This is my son Eric Blackwell," said it with pride, like I was somebody important. "This here is my son, this is my youngest boy, Eric." Even today, when I walk through the streets of my old neighborhood, people ask me about the different projects I'm working on and how I'm doing and they know what I'm doing because my dad talks about his son Eric.

During those walks home with my father I got to see him the way he wasn't at home. At home, my mother controlled the house. When we were out together, it was Dad and me, and he was in charge. I got to witness that and how people treated him. He was special in ways that I didn't get to see at home. Looking back, it was important for me to see that. I grew up in a place where a lot of the kids didn't have fathers. But I needed to have a father even more than most kids because I was still having trouble going out and facing the big-head remarks of the other kids and their rejection.

I never had to wonder who my dad was because he was there with me. I never had to wonder where he was, why he didn't want to be home with me, because he was always at hand, with me. And on top of everything, he liked being with me, big head and all. He said I was good company for him, made him smile and made him laugh. I was all right. Of all the people he could be with, he was with me.

We spent hours together talking about anything and everything, except one topic. We never talked about his drinking, not because he wouldn't have talked about it, but because there was nothing to talk about. He never hid it from me; he never made excuses for himself; no matter how critical of him my mom was, he never criticized her for criticizing him. Athletes talk of a certain kind of ballplayer as an excuse player. If he doesn't make the play, sink the shot, he'll tell you what happened that caused him to miss it. He was fouled, the sun was in his eyes, the grounder hit a pebble and took a bad hop. He thinks having a good excuse for not making it happen is as good as making it happen. My dad was no excuse player. He did what he could, and when he came up short, you never heard an excuse from him.

I remember once, he had just come out of a fight with Mom over his drinking where she really tore into him, and later I couldn't get it out of my head and told him, "I hate her!" He said, "Don't ever let me hear you say that again. Don't you ever say you hate your mother. Your mother keeps this family going, you remember that."

"But you make more money than she does," I said through my tears. "Who has the cash has the lash," I recited to him, giving my father fatherly advice.

"It ain't just money," he said. "Your mother does things for all of us, things I should be doing."

Anger was just not his way. Nor was defending himself by criticizing my mom. He was a gentle soul, too, not just a man to lay his failures on others. And he loved my mother.

My mother tried to raise me by staying on top of me, by making sure I was dressed right and got to school on time, toed the line. My father was incapable of doing what she did, even if he wanted to.

But he wasn't incapable of being a parent. He was not afraid to kiss me and hug me, to show me that I was lovable, big head and all, and he continued to do so until I got too old to want my friends to see him do it. Sometimes in the middle of walking down the street with him or after a game of basketball, he would say, "You know son, there ain't no stopping you. You have a lot of fight in you." "That's right," I'd say. "I learned it from you." But the truth is, any fight I had in me I didn't learn from him. I learned that from my mother.

But that was a great part of our relationship. I learned from his strengths, and I learned from his weaknesses. I saw what happens to good people who have no fight. And I learned not to be an excuse player. Slowly, during those endless walks, I began to forget that I was once Eric with the big head, and instead became Eric Blackwell, my father's son. I can't say his drinking didn't bother me. There were times when his speech was so blurry that I couldn't make out what he was saying. And I also knew that many nights when I peeked into the room where he slept, there was a bottle on the floor beside him nearly empty. And that my mother used to say to him, "Admit it, Willie. You're just a drunk."

Yet somehow, who he was shone through his weaknesses. My mom would argue with him about beating us. He would say, "You better beat them yourself." She would literally have to make a case for why he owed us a beating. But he never wanted to beat me. While some fathers might teach their sons how to defend themselves in the streets, to face trouble head-on and, if trouble was coming, to make sure you get in the first punch, my father was not afraid to teach me to walk the other way when violence broke out. There was no macho in him at all. And that made me feel better about myself, because I was a little like that too.

But not being macho does not mean you have to make a doormat of yourself with your wife. As I got older, I remember being mad at him because he wasn't handling confrontation with my mother the right way. They used to fight all the time about his drinking, and she used to really lay into him. I used to get so mad at him because he didn't fight back. Which made her even more angry.

I remember being angry with my mother too because as the years went on she was losing more and more patience with my father. He was disgracing us, the whole family, she'd scream at him. Much later I learned things that finally made me understand why she was so fixated on what people might be saying about the family, why it was such a source of pain to her.

Although they met in New York City, both my father and mother were country folk, born and bred in the South, products of farm families from Arkansas and North Carolina. It took me years to figure out why they were ever attracted to each other. When I finally found out, it was a story I would never forget.

My mother was raised in North Carolina by her maternal grand-mother, Ida, and her daddy, my granddaddy James. Her own mother had died when she was very young. Her grandmother told her about her mother, endless stories about her, about how she had long silky hair, high cheekbones, and that special caramel skin my mother inherited, part copper Indian skin and part rich satiny black skin. But there was one story she never told: that her mother's death had come at the hands of her own husband—my granddaddy James, my mother's father.

Years later, with James's death, we would learn, from letters found folded into a silver box, what the whole thing was about, what he had done, why he did it, and what it had really done to him as well as to his victim. They were prison letters, written from a small cell in a small county jail that had become Granddaddy James's whole world. In letter after letter, he retold the events of that day when he found her—his wife, the love of his life, his only heart, the woman he had defied his parents to marry—lying in the heat and sweat of sexual passion with another man. And how he snapped and did that totally irrational but most human of deeds—he killed the thing he held most dear.

It was all so strange. By any standard, Granddaddy James must have been considered a prize catch as a husband in those days. You had to wonder why my grandmother would risk such a marriage for a few mo-ments of forbidden lust. He was from a well-to-do Southern black family. They had property and just about as much money as black people were allowed to have back then. And they had something as important—community respect.

Granddaddy's family was considered to be among those Negroes who had made it, a model of hope for those others who had a thousand good reasons to doubt good things could ever happen to people with dark skin. When he was jailed for the crime of killing his wife, he was stripped of his property and money, which was a customary practice in the South; and the respect his family had worked so hard to achieve and had valued so much was taken along with his freedom.

Granddaddy James served his sentence, and it was a good thing for him in some ways, because he was spared the stares of his neighbors, relatives, and busybody know-it-alls who smelled blood whenever they said his name and talked about him as a boy who had been given too much and had gone real bad. Some were even glad in a strange way to see his fall from grace, being from an uppity family and all. Irony of ironies, the gossips chortled, this snooty family had produced one of the most violent men their little town had ever known. And that was Granddaddy James's legacy—for the rest of his days on earth, to be known as the most violent man his town had ever produced.

His one friend during his incarceration remained his mother-in-law, my great grandmother, who, when the right time came, simply went down to the jail and requested that her son-in-law be released into her custody. She saw him as "a good boy who had done something terribly, terribly awful." Amazingly, she convinced the authorities to let him come home with her. She took the man who had killed her daughter into her own house because, she said, her granddaughter needed a father. In that role at least, her son-in-law did not disappoint her.

Every night, without fail, he ate dinner with his daughter; every evening he tucked her into bed and told her stories. At first, my mother recalls, he was completely engaged and engaging, listening with the infinite patience only a loving parent can have for the conversation of a child, playing the kinds of games that only children know the rules to.

At these times, she said, he seemed not to have a care in the world. He taught his daughter how to read, and he even passed onto her, as if she were a son, the things that men need to know to deal from a position of strength with other men, with the world—like how to take no mess and how to laugh at her fears. As far as the first goes, I can attest that he taught her well.

But there was another side to him, a side that gradually came to dominate who he was. This disgraced man who had fallen from so high would be sitting in his rocking chair, in the middle of a conversation with whoever happened to be there, family or not, and just drift off to someplace only he could enter, rocking back and forth, back and forth, lost in memories that did not include anyone else, all the while stroking the barrel of the .45 he kept in his waistband. When my mother learned the truth about Granddaddy, she looked back and realized that during these moments, which came with increasing frequency as he grew older, he must have been prodding at the burden he carried, like pushing against a bad tooth with your tongue to be sure it's still there. He was a man with the seed of violence in him, a man who had killed his wife, a sin for which he could never be forgiven, least of all by himself.

Over time, the teenage Bebe watched this distant, lonely ghost of a man take over her father. And soon, rather than engaging him in conversation, she spent hours just watching and listening to him. Sometimes she'd watch him from the dining-room window. His rocking chair on the porch was always positioned just to the left of the window, so her view of him was unobstructed. Her gaze was often drawn to his face, a face increasingly lost in guilty thoughts, one hand always poised near that flat silver box he kept next to him in his lap or at rare times on the little table that held his glass of iced tea. Once when she asked him about that silver box—which as long as he lived was always so shiny and clean that you could see the reflections of objects on the porch in its top and sides—he grabbed it and put it inside his bosom, and buttoned his shirt all the way to the neck, saying nothing to answer her question, just rocking in his chair, looking past her but not at her.

When I was sent South to visit him, my mother warned us about this. "Granddaddy James sometimes just goes quiet. When that happens, just leave him be." And that's what we always did.

Many years later my mother told us she learned the truth about how her own mother died when she was about eighteen—overheard it while visiting out-of-town relatives. There will always be people who think a child should know the worst there is to know about her parents, and these relatives did the dirty deed. My mother was lost with her new knowledge, she told us, unable to reconcile the truth of the violent person she had heard described with the person who had shown her profound love for as long as she could remember. In some ways, he had been both mother and father. "Did you ask him why he did it?" I asked her.

"I intended to, as soon as I got home," she said. Arriving home after weeks of being gone, she saw him watch her slowly climb the front steps, like he knew that she finally had learned the truth. She wanted to throw her anger at him, jump on him and strike at him for robbing her of her mother. But seeing him sitting there, a shell of the man he had once been, acknowledging her presence but not stirring to meet the barrage he must surely have expected, she could not lash out at him. All the accusations, anger, pain, and confusion, that big question too, stopped in her throat. She passed his chair to enter the house, and he reached out a hand to grab at one of hers and, holding it, touched it to his face. She stopped only for the time it took to wrest her hand from his grip, and went on in, tears filling her eyes as she realized the hand she had pulled from her father's face was wet with his tears.

It wouldn't be until after Granddaddy's death that my mother, already a woman herself, would find the silver box and get her answer. It was in the bottom of his closet in a sack stuffed with his clothes. The silver box, whose top and sides were now dull and brown from the lack of handling that came with the passage of time, was stuffed with letters written in her father's own hand addressed to himself. When she read them she finally understood—not forgave, but understood—some of what went into the act, and the price her father paid for that one mad moment.

But on the day she returned home from her visit to relatives, she did not yet have the letters. So she did the only thing she could do. She packed her things and left, went North, to find what life meant for a girl from the South, raised in a family with such a tragic past.

And then she found my father. He was singing in Harlem nightclubs. He was gentle and charming, no seed of violence in this man. She always said she fell in love with him because of his voice, which, as she put it, was "angelic." But if you ask me, there was another reason she fell in love with my father. He was completely opposite of Granddaddy James. She didn't know yet about her father finding her mother with another man. In wondering why he had killed her mother, she may have speculated that it was because her mother had had the same streak of stubborn independence she had, and her father wouldn't have it. This gentle charmer with a voice like an angel was perfect for my mother, because he would never interfere with her need to be fully her own woman.

I would be the first member of our family to graduate from college. I would never have made it to college if my mother and my father, each in their own way, despite the very real problems in their own marriage, had not been there for me as parents from the day I was born. There were lots of problems in my family, but tell me about a family where there aren't problems. I just know that in countless ways my parents were there for me—my mother, by teaching me that making something of myself started with managing my own life day by day. My father, by helping me to believe in myself, that I could be whatever and whoever I wanted to be.

We never had a lot of money. When I was twelve years old, I asked my parents if we were middle class. You see, once I accepted myself for what I was and stopped looking for validation in the streets, I grew up enjoying life—along the Brooklyn waterfront, playing under the Brooklyn and

Manhattan bridges, feeding bread to the seagulls, rapping with my friends with my feet dragging in the water, and finally running home, stopping at R&S Licorice Factory where we got free licorice, and then coming home to the incredible meals my mother had waiting for us on the table. To me it was a Huckleberry Finn existence. But when I asked them if we were middle class, my parents exchanged a look between them and laughed and said, "No son, we're poor." And I couldn't believe it. Poor? How could it be? I felt so fulfilled by the childhood I was living.

So in my senior year of college I decided to do something for them. All during my senior year I spent quite a bit of time thinking about the fact that I wanted to stop my father's drinking. It would be a gift not only to him, but to my mother as well. My siblings and I came up with a plan that would show my father how much we all loved and needed him, in order to support him enough so he could stop drinking. We planned a surprise party for his sixty-first birthday. Up to this time he had been a practicing alcoholic for at least twenty years of his life, so we had to face the possibility that his stopping was small at best.

That day, we packed into our three-bedroom apartment nearly one hundred people, all of whom knew him from some part of his life. The whole family was present—his brothers, sisters, cousins, children, my mother, of course, and countless friends gathered together to honor him on that day. I had just graduated from college and had my mind set on getting him to promise me that as a graduation gift he wouldn't drink anymore. There was an almost palpable sense of something about to happen in that crowd of people crammed into our little apartment. Following hours of celebrating his birthday, I got everyone's attention. Jumping on top of a table, I said, "Hey, everybody let's go." So almost on cue we gathered around my father, making a circle. Each of us took turns telling him how we felt. Each person had a different story to tell or words to say how important my father had been in each of their lives. Some said how much they loved him: "We love you Pops, we want sixty-one more years for you, we need you to keep on keeping on," and other things that only he and the person speaking knew the meaning of.

We started our circle activity at 4:00 in the afternoon. By the time we were done, it was nearly 8:00 P.M. My dad, who at the end of it understood exactly what some of us had been saying and trying to say, basking in the love that pulsated around him and without a moment's hesitation, fell to his knees and cried like a man who had been given a reprieve from death. In a crowd of one hundred people who knew him, he cried his heart out, tears running down his face, soaking into the front of his favorite party suit.

Shortly thereafter my father stopped drinking, never drank again. Yes, believe it. He never drank again. My mother assumes he was delivered from his fascination with the bottle by the hand of God. But, for whatever reason, it's been twelve years and he hasn't touched a drop since then. And during those years he has taken care of my mother, who finally got sick herself.

Watching the faces of the people surrounding him at the party that day, I was reminded of the times in my childhood when my dad worked his magic on me. My father, through all his weaknesses, taught me how to be a person. "Regardless of the stuff that happens around you, be a person first," he once said to me.

"Everybody's a person," I remember answering, and he said, "Yeah, but you got to be your own person, a person you can be happy being."

"But how can I know what will make me happy?"

"You know, son, every bird has his own tune to sing. Except the mockingbird. He tries to sing the other bird's song. Sing your own song and you'll be happy. Because if it's your song, it will be beautiful, and singing it will make you happy."

∽ *Eric Blackwell is an associate professor of urban studies at the Long Island University in Brooklyn. He and his father were best friends until his father's death in the spring of 2000.*

Moms—Thelma Ganious

Me and Moms, 1982

The Sweet Sound
of Respectability

❧

I am a little boy, so little that wherever we go, my father is holding my hand, like I might get lost if he didn't. Those days, the days he still lived with us, are indelibly preserved in the scrapbook of my mind. And yet most of those pictures are not of him and me together, but of me watching him.

I liked to watch my father, especially the way he entered a room, confident strides bringing him through the door, where he'd stop, holding himself tall, apart from everyone else. Once he walked through the door, he'd pause and look around to see who was there, his face lighting up each time he spotted a pretty woman. He used to say to me, "Look at all that meat and no potatoes, Booby. Don't forget, we're the potatoes." "Booby" was his nickname for me, and I was caught up with him at that moment in time, when he took notice of me, bringing me into his world by calling me Booby, reminding me that I was his son and we were together.

Whenever he walked into a room, friends and strangers alike reached out to slap him on the back or give him a high five or "Hey man," and it wasn't long before everyone stopped what they were doing to say "What's happening, James Albert?" Or to say something about his cool clothes. My father liked that, to create a buzz in the room. Always dressed to kill, he'd make a casual stroll through the room, moving from one little group to the next, shaking hands and giving out kisses to all the ladies. Sometimes, when I was alone, I would imitate the way he walked, the way he cocked his head like he was the coolest cat in the world.

How differently those same folks acted toward my mom and me when my father wasn't around. He knew how to get respect without asking for it, just by the way he walked down the street or entered a room. And perhaps, without really trying, that was one of the things he taught me before he died.

When I think of the beginning of my life, it is the memory of my father that stands out most clearly, because when he was present, everything that happened to us revolved around him.

Our life together began to change when I was four years old. That's when I remember my little sister being in the house with us. The funny thing is I had no idea where she came from. I don't remember my mother being pregnant or in the hospital like she said she had been with me. All I know is that my sister just appeared in the house, and there I was handing my mother diapers and stuff. When my sister came, my mother seemed to be constantly bathing, changing, and feeding her. Sometimes I watched, and there were other times when I helped. I never remember my dad helping, even though he was still living with us. But by then, my father was no longer the main event in my life. Between my sixth and seventh years, my father started staying away. First he would be gone just for a day or so, but then the days became weeks, and I wouldn't know why until years and years later.

But in the beginning, while we were all still together, we lived in an apartment on Nostrand Avenue, in the Bedford Stuyvesant area of Brooklyn. It was a tiny one-bedroom apartment with a small alcove that was just big enough to hold a bed for me, with room to spare for my toys. The apartment was on the second floor, on top of Mr. Hart's meat market. Mr. Hart was this round and happy old white man who owned our building. He sometimes offered to have someone from his market help my mother carry her bags of groceries upstairs, especially when she bought a lot of stuff. I liked whenever he offered to do that, because it showed that he was respectful of my mother. And I used to think that my mother returned the favor when I watched her carry a dish of her famous peach cobbler down to him. What I didn't know back then was that it was a sign that the rent would be a few days late.

Cleanliness was a big thing in our home. Both of my parents were neat freaks, and our apartment was always spotless, although we did not have fancy furniture. I loved their neatness, which was a source of pride to me, especially when my friends came over to play.

Once, my father decided to paint the apartment, and because it was so small, Mom said she never expected it to take him so long to finish. You would think he was painting the White House. My mother used to say he was like an artist, always admiring his work, stepping back to make sure everything was just like he wanted it to be. He was meticulous and always very careful not to make a mess.

Watching him paint is one of the last memories I have of my father truly being at home with us. After that, he sort of circled around us but wasn't a part of our lives. He was physically there, but I got the feeling that he lost all feeling for the things that went on around him. He became a master of moving through situations and avoiding the kind of commitment that I would later learn was essential to being a good father. His was a skill that I would see time and again as I grew up without him, in the fathers of my friends who would come and bring little gifts, but not really give very much of themselves. And because he was in and out of my life, I didn't have all of the experiences that help a son to develop into a man.

My father's name was James Albert. He was tall, with bushy eye-brows that seemed to stretch from one side of his forehead to the other. His skin was the color of a bright copper penny. Two things are most prominent in my memories of him: his love of clothing and the way he threw a baseball. My father knew how to wear clothes. He had a long black furry jacket that was belted at the waist. Its collar stood up stiffly when he turned it up, and the fur had a zig-zaggy pattern that never seemed to be disturbed no matter how often or how long he sat down in it. When he wore that coat he was a sharply dressed man to be reckoned with, and those who saw him would nod their heads in appreciation of his style.

When it came to baseball, well, he was prime grace on a ball field, at bat or in the field. Especially when he was gliding over the outfield grass to get under a fly ball. It was almost like he was whispering, "Here ball, here ball," and the ball obeyed and came and settled in his glove.

At the last family reunion he attended before he left us for good, my father arrived late, which wasn't unusual. His lateness allowed him to make a grand entrance, and that was okay with everyone because no party ever really started until he arrived. Anyway, at the reunion we were all sitting around—my mother and her sisters, cousins, and uncles—in Prospect Park in Brooklyn, waiting for him. Food was cooking, people were talking and laughing, my mom was jiving with her sisters, and my older cousins were playing baseball. I wanted to play with them, but they were older than I and said I couldn't play because I was too short. But then my father arrived. I saw him at a distance, walking through the park, and knew that when my father got there, my cousins would let me play, because they always wanted him to play with them.

My father's reputation as a baseball player was legendary in our fam-ily. From a young age, he had a gift for throwing and catching a baseball. In fact, my father often said to me, "You know Booby, I had a shot at the Negro leagues, but Willie Mays took my spot." There was some truth to his story, because my mother always confirmed what he said. "He let that damn bottle get in the way in the end," she'd say. So he lost out but man-

aged to pass along his throwing and catching abilities to me I guess, because after high school, seven colleges offered me scholarships to play
baseball for them.

Playing ball together is one of my fondest and dearest memories of my
father. It was an experience that I miss now. He picked up my glove in a
way that I never did. He looked at it with longing, touched it tenderly,
like they both—he and the glove—knew things I didn't know. And
whenever he picked up my glove, it was a silent signal to me to run
and get my bat. I never asked him if we could play. Rather I waited and
watched him go through his ritual of picking up my glove, pounding his
fist into the pocket a few times, and then he would arch his thick eye-
brows at me and wink, and we would go play. Whenever he played with
me, I felt this energy inside and was able to soar a bit with him. And his
love for baseball was one of the gifts he passed on to me. A gift that he
gave to me freely, without asking what someone thought about it.

My father liked to give me presents. He said he liked the way excitement welled up in my eyes and the way a shy smile flitted across my
mouth when he handed me a gift. But thinking about it now, I'm not so
sure. There were often times when he gave me a gift and then would ask
me what other people, like my mom's friends, or his friends, thought
about it. "Hey Booby," he'd say, "what did Fats say about the bike I
bought you?" Or, "What did John say about that new toy? What did he
say about that?" But as a kid it didn't matter so much. And even now, I
know he meant well, because one of the things he passed on to me was the
joy of giving things to people to make them happy, and I know he wanted
to see me happy.

Another lasting memory of my father is of the weekends, when another, very different side of him came out. It begins on Saturday morning
with Moms (I always called my mom, "Moms") cooking breakfast,
scrambling a whole bunch of eggs, and making biscuits and grits. Those
breakfast smells would drift into my alcove and tickle my nose, gently
easing me out of sleep. By the time I got out of bed, my dad was already
outside talking to some of his buddies, yelling and laughing and cussing,

which we could hear through the window that Moms kept cracked open, rain or shine, winter or fall. "I'm lettin' some air in" she'd say, when sometimes I'd find her sitting there, silently looking out onto the street. Although we were on the second floor, it was easy to hear the hum of the voices of the men gathered on the street down below. They were talking mostly about numbers. My dad was a big numbers player. For hours on end, it seemed that's all he talked about, numbers—playing numbers and running numbers. On those Saturday mornings, when he didn't have to go to work, when he could spend hours talking on the corner with his friends, he would ask me, "What'd you dream Booby? Did you dream any numbers?" Just to put myself in the center of his life, I would say yes and make up a number. A couple of times my made-up numbers made a hit, and he gave me the money to give to Moms. But win or lose, every Saturday, hours at a time, that's all he ever talked about. I cannot remember him ever talking about racism or politics or white people, or even that there was a place just across the river called Manhattan.

You see, our lives back then were lived in the moment. What we were doing that day, that moment, that second, was all that mattered. No past, no future. None of that talk, "I'm gonna do this one day" or "I'd sure like for this or that to happen one day," like other people talked. You'd think a gambling man would dream about what he'd do with a lot of money if he ever won big, but if my father ever thought about that, he kept his dreams to himself. The way we lived our lives was in the present.

No one ever talked to me about making something of myself, per se. Education was about being able to go to the store and being able to count your change. God? God did not enter into the conversation. The Church did not exist, not because my parents didn't believe or want us to believe, but because back then, at that time in their lives, the moment was what mattered the most, and the Hereafter was part of the future. There was this pervasive sense of just being, existing in the moment and living life just in that fraction of time. And that sense of instant living was so dominant in everything that happened to us as a family. There was no pressure to do anything, but just get through the day.

My father and mother never let us know that they didn't have enough money. Or that my father was struggling to find a job that paid him well enough to take care of us. I'm not even sure my parents really understood it themselves. If they did, I'm not sure they understood that it was something they could have changed, with just a little planning. Or, if they did understand, they buried that understanding of how they could plan for our lives to be better so deeply inside themselves that it had no chance of unexpectedly reminding them at odd moments of all the dreams they once had. That was how we lived. Saturday morning was a good time in our house because my father and Moms saw it as a day that was meant to be lived just in the moment. And that's how they lived it, all the years of my growing up.

Saturday morning would drift into Saturday evening, and on one particular Saturday evening, although it wasn't a special birthday or celebration that I can remember, many extended members of our family and neighbors were crowded into our living room. I was sitting in my bedroom, with my toys gathered around me, watching everyone and everything in the living room. I did that often—just watch and listen to conversations. Whenever my mother's friends came to visit, I hid behind the sofa and listened to them talk about everything. I really liked listening to adults talk, with them not knowing that I was there. I heard what was going on in the neighborhood, who was cheating on whom, what father had left his children, who had lost their job, and so on—things young ears wouldn't normally hear if they weren't in the wrong place at the wrong time. And although I didn't understand everything, I learned a great deal about my family and our world.

On that particular Saturday night, there was music, loud music. But as loud as it was, it became background noise to the adults talking over each other. There was plenty of beer drinking and numbers picking, and smack in the middle of everything was my father. By then I knew that, for my father and for most of the people he hung out with, drinking was an essential part of their lives, sort of like watching the news at 6 o'clock every evening right after work. It was a way to distract yourself as you passed the day. It seemed everyone who hung out with my father drank, everyone except my mother, who as far as I knew never took a sip of liquor in her life. In those days, I never connected my father's drinking with him getting into fights or getting beat up or being jealous or argumentative. That would come later. On that night, they were just a bunch of people hanging around, living for the moment, talking about what we're doing now, *"Hey ain't this cool?"*, moving about the room, traveling, without getting anywhere. My father too seemed to be always moving, although the life he built around him seemed to remain still, not going anywhere.

After hours of talking, laughing, and cutting up, he said to everyone in the room, "Let's go across the street to The Baby." My father took my hand and said, "Come on Booby, you're going with me." And off we went across the street to The Baby.

The Baby was a bar called The Baby Grand, and it was almost directly across the street from our apartment. The minute the door opened, a whiff of musty air hit you in the face. The air was thick and heavy with the smell of beer, as if the mop water used to clean the floor was actually beer, or at least flavored with it. For as long as I can remember, all bars have smelled like that to me.

Once inside, surrounded by the musty smell and a soft haze of smoke, my father took me around and introduced me to each and every woman in the bar, saying, "Look at my son. Look at my son." I knew he was proud of me. And it made me feel good to be with him. Many of the women said "He is so-o-o cute, James. He's gonna be a lady's man just like his father." And then they all laughed. Some of the women even gave me money, a dollar to buy some candy, they'd say. We stayed at the bar a long time that night. After a couple of hours I wanted to leave. I kept looking at my father, hoping he would see how tired I was and take me home. But I knew he would not get up until he was ready. And that wouldn't happen until he was too tired or had too much of his favorite drink.

As soon as we hit the street, he asked me for the money the women had given me. Maybe I had four or five dollars at most, and I wanted to give it to my mother. But my father was insistent. As we climbed the steps to the apartment, he was still demanding that I give him the money, reaching for my hand, which I pulled away from him easily because he wasn't trying very hard in his mellow state. The next thing I remember, we are in the apartment and he is trying so hard to get the money he is grabbing at me, and he is so out of it that I can't make out a word he is saying. And then I hear a thud, and my father is lying in a heap on the floor. My mother has banged him over the head with the top of an ice bucket.

I watch my mother wedge a pillow under his head and put a blanket on him and then she puts me to bed also—first her husband then her son.

Come Monday, however, my father is back at work. For all his drinking, and all his attempts at making it big with the numbers, he is a very hard and steady worker. At first he worked in a candy factory and would come home smelling sweet, like a piece of candy. My mother would get real close to him when he came home. She didn't hug or kiss him, but she smelled him, his clothes, and his hands. And he stood there and let her smell him. It was their ritual. And he often brought home candy for me.

Unfortunately, the candy factory job didn't last for a long time, and it was followed by a series of others. The last one he had when he was living with us was in a factory that built toy banks made out of plastic. They were shaped like gorillas, monkeys, and pigs. There were plastic animal-shaped banks all over our house, but they never had money in them. If he didn't come home with one of those banks, he came home with something else, a new toy for me or Chinese food, but he never came home empty-handed. Those were good times for us. But that all changed when my sister was born.

Once she arrived on the scene, even when my father was at home, it felt like he was half there. And from then on, I heard him talk to my mother differently, really short in his answers and rarely teasing her the way he used to. He stayed away more and came home later each night. One night shortly after my sister's arrival, he came home so late that my mother, worried, asked him, "Where have you been?" He had come home late before, and she was usually not one to ask him to account for his time, but he had never come home this late. And he said, "It doesn't matter where I've been. It's where I am." He had come to stand in my alcove. I had been asleep, but he picked me up anyway and took me over to the kitchen cabinets and stood me up on the counter so that I could play the drums on the cabinets. He held me steady so that I wouldn't fall and said nothing more to my mother.

My mother's name was Thelma May, and I liked to call her Moms. When I was young, she had soft hair that was nearly shoulder length. She once told me that she smoked since she was three years old, although I had no way of knowing if that was true. She was the oldest of seven sisters and came to New York City, with five of her sisters, hoping to make her dream of being a nurse come true. They were all able to find jobs cleaning houses in New York City. But, instead of putting that money aside to pay for the education they needed to have the careers they wanted, they went out every night, going from club to club, partying. That's how my Moms eventually met my father. And once she met my father, seems she somehow misplaced her dream.

Everyone called my father a lady-killer. His angular face and red-copper skin, his strong forehead dominated by thick eyebrows, made all the ladies, including my mother, think he was handsome. He was very much aware of his looks, which Moms said her sisters warned would cause her plenty of trouble later on. My father also did a great impersonation of James Brown, who was my mother's idol. When he did his James Brown impression, that was it for her; she was convinced that he was the one. She said it was one of the reasons she had such a thing for him, because she loved James Brown, and my father reminded her of him. And that was part of the problem. We all rallied around when my father did his James Brown thing. He used to stand up there and hold his cigarette and do that famous JB slide. I loved to watch him do that, not because I loved James Brown, but because it was one of the things that made my father happy. There's nothing for a son like having a happy father, one he can look up to and laugh with. But afterward, when things got serious, my father used to say to my mother, "I ain't James Brown."

After that night at The Baby, everything changed. My last happy memory of my father in our house is of him watching TV and wrestling with me one Saturday morning. He really got into wrestling. It was violence without anybody getting hurt. It was all an act, he told me, and he loved it. He used to laugh out loud at what was going on, and I liked to hear him laugh, because when he laughed, it felt like everything was going to turn out all right. Somehow, he would come back to us, I thought for years. But for all my wishing, it didn't happen that way. Life's not like TV wrestling; it doesn't follow a crowd-pleasing script.

I learned he was gone for good on the day that my mother, my sister, and I went to his job to pick up some money. He was still working in the plastic factory. We walked into the factory and waited for him at the foreman's office. When he came, I saw his face, and he wasn't smiling. He didn't even say hello to me. He didn't turn to face us, and he didn't talk to me at all. It just felt strange to be in his presence; he was not at all like the father I knew. I felt this thick sadness around us. We were in the middle of a throbbing busy factory, yet between my father and mother, it was quiet. Not even my sister cried, which was not normal for her. Standing there with Moms on one side and Pop on the other, it felt like there was this thing between them, as though they were standing in two separate worlds. And by the three of us coming to him there, we had somehow invaded my father's world, something that had been private and his alone. I felt like saying, "Moms brought me here! I didn't want to come!" He didn't once look at me during the exchange with my mother, and it wasn't until we were walking away that something in me said, "Turn around." I did, and he gave me this real quick glance, and it seemed like he was sad. Just a quick glance and then his head went down and he turned away. I felt really heavy in my chest, and I knew he felt the same thing too. I just sensed that something was bad between him and Moms.

It's funny, because I couldn't have been very old then, but I just knew. When the two people who gave you life aren't together anymore you just sense it. There doesn't need to be an argument, or for someone to slam the door. It's a sensation, the way the air feels around you in their presence, and I felt it that day in the sad glance from my father. And each time I saw him after that I felt his sadness.

But I knew something else in that moment, I knew that my father loved me. With that one quick glance at me, I felt that he was trying to tell me he was sorry, sorry because there was nothing he could do to make things right. Which made me feel even worse, because I felt I had to take a side. And I had to be on my mother's side. It was a natural thing, because I was with my mother, I lived with her, she was with me all the time, and she needed me. She was my mother. And I knew he understood that. His feelings, the pain I saw in him that day, made me know that he understood the choice had been made for me.

Once we left the factory that day, my mother took us to buy food, and then we went home. But from that day forward, my mother never really talked about my father to us, or explained what had happened. After that day, he came over to see us, but he no longer lived with us, and whenever he visited, he was never quite all there. Sometimes he would come over and be a little tipsy and at other times he would be on his way to being completely and totally wasted. He rarely came over sober. And if he sobered up while with us, he would leave.

Unfortunately for all of us, on the day he got us kicked out of our apartment, he took longer than usual to sober up. It was a Saturday, cold, bright, and sunny. Back then it seemed as if everything important happened on a Saturday. My father started arguing with Mr. Hart and, of course, threatened him as he did everybody when he was drunk.

He got into that argument with Mr. Hart for silly reasons, he and Moms later agreed. Apparently, Mr. Hart said something about my mother's cooking, which my father thought was the best cooking he had ever known. Mom had given Mr. Hart something that he didn't like, and he dared utter words about the food not being prepared well. My father got upset because Mr. Hart didn't give Moms the food to cook. She bought it from him, and he was selling that food to his customers. So, my father said something to Mr. Hart, who didn't like what my father said, so he told my father to get out of his store. And then the arguing really started. Upstairs, Moms and I just heard them yelling. We couldn't hear exactly what was being said. By now I had come to learn that whenever my father had a few drinks, he was the biggest and the baddest man around and he could beat anybody's butt, even though when he was sober he couldn't kill a roach without scrunching up his face like he was in pain.

The rest of the events of that day are hard to forget. Mr. Hart and my father arguing downstairs, my father eventually coming upstairs, cussing and fussing. My mother yelling at him, "What are you doing, what are you talking about? Leave that man alone. He is my landlord." And then the next thing I remember is the four of us walking down the street in the bitter cold looking for a place to live. My father is walking with us, even though he has long ago moved out.

My mother is pushing my sister in a stroller down Dean Street in Brooklyn. It is a long row of brownstones that were beautiful and quiet in their elegance. But none of those brownstones were waiting for us to come and live in them. My father is walking behind my mother, and I am walking with him. Everything is quiet except for the crunching his shoes make on the pavement, his long strides, outstretching mine. I am tired, trying to keep up with him. Who knows why, but suddenly I just stop and say, "I'm not going nowhere." "What did you say?" he asked. And I said, "I'm not going nowhere, I hate ya'll." He turns to me, takes his belt off to hit me, and I pull away. As I do, he swings the belt and it misses me except for the buckle, which hits me on the tippy tip of my thumb. And because it is so cold, the pain from that contact shoots through my entire body, and I feel it throbbing to my core. I am quiet for the rest of the day.

We go to each of Mom's sisters. We walk from house to house, but they all put on the same face that says they don't have space for us. My father then takes us to a whole bunch more "friends," who also don't have space for us. What hurts most is that their faces don't say, I feel sorry for you, but rather their faces seem to say, I feel sorry for me having to deal with you, for having to deal with your problem. And I feel sad inside because of that face. I hated having to go from door to door and then being turned away. Years later, however, I realized that this would be the last thing we did with my father, the four of us as a family together walking down Dean Street in the cold looking for someone to take us in.

Finally, my father took us to a woman named Gloria, who turned out to be my godmother, although I didn't remember ever meeting her before that moment. When Gloria opened the door, her face was different, like resignation with the inevitable, "Yeah, all right, I'll do it," with a smile. We went into Gloria's house, and it was dark and I bumped into things as we walked into the living room. My father took Gloria aside to speak to her, and the next thing I remember was my parents leaving me and my sister there and Gloria putting me to sleep on her sofa. I closed my eyes but I couldn't sleep. Not even a little. I stayed awake all night, thinking about what had happened to us, walking down the street, that belt buckle hitting my finger, which was still sore. That night seemed to be the longest I had ever known. I felt ashamed and confused inside. I felt my mother's shame when she came back alone to get us. I couldn't wait to get out of there, and I had my clothes on long before she came back. I was sitting up ready to go when she knocked on the door.

We went back to going from sister to sister, and still none of them had room for us, so we ended up in a homeless shelter in Brooklyn.

The shelter was really a hotel. Our room was very small and seemed to be dominated completely by the bed in the center of it—the biggest bed I had ever seen in my life, covered by a green padded bedspread that fell halfway to the floor. I bent down and looked under the bed and saw a red fire truck. I don't remember how we walked to the building, I just remember being on the seventeenth floor in that small room with the big bed and some other kid's toy truck, looking out the window.

I leaned over the edge of the window and looked down. There were yellow cabs darting around traffic in the street below, and I saw the big clock that stood in the middle of downtown Brooklyn. It looked so far away. I leaned over as far as I could and spit. I watched the ball of spit break up as it fell from my mouth and headed down to the street below. I hung over the ledge and remember thinking I shouldn't be doing this, as I watched the spit fall and break up. Then my mother called me to come and take a bath.

It happened so fast. My sister and I washed and my mother dressed us in our pajamas. Although I was nearly six years old and three years older than my sister, I wasn't a big kid, and Moms could still pick us both up. Wrapping an arm around each of us, she picked us up and walked toward the window. I don't know how, but she stepped out onto the window ledge with me in one arm and my sister in the other. We were all together out there, on that ledge, in the still, cold night air far above the city. I don't remember how it felt to be so high up off the ground. It really wasn't clear to me what was really happening, except that it all felt wrong. I was standing on the window ledge with my mother and sister, and I felt like my father was looking up at us. I don't remember leaning over and looking down, but I had the feeling that he was there on the street, looking up at us. It seemed like we were on that window ledge forever. And then my mother looked at me, and I said, "Ma, I don't want to die." Without saying anything, with one swift move she pulled us back into the room and cried. She sat on the big bed and cried and cried and cried.

After that night, Moms never left us and we never went hungry. Whenever we went outside, the first thing my mother did was call my father from a pay phone. I would hear her say, "Okay, as long as you are working on something." I never thought he abandoned us. I knew he hadn't. I just knew it. Maybe he wasn't being too successful, but he was working on something.

Soon, somehow, through my father, we got an apartment on Gates Avenue. It was in Bushwick, another section of Brooklyn. The street we lived on was divided between the haves and the have-nots. We lived on one side, and the haves lived on the other. My father came over every other week. He was sometimes tipsy when he arrived. But by then, I couldn't wait for him to leave, because by then I didn't like my father for what he had allowed to happen to us. I was angry with him, and I was ashamed of my mother. As I look back on that time, it makes no sense but that's how I felt, angry with him and ashamed of her. He had done this to us, but she had let him.

The "this" was that we were on welfare. I was old enough to know what that meant. I didn't like to go to the welfare center, and one day I said to my mother, "Ma, I don't want to come here. I don't ever want to go in there again. I hate this place." My sister just stood there waiting while my mother stared at me. She didn't say a word and never tried to explain why we had to go to that center, but that day, standing in the street with a son talking nonsense, my mother said, "Ganious, go play with your friends." After that day, she never made me go back to the welfare center, and each time she had to go she made arrangements for me to be somewhere else. She didn't give me a hard time about it; nor did we ever talk about it again. I just never went back. Of course I ate the food bought by the money she got from those visits, but I never felt like going with her was something I had to do.

Our first Christmas on Gates Avenue was one of the hardest I had known. There was no money—zero. The first humiliation came on Christmas Eve in the form of my uncle Donald, who came over to see my mom and caught a glimpse of our Christmas tree. It was very Charlie Brownish, sort of pathetic and anorexic. The balls were hanging off skinny, bent limbs, screaming for help. Uncle Donald was sitting at the kitchen table, and my mother was trying to find him something to eat even though she knew we didn't have any food that she could proudly give to company. She didn't know how to tell her own brother that she didn't have any food to give him. But then, he started to talk about the tree, and he laughed at it. When he laughed, I saw something click in my mother. She laughed with him, but I saw how her body stiffened. I could hear her laughing with him, but I could tell she wanted to cry because I felt that way too. Ever since that moment, I haven't been able to look my uncle in the eye.

That night, after Uncle Donald left, we spent the rest of the evening wrapping gifts. We were all going to spend Christmas day at my Aunt Bouchie's house, because my grandmother and grandfather had come up from the South to spend Christmas with the family. We couldn't afford to buy any gifts, so my mother had us wrap whatever we could find in the house, mostly gifts given to us the year before. We spent the whole night washing statues or ashtrays or dishes, and we wrapped them up in whatever wrapping paper we had. It got to the point where my sister and I hid the things that we really liked because we knew if we didn't, they might end up being wrapped as gifts for someone else. But after a while, when there was nothing left to give, we both told Moms she could take our hidden stuff. I don't know who felt worse when she took them, our mother or us.

On Christmas morning, I wore nine pairs of nylon socks, and I was still freezing as we waited outside looking for a cab to take us to Aunt Bouchie's house. I felt so cold, but most of all I remember feeling so terribly sad for my mother. I was looking up at her, and I felt this sadness, this shame, coming out of her whole body; she just seemed so ashamed. She was looking down at the ground; she never looked me in the face. I tried to take her hand as we waited but she wouldn't let me. She didn't help me find a cab but stood stiffly in the street with my sister at her side while I looked for one. When we got to Aunt Bouchie's place, we didn't have any money to pay the cab. My mother looked at me, and I opened the door and went to the house to get my aunt to come out to pay. I knocked on the door but it took a long time for anyone to answer; it was still early and everybody was sleeping. The shame that I suspected filled my mother now welled up inside of me. Before you say Merry Christmas to your aunt, or even good morning, you have to ask her to come out and pay the taxi that brought you to her house for Christmas breakfast and dinner.

I waited on the steps for Aunt Bouchie to come out and pay the driver. Then, once she had, my mother and sister got out of the car. The whole time, my eyes were on my mother, who seemed to grow smaller before my eyes. Her head hung lower, her shoulders slumped, and she didn't even look at her sister. For the rest of that day, I don't recall her looking directly at any of us.

That whole day everybody seemed to be looking out for us, feeling sorry for us by the way they let us go first whenever meals were served. We went first when it was time to open gifts, and I saw the way my mother's sisters looked at each other whenever they mentioned their husbands, as if to say *watch it,* so that my mother wouldn't get upset. They all seemed to act careful around us, and I just remember looking around the room at everyone, and for some reason this strong feeling of anger came up inside of me. I was angry and ashamed at them for how they responded to my mother, but at the same time I felt angry at them for what I was going through, even though it wasn't their fault. I didn't know whose fault it was, I just knew something was wrong with the way we were living, having to struggle just to get by. Even though my mother was getting money from welfare, it didn't last. It never seemed to be enough.

Things got even worse that day when we started opening the gifts. The floor beneath the tree was covered by beautifully wrapped gifts, except for ours. Finally they got to our gifts, and my Aunt Bouchie tried to be nice when she opened the ashtrays that my sister and I had wrapped, but the look on her face said it all. It was easy to see that same expression on my cousins' faces as they opened their gifts too. It was pretty painful for me to watch. And then we opened their gifts to us, and they were like these *care* packages—dried peaches, pinto beans, Fruit of the Loom stuff, not really Christmas gifts but useful things to help us survive. Stuff that you gave poor relatives when you couldn't take them in.

Every Christmas wasn't a total bust. Even when he wasn't around, my father brought us gifts, and it was always stuff I wanted, never junk. One year he bought me a set of drums that lasted one day because I banged on them so hard I ripped a great big hole in the top of them. Another year he bought me a black-and-white TV, and I wrote my name on it in big bold letters, so that everyone would know it was mine. Somehow, through all the troubles, my father always managed to bring me something for Christmas or for my birthday, even if it was late. But the most important thing about gifts my father gave me was that he had to be there to give them to me. And my mother knew that I needed all of my father, all that he could spare me. So, no matter what happened between my parents, she made my father feel welcome when he came to see me, and that was her gift to me.

Actually, my father came around whenever he could. And in his own unique way, he showed me that he loved me and was proud of me. He continued to take me out with him once in a while—although I was older now—to show me off to his friends. At the end of the school term, I could count on him to come and get my report card like clockwork and stuff it into his pocket to show to his friends later. He collected them along with all of my school awards. He was very proud of me, but he was also very proud of himself for being my father. And that's not a bad thing for a kid to see. You made your dad a little bigger, and that made you bigger.

Although neither of my parents understood how to make their lives better, somehow they both understood that their first priority was my sister's and my well-being. They were very consistent about us being okay first, no matter how things were between them. No matter how little money they had, we always had something to eat and school clothes— even though I had to wear my sister's corduroy pants that were at times too tight for me and itched in the wrong places. And in their own strange way, my parents were very responsible. I could never go out to play until I had done my homework, and by 7:00 P.M. every evening, no excuses, I had to be home, whether it was still light outside or not. I could hear my mother three blocks away on any given day: "G-A-N-I-O-U-S, get your butt up here!" And no matter how often we asked, we weren't allowed to stay up late. We had to be in bed at a certain time no matter what, so we could go to school with a good head.

Even as kids, especially through the really tough times, my sister and I realized that my parents loved us, and we loved and respected them. I always tried to be a good kid. I studied hard and did well in school, and I listened to my parents even though I sometimes didn't like what they had to say. The one time I talked back to my mother, she said, "I'm gonna tell James"—that's what she called my father—and I remember feeling good because that meant I would get to see him. It had been a while since he had visited, and many of my friends didn't have fathers who were close enough to be called to come and discipline them. That same day, I had talked to my friend Tyrone about his dad, who had sent him a radio but never came to visit. On that particular day, whatever I had done, Moms said, "I'm gonna tell James," and it made me feel good. My mother could tell my father and he would come and whoop my butt, because that's your daddy's job, and I could live with that.

A few days later, my sister and I were playing with a ball in the house and it rolled under the bed. I struck a match to look for the ball, and the bed caught on fire. My mother was sleeping in it, and my sister was calling "Ma! Ma! Fire! Fire!" I was so scared that my mouth felt frozen shut. I couldn't say anything, I couldn't even move. Finally, my sister was able to wake my mother up. "What's that burning?" she asked, and I could finally speak and yelled, "It's the bed! It's the bed, the bed that you're on! It's on fire, it's on fire!" She somehow managed to pick the mattress up off the bed and throw it out the back window.

Then she called my father, who came over, took me in the back room, and said, "Act like I'm beating you." I didn't understand why he didn't beat me, but was very happy to pretend with him, dancing around the room, pretending to cry and scream, like I was getting a beating. That was the most fun I ever had getting a beating. Later on that evening I said something smart to him, sucked my teeth, and he took me in the back room and whooped me big time for burning that mattress.

It was shortly after that evening that I found out why my father never came back and lived with us permanently, despite the fact that he and my mother often laughed a lot together and we all had good times. He was married to another woman. One day my mother just decided it was high time we knew the truth and took us over to his house. We went inside and I heard him yell into the room, "Booby," and this big, big boy comes out. That was the day I learned that my father had another son he also called Booby, a name I thought was special for me. Without me ever knowing anything, he had been living with them the whole time he was married to my mother, even when I was a little boy. I didn't know, couldn't figure out, how he could do that. I realized this was where his energy had gone. I felt many things at that moment, but most of all I felt a lump in my chest, so hurt that my brother had his own room, games, football equipment, things that I didn't have. Things I thought I needed. Goodness, he even had a dog. And their house was filled with pictures of him with my father, and I could see they had been places together, places he had never taken me.

Later on, I learned that my brother's mother had died and that my father was a single parent. I also learned that my brother was sick with a chronic hormone condition that caused him to grow too big for his age. He died when he was twenty-five. Was that why my brother got so much more of our father than I did? Or was it because he was a better son, knew things to do or be that I didn't know? And the worst part of the whole situation was that no one talked to me about it. No one ever asked, "Ganious, are you okay about this? Is there anything you want to say about this, Ganious?" It was a major blow to me—I felt like I lost my place in life, like I lost my special relationship with my father—and I had to deal with it on my own.

When I was nearly twelve years old, a man named "Fats" Brown came into our life, and it seemed as if he would change everything for us. He was a WWII veteran, an ex-marine sergeant. People said he was a hero in the war, in Europe, where there were some all-black fighting units. But then he came home, and there was no decent work for a black man, not even a black hero. "Thank you, boy, and for your reward you can have any of those Negro jobs you might have had before the war, shining shoes for chump change, or in a bank, mopping the floor after hours." So he became a hustler, earning money any way he could and my mother never told us how. But he always had money in his pocket. Fats was like a brother to my mother and seemed to always treat her with respect. He took me on as a surrogate son, and he looked out for me and bought me things and became a consistent male presence in my life, something I had been missing since learning about my father's other family.

Fats had a soul food restaurant that he wanted to sell, and he knew my mother was a good cook. So he decided to sell it to her for one dollar. And that started a new phase for us as a family. It was some of the best times; we had money, my mother was cooking everyday—something she loved to do, and people loved the food. For once, it felt like life was indeed good for us. Those were happy times, seeing my mother get up and open that gate to her own business, hearing the sound of that gate rolling up, the sweet sound of respectability.

Owning and running that restaurant was my mother's first job, and she was good at it. When she had the store she was the happiest I'd ever seen her. She didn't have set prices on her menu; she'd say taste it first and tell me how much it's worth. And her customers would do so and go "Hm hmm hmm," and she would say, "You know, that's a five dollar hm hmm hmm."

I loved my mom before she opened that restaurant, but I was especially proud of her during that time. She acted like she was worth something. I saw it in her face and how she walked straighter and talked to people more readily, holding her head up more often than she did before. She even had her name in the window, "TOOTS." It was a little hole-in-the-wall restaurant, the kind where you know the food couldn't be anything but good. After school, I'd often come with one or two of my friends and it felt good to be there with her, making food and serving customers.

People must have paid for their meals, but the funny thing is I don't remember seeing any money ever changing hands. I never saw money being passed along in that place. But the restaurant didn't mean money to me. It meant my mother was happy, a respected store owner, doing her special thing. When my father came over, he seemed proud of her and that restaurant too.

But in the end, we were only able to keep it open for one year. There was something about past bills owed that my mother couldn't pay. Or at least at that time she thought she could never pay them, and we didn't know what to do or where to go to get help. So the restaurant was closed. A little while later when the place was sold to someone else, we found out that the past bills were just old utility bills that could have been taken care of. We could have worked it out, paid them off over time with the place's earnings. But nobody told us how to do it, and we didn't know who to talk to, who you sat down with to work it out.

And that was where my mother's lack of awareness came in. She had never seen a problem and then faced it, sat down with whoever she was having the problem with and said, "Hey, how can we work this out?" Life had taught her that there was no use trying to stop bad things from happening, just let them happen and deal with it. She was just too damn used to letting life happen to her. It hit my mother hard when we had to close the restaurant. So damn close we were, and then no more.

I started to figure things out about life when I made friends with kids who lived on the other side of the street. You see, before that, my home, my parents, they were the world I had made for myself, a tiny circle. It was like culture shock interacting with people outside of that circle. My mother had her own way, her own language. She would create sounds. She was almost a country unto herself, with her own laws. And she didn't do many of the things that other people did, like using utensils regularly to eat her food. She used any piece of bread that she had to eat with and clean up her plate. She never used a knife, just speared the meat with a fork and tore off a mouthful with her teeth. That's how I ate too until I made friends with Charles, who lived on the other side of the street. Spending time with Charles I learned to cut meat with a knife.

Charles and I became friends after his bike was stolen by one of the bullies on our side of the street. We played together nearly everyday. I was one of the few kids able to play equally well with people on both sides of the street. I remember that when Charles and his mother came to our house I was embarrassed about our furniture. I had been to his house and it was nice, with a color TV, a telephone, and stuff, and what I thought was nicer furniture than what we had. It was kind of sad and funny because here we were right across the street, and our living room was in the kitchen, we sat in the bedroom, everything was sort of all together, even though it was clean. Charles came over with his mother, and my mom was eating dinner. When Charles and his mother came in, my mother stopped eating, took out a knife, and put it on her plate. But she didn't go on eating.

My mom invited them to eat with her. Our neighbors and friends often came over to eat because of my mom's good cooking, so it was normal for her to offer food to everyone who dropped by. But Charles's mom said no, she didn't want anything. And I thought she said it in a high-handed sounding way, as though she looked down on my mother's offer of food.

And then I watched my mother change toward Charles's mother. Her spine just straightened up and she said, "Oh sweetie, whoever stole his bike will probably not bring it back. Why don't you just sit down and have something to eat." She became very proper. When it was just the three of us at home, my sister, Moms, and me, we sometimes didn't completely pronounce a word. We called it "saving syllables." But with Charles's mother, Moms put all the syllables back into her words. I thought at first she was playing with the lady, but then I realized she was trying to do some serious impressing. And that feeling of being ashamed again welled up inside me. I hated that feeling. And I didn't lose that feeling until I became an adult myself and became a spiritual being, which allowed me to begin to look at both my parents very differently.

When I began to believe in God, my image of my mother completely changed. I was no longer embarrassed by the fact that she had let herself go physically, that she didn't pronounce all her syllables, or that she didn't use utensils the way everyone else did. I stopped feeling ashamed that she had never fought to become the nurse she wanted to be or that she had the most unrealistic view of my father and of her own life. Instead, she just became someone who was beautiful to me. And all that she had been in my past, everything she had done, I could finally see clearly without pretense and it became beautiful, even the yelling at us. And maybe my forgiveness of her allowed her to forgive herself. All those years I was growing up she was never overly affectionate with me, maybe because she didn't see herself as having earned the right to be affectionate with her children. But when I started to look inside of myself for answers and acceptance, it was as though without saying a word to her, she knew. And whenever I saw her she would grab and hug me and say, "My baby, this is my baby."

When I finally left home and started to live on my own and worked hard to begin living some of my dreams, she started to say how proud she was of me and that she knew I could do anything I wanted to do. She wrote that in a letter to me, and I still have that letter.

It wasn't long after I left home that my mother started declining physically—although I didn't know the full extent of it at the time. She developed cataracts and couldn't see very well, and she gained a lot of weight. She was eating too much and often sat in the window of our house and watched people pass by on the street below. From that point on, she lived life through that window. She hid from me that she not only had cataracts but also by then had cancer and was in need of money, and just how lonely she really was.

I lived with her until I was twenty-two, but I never moved very far from her. I could tell by the sound of her voice on the telephone that she needed me. At first, I thought I felt so tied to her because she didn't jump off the window ledge that day and take my sister and me with her. But it was more than that. My mother never bought herself anything, but she got us everything we needed. We never lacked anything really important, and she never stopped telling us that we had to be good kids. We had to do well in school, do our chores in the house, and not get into trouble on the street, because that was the one way we could have a chance to do other things. Staying out of trouble allowed us the chance to dream about a bigger world than the world we lived in.

I used to think my mother and father never wanted to be or do anything. And that confused me. I couldn't imagine not having any aspirations or settling for making just enough money to get to the next week. Maybe that's why I took to traveling once I was old enough to do so. I got my passport and made it my business to travel whenever I could, for work or pleasure, because there was a time when I didn't think I would get past the square block that we lived on. Once I started traveling, I kept going, and my mother would just wait for me to come back and would tell me how proud she was of me. It was after one of my trips that I brought her an autographed picture of James Brown, and of course she flipped. When she got sick with cancer, one of my friends introduced me to Isaac Hayes and I asked him to write her a letter. These men were her idols.

It was only when my father also got sick with cancer and was dying that I realized I had to do my own thing and not try to make up for what he hadn't done with his life. It was the same with my mother. When I recognized that she was settled in herself and that sitting in front of the window in her apartment and watching life go by made her happy, I stopped trying to live my life the way I thought I had to.

I went on to film school because it was something that I had wanted to do since high school. After film school, I had some great experience working as an art assistant on films like *Malcolm X*, and learning that I had to have something inside of me that pushed me to move forward. I spent a lot of time in my teens and twenties working hard, trying to do some of the things that I thought my mother wanted, like buying her nice clothes and jewelry. But she never wanted those things. She was happy where she was. She enjoyed living where her friends were, and she had her routine. It was my happiness she wanted, and that could have been me doing anything as long as it made me happy.

When my mother was dying from cancer, I had to spoon-feed her. She was in major pain. She only wanted to hear the Bible, and I read it to her. As I read she could only say, "Yes Jesus, yes Jesus." I was never into the Bible myself, but I got into it to help her. At first, I didn't believe what I read. I just wanted to help her, and that was my last-ditch effort to do something that she wanted me to do for her. I had to help her. But somewhere along the way, watching her and trying to help her, I knew that I had to understand what and who Jesus was for me, in order to understand my mother's dying. Even my father eventually found Jesus in the end. Before he went into the hospital for the last time, he used to answer the phone by saying, "Jesus loves you." Watching him, I knew I didn't want to wait until the end of my life to find God.

Understanding my mother and father as they truly were came only toward the end of their lives—when I was spoon-feeding my mother while she was dying and shaving my father before he passed on.

I loved my father because I saw early on that he had so much to give. I never deluded myself that he had made a success out of his life. But there was something special about him. He just lit up a room. When he walked down the street, he talked to everybody, and everybody knew him. Whenever he arrived on the scene, everyone's mood changed. He had great energy. It was just harnessed in a way that didn't always serve him well. He was very free in the way he lived and couldn't be told what to do. He did what he wanted. He took risks and loved it.

When he died, I thought he had left me without telling me the whole truth, and I would have to discover it using whatever clues he left me. Who was this man, my father? I knew he loved me. Every time I ever looked at my father I knew he loved me. I was surer of his love than I have ever been sure of anything else. I felt it in his energy whenever we were together. And I think my mother did too. Looking into their eyes was like being home, and I haven't felt that in a long time.

Through the rough times of my growing-up years I never doubted that my parents loved me. They did the best they knew how to do. Everything they had ever done for me, all the moments and events of my life with them, I can string together, and they tell this story: I was blessed to be their son. Everything they were afraid to do, I am free to do. And they are the reason why. They gave me the two most important things parents can give their children. First, they loved me. And second, they gave me themselves to love back.

ᏈᎦᏌᎦᎧ *Ganious is a poet and an aspiring filmmaker living in New York City.*

"Deddie," 1999

Early days—
(left to right) Vuyo,
Mama, Andile, Dad, and
me in Manzini, Swaziland,
1971

A gathering of family from South Africa

The Way Things Were

❧

Everybody's story starts with that person's earliest memory, and I have many early memories. But, in another sense, my story begins even further back, before my birth. For mine is a story of a destiny, my own and my family's, and the destiny of my people. A destiny that my father knew and served long before he thought about my birth. How do I put into words those signals given me, some subtle, some not so subtle, that taught me I am of a people? I am anchored by these threads of memory— my own and those that my parents passed down to me—memories that I am happy to hold on to. Some are elusive, like tattered pieces of cloth, while others are as vivid as the very real events that formed them.

I was born in a little country called Swaziland, while my parents were in exile from their home in South Africa, and so in my earliest memories we are living in a country not our own. Over time, this fact would come to define how I saw myself as I grew into womanhood—always as an out-sider. We had to move from Swaziland to Mozambique when I was still very young, and even there I was an outsider.

I have many vivid childhood memories of my life in Swaziland, which borders South Africa. I remember a family feast. I am about five years old and there are many people, many voices, and many smells. It is a gathering-together meal, repeated at least once a year, I would guess, but this is the earliest I recall.

My mother's family has come to visit us in "exile." People are laugh-ing, and there are the sounds of voices, with smiles and furtive glances exchanged, kisses of welcome, and the embraces for and from each new-comer, reminding me that I was missed, that even in absence the little five-year-old still counted with these people who are my relatives.

Through my child's eye I revisit the day. I am all dressed up and so is Mama. And so is everyone else in the house. The house is filled with people and with noise. Too much noise. And Mama has no time for me. Through the window in the kitchen I see Deddie in the backyard, stand-ing under the papaya tree, bent over, his back to me. I am thinking I will go outside to be with Deddie, when I see another man is with him, hold-ing all four of my dog's legs in his hands. My dog is not really a dog, my mother has often had to remind me. It's a sheep, but I call him my dog because my friends have dogs and I want one too. Why is the man hold-ing my dog? Why doesn't Deddie tell him to let my dog go?

Now the stranger bends lower, and so does Deddie. Deddie is press-ing down on my dog's head with one hand. I think he is hurting him, and I want him to take his hand away. Then I see the knife, a long knife. I cover my eyes and run to find my mother.

I hear my mother's voice, but there are so many people in the house I can't get to her. I want to tell her about Deddie and the stranger and what they have done, but as I get closer I see she is already crying. I know she is not really crying sad because I hear her say over and over again, "Oh it is so good to have you here. It is so good to have my family with me again."

People call out my name, Phola, and pull me to them, hugging me, and telling me how much I have grown up. They ask me if I have started to go to school, and I shake my head no. I say I am five years old, and school does not start until you become six. But no one is really listening. They are all busy hugging each other and talking about "back home," and I wonder where "back home" is. I want to pull my mother away, but I can't. I go back into the kitchen and wait for her, hoping no one else will find me first. I am afraid to look out the window because I am afraid of what I will see.

Finally she comes back in, and I tell her about the dog, about Deddie and the stranger and the dog. And I start to cry again. She hugs me and dries my face with her shirt. She tells me not to cry, and not to worry, that it is a sheep, not a dog. That people raise sheep to provide food. And that I must not cry because today is a day of celebration, a day to welcome Mama's family, who have all traveled a long way to be with us in Swaziland, all the way from South Africa. She explains to me that the man had to kill the sheep so that she can make a welcome meal that will honor our guests. It will show them, she tells me, how much we love them and have missed them.

My mother tells me to go back out to the living room, and as soon as I do, one of my aunts pulls me to her, telling me again and again how much she has missed me and how beautiful I am. One uncle, who is very tall, lifts me way up in the air before bringing me down and hugging me. He points to some kids and tells me that these are my cousins, but they are all boys so they will not be much fun to play with.

My father's fellow teachers and our neighbors who live alongside us in Swaziland also come to the house to greet my relatives. There were no formal invitations sent out. People just came. You demonstrated your humanity by sharing everything that you had—your table, your food, your pain, your joy. That was the custom. People just came whenever there was something happening at a neighbor's house.

Another knock at our door and I run to see who is there. It is other teachers who work with Deddie at his school. My mother comes up be-hind me and puts her hands on my shoulders. "Come in," she says. "Come and join us." Every time we hear a knock at the door, I run to the door to open it and my mother comes up behind me. Even the funny lit-tle Indian man and his wife from #3 down the row come. The wife is holding a big dish of food in her outstretched hands, and they come in and sit with us and laugh with us and suspend time for a moment, forget about the daily weight of life's struggles, while we make welcome these relatives of mine from a home that goes back to before I was born, to a country that was mine by heritage but not by birth.

My aunt takes my hand and says, "Let's go see what your mother is cooking." She leads me back to the kitchen and tells my mother, "We've come to see what all these delicious smells are." She holds my hand as she lifts lids off pots and lowers her face to smell the bowls of food covering the table. "Oh my," she says, "that *umqgusho* smells delicious." I know what she means. I love the tiny white kernels of corn, or samp as my mother sometimes calls them, and the tiny carrots and potatoes sitting on top of big pieces of onion. I hear my aunt lifting lid after lid and calling out, "Just look at that beetroot salad, Phola. Your mother knows that is one of my favorites. And how could I forget that your mother makes the best roasted chicken in the family and she never gives me her secret recipe. Look at all this food, the pumpkin, and the lamb, all the things we enjoy. My dear Phola, this is a welcoming. Your mother is a fine cook."

Finally, we are all crowded around the table, and I can barely move my shoulders because there are so many people at the table. And then Ded-die begins to say thank you and welcome. I am sitting in my mother's lap and someone takes my hand as everyone around the table takes the hand of the person next to them. We all turn to Deddie, who is standing at the head of the table. The humming of voices gets less and less as Deddie's deep voice says, "Welcome to everyone, welcome one and all! We are so happy to be together with you here in Swaziland. This lovely country, which is not our own, has given us refuge so that we can continue to hope and fight for the freedom of our beloved South Africa. Today, we are happy to be with you, but we are sad too as we remember our fallen brothers and sisters of the ANC (African National Congress), who have paid the highest price for the freedom that will one day be ours. We must continue the struggle for their sakes, and the sake of our children. One day very soon we will be blessed to celebrate the freedom that we have fought for long and hard, and we must remember, comrades, that God is with us."

And that is where my second memory starts. It comes back to me like an old friend who thinks I have forgotten her. It is one of shoes. Pairs and pairs of shoes, lying all over our tiny hallway, spilling into the living room, as though searching for places to hide themselves, forgetting their owners for a moment as they rest from the weariness of the journey. A ragtag army of shoes paused in their long march, combat boots alongside sneakers, flat black shoes and brown ones, men's shoes and women's shoes, all sizes, the toes of one pair touching the heels of another, at times nearly covering the entire floor. There are big shoes, little shoes, shoes that are brown with mud, shoes with holes in the toes. They are jammed into corners, some on top of others where there is no longer floor space, and under the couch, as if these had sought out a quiet haven for their rest. When no one is looking, I put my feet into as many shoes as I can.

I must be older now because I associate the shoes with getting dressed for school. Sis Thoko lives with us and takes care of me and my brothers and helps Mama with the house. She fights with me to get into my school uniform in the mornings. It is a boring brown with a green stripe. But once I agree to put it on, Sis Thoko always lets me pick out my headscarf. I love my headscarves and wear one everyday. One of my nicknames soon becomes "Doekie," an Afrikaans derivative of headscarf.

Sis Thoko takes me to the bathroom and watches me to make sure I fully brush my teeth. "Don't forget to rub Vaseline on your skin; it will get dry and crack if you don't," she reminds me. So I do as she says and rub Vaseline all over my body. Now we are finally ready for breakfast. In the kitchen, while I eat my porridge and brown bread, I finally see why there are so many shoes in the hallway. The room is filled with men and women I do not know. They are all barefoot.

My mother kisses me and watches me eat breakfast. The other people smile and look at me too. Some talk to each other but most stay silent. My mother introduces all the men as *Buti* and *Sisi,* terms of respect for an older brother and older sister, but she calls everyone "comrade," and that is what they call her. At first, I wonder who will be here when I come home from school. But after a little while, I am so used to someone being here, or even lots of people being here, that I barely notice who has come and who has gone since I left the house. These visitors are part of our household, like Sis Thoko. It never occurs to me that this isn't the way "normal" families lived.

I cannot say when I started to understand that our family was different from all the other families I knew. It all happened so gradually. First I realized that my father was the only father who had two jobs. During the day, he is a teacher of literature and language at a local Catholic boys' school. By night he is what my mother and he call a "freedom fighter." I don't fully understand what he does, but I know that he is fighting the Boers and that the Boers are cruel and mean to all black people. These people who come in the night are "comrades in arms," fighting with him.

"You have lots of brothers and sisters," my school friend says when I bring her to my house to play one day. "Yes, she does," my mother says. I say nothing. Later in the day, as soon as I say good-bye to my friend, my mother calls me into the kitchen and tells me she has something to talk to me about.

"Don't talk about the fact that there are lots of people staying here or that there are meetings here," she says. "Or that we call each other comrades. Everything that happens in the house is not something you should tell teachers or your friends at school. When you are a little older, I will explain everything to you." I remember how different her voice sounded when she said that to me, but then she hugged me and her old voice returned, and I knew that everything would be all right.

From then on, I just accepted that in our house there would be lots of people coming and going. That when it was really crowded we would sleep on the floor of our parents' bedroom or all together in my parents' bed. And that when the house emptied, we would go back to our own beds.

Most evenings, after we finished our homework, we would quietly go into the living room where all the comrades would be gathered, each one with a story to tell. We kept hearing about a place called Soweto. To us— my brothers and me—it seemed like such an exciting place, where men were chased by police dogs and had to jump over fences. I remember being told that there was some kind of war being waged there by my Deddie and these people who owned the shoes.

And then, finally, late at night, after we had gone to bed, there was always activity, and Deddie was often out of the house. Long after I'd gone to bed, I remember the sound of the door to the spare bedroom opening and closing. I don't know how I knew by then that there was something or someone in there that we mustn't know about or even ask about. All I knew is never to go into the spare bedroom. And never talk about it. At night, after bathing and storytime, my brothers and I filed past the spare room, casting quick glances at the door, but we never asked our mother who was in there. Nor was the door ever opened when we walked by, even during the day when we came home from school.

Although there was lots of additional activity in our house, my parents tried to structure our lives as much as possible. In the morning, my father got ready for work; my mother drove us to school in her VW, and then went on to her job. Sis Thoko greeted us when we came home from school with juice and delicious peanut butter and jam sandwiches on brown bread. Then I changed out of my school uniform and went outside to play. At night, first we did our homework, then we listened to the stories of Soweto, and then we brushed our teeth and went to bed. To us it was a perfectly normal life. After all, we knew no other way.

Still to this day, when I see shoes lined up at the door, like after a rainfall, I tense up. It is not a rational tension. But I know it is there, disturbing me. But if you ask me was I frightened back then, I would say no. I never remember being frightened in those early years because the way we lived seemed so perfectly normal to us. Except for the evening when Bobby's parents came to talk to my parents about something I had said.

When I heard the knock at the door I ran to see who was there. It was Bobby's mother and father. They said hello to me, but they weren't really friendly the way they were when I played with Bobby. They asked me if my mommy and daddy were home. By then my mother was already coming to the door.

Bobby was a boy I played with at school. He was an American, he said, and his parents were in something called the Peace Corps, he told me each time I asked what they did. I liked playing with Bobby, but I was also confused because Bobby was white and all the Boers were white.

"Your child has called our child and us pigs," I heard Bobby's father say. "Where does this come from?" I didn't wait to hear what my parents would say. Instead, I ran into their bedroom and got under the covers and stayed there until I heard the front door slam. My mother then opened the door to their bedroom and sat down on the bed.

She was quiet, and I said, "They are white people, like the Boers, and the Boers do bad things to blacks." All of the people who came through our home and belonged to the shoes were black and Indian and colored, so the enemy must be white, I thought. My mother hugged me and told me that not all white people are like the Boers. "You must never say that again," my mother said, over and over again. "These people came here to help, and you must learn to judge people by their behavior and not their appearance. We don't hate white people." Then she began to explain to me something that I had never really understood: that we were fighting the Boers because of what they did to blacks and not because they were white.

She told me the story of my father, how when he was just a few years older than I was, he lived in South Africa, where he was born. To help earn money, he worked along with his father picking oranges on the farm of a Boer farmer. One day, tired and thirsty, he ate one of the oranges.

The farmer accused him of theft and hit him on the side of his head and burst his eardrum. My mother, with tears in her eyes, told me there was nothing my father or his father could do about it because in South Africa there was no justice for blacks who were treated badly by whites. "Your father grew up young and black in South Africa," she said. He learned about apartheid firsthand and watched his father struggle as a sharecropper to feed a family of seven. His family had to move from the farm to the townships—places outside the city limits that the whites had carved out for all the blacks to live on. "Your father wasn't even allowed in town when he wasn't working. And he had to carry papers, called a pass, which said who he was and where he lived. He could be stopped at any moment by the police, taken in, questioned, and even hurt. He couldn't even move around without a pass." Even when he went on to mission school, my mother said, some of the priests were cruel to him. That's why, my mother told me, when my father's family moved to the townships, he was ready for an outlet, and it became politics. "From the age of fourteen," she said, "your father became an active member of the African National Congress, the ANC, to fight for freedom, for racial justice for his family, and for all black people."

It was that night that I slowly began to understand who my father was and why we were living the life we were living. In a very simple way, I understood that Deddie was a freedom fighter and that, with my mom, he helped to fight "apartheid," which she described as cruelty and injustice by the Boers to black people. This was why, she now explained, there were all those shoes in the hallway and people in our house at night. They were also freedom fighters in the struggle, fighting apartheid any way they could. That night I slept with my mother and father in their bed, holding on to my mother as tight as I could.

Soon I could not remember a time when there were just the five of us—my two brothers, me, and Deddie and Mama—in the house alone. By then, Deddie began working late into the night. Sometimes I wouldn't see him at all during the night. And then I began to worry about my parents. I remember going to primary school and coming back home wondering if either Mama or Deddie would come home at night to be with us. And then somehow I learned that Mama was being followed. That's when I became even closer with my brothers. I tried to do everything with them because I felt better when we were all together.

But things got worse, and I couldn't shake the feeling that something terrible was about to happen to us, to my Deddie. Each day it seemed like something frightening happened to someone we knew who had been fighting alongside Deddie in the struggle, and it was just a question of time before it would happen to us.

And then the car was moved. You see, one day we went out to go into town, and our car was gone. We finally found it, just a short distance away from the house, but everyone was upset. My father, I learned, had just installed a new alarm to make sure that, if it were stolen, we would know about it. I asked my mother who took our car, and she said she didn't know but believed it had been moved as a warning. "A warning about what?" I asked her. She took my hand and held it tight but she didn't answer me.

That night I listened to her conversations with the other comrades in the house—by then, I realized you could find out a great deal if you just listened to those discussions. The South African police had moved the car to scare Deddie. From then on, whenever the alarm went off in Deddie's car, which happened often, my job would be to run upstairs to my room to see if the person who had done it was escaping across a sandy patch of ground visible only from my room. I used to feel so cold up there alone. And afraid, afraid that I would see someone and that someone would be running away only to return a few minutes later, except this time he would not be alone. I made up this story in my mind that the alarm going off was just a signal to tell our enemies that we were home. I even started having problems sleeping through the night.

Then there were the bombs. It sounds so strange to say it now, but by then, from listening to the comrades coming in and out, I knew about bombs, grenades, and guns the way other children knew about kites and rollerskates and dolls. And I knew about the tricks that the South African police used, like booby-trapping cars and sending parcel bombs, things that many adults didn't even know about. One day, I came home from school and my mother pulled me aside and told me that for the next couple of weeks, two of the kids we played with from the neighborhood were going to be living with us. Something terrible had happened to them, she explained. Their parents were part of the movement, and they had been killed by a car bomb. She didn't give me the details, and I don't know how I learned exactly what had happened—probably the way I found out everything else, from listening to the comrades—but they saw it happen, those two kids. "Come on," their mother must have shouted, the same way Mama always said to me when I was late. "Hurry to get in the car," she must have called out to them, as one behind the other, brother and sister ran from the house to get into the car. And as their feet touched the steps, their mother watched them come, smiling, as their daddy turned on the car. And then the car burst into a fireball. Replaced by red and yellow flames with thick black smoke pouring from the flames. Somehow, miraculously, neither child was hurt.

After that, calmly, almost matter-of-factly, Deddie told us to be extra careful around the house, especially if we saw anything that looked unfamiliar in the yard or near the house. He also showed us how to search under the car for unusual looking stuff before getting into it.

And then there was the mail bomb intended for Deddie. It had been addressed to him and put in our mailbox. Ordinarily we kids collected the mail, or Sis Thoko. But that day it was someone else, because our mailbox was used for ANC mail as well. The man who picked up the parcel opened it, losing his arm in the process.

In the midst of all these horrible things, my brothers and I played a trick on Deddie, a trick all kids play, but one, in our situation, that we should have known better than to try. But we were still kids, and despite all the worry, we believed that nothing was ever going to happen to us because our parents always had this way of making us feel safe and secure. Maybe it was the calm way in which they delivered bad news. Maybe it was the feeling of goodness that comes from helping other people in need or the gentle way my father had of speaking to everyone. I don't know. I just remember that one night, while my brothers and I were getting ready for bed but not asleep, we got the idea to go outside and scare Deddie as soon as we saw him walking toward the house.

Our plan was simple: run outside and hide behind the bush next to the front door and jump out at him just as he came to the door. We stayed absolutely still, my brothers and I, hushing each other so our giggles would not give us away. And then, as planned, as soon as Deddie came near the door, we jumped out at him. And there it was. A gun. In Deddie's hands. Pointed at us. We screamed in terror. "Deddie! Deddie! It's us, Deddie, it's us!" I will never forget the look in Deddie's eyes. He dropped the gun and grabbed all three of us. I think that was the moment that did it for him. The next thing I remember I was sitting on the stoop crying with my brothers because we had just learned that we were going to move to a new house in a town called Maputo, in a country called Mozambique, about three hours away from Swaziland. And we would have to go there ahead of our mother and without Deddie. They both would take us there, but we would have to stay with the ANC representative in Mozambique until Mama found us a house. Deddie would come to visit when he could, but not to stay. With that news, my brothers and I sat down and cried.

It happened so quickly, the early morning when we left Swaziland. Mama and Deddie drove us all the way to Mozambique. There we pulled up to a house and sat in the car and waited. Shortly thereafter, a man and a woman pulled up in a white car, and we watched them get out and walk toward us. They smiled and looked happy to see Deddie. They were from the ANC, Deddie told us, and they would take care of us until Mama could come back. My mother kept saying that she would come back soon, but I kept asking, "How soon will you come?" and she kept telling me, "Soon, Phola, very soon."

They left and I cried watching their car pull away, until the woman took me inside to the kitchen. I got absorbed in the kitchen, wiping the counters and cleaning, and I didn't cry for very long. At home, Mama let me clean the kitchen even though sometimes I didn't do a very good job. She knew I liked to do it and let me.

My brothers and I were afraid of the woman we stayed with. Mostly because she wasn't very nice. And all she seemed to eat and drink were dry bread and tea. Was that all we were going to have to eat until our mother came? We were ecstatic the day Mama came back. We couldn't stop talking and jumping into her arms and trying to get close to her. Our Mama had come to get us.

Mama drove us to a house not far from where we had been staying with the lady. It was a tall, narrow house with an upstairs. I later learned it was another teachers' quarters. We stayed in that house less than a year. Then we moved to a bigger house, one with three floors and lots of gardens, and each one of us had our own bedroom. All of a sudden we lived in a house with plenty of room, and all the shoes were our own. We had bicycles and rode them to school. Our mother was there almost all the time. When we were at school she was at work, but when we came back for lunch, which was a two-hour break in Mozambique, she was there also. And then, like a special bonus, we had her in the evenings as well, all evening, just to ourselves. And on weekends she often took us to the beach or to the lovely terrace gardens of Mozambique. Always some-place fun. And there was no talk of bombs and no other people staying in our house. It was just us, the Mabiezelas, and for the first time that I could remember a calm fell around us. And we were happy.

There were still people visiting us but not living with us all the time. Our lives now seemed to be the way my friends lived. Normal.

My brothers and I started school, even before my mother returned. It was an "international" school, with children there from many countries. All the classes were taught in English, which we had been speaking since we were born, although the children we played with in the street spoke Portuguese. And then I found out that a couple of the teachers—my biology teacher and my geography teacher—were South African. They even knew my father, and I called them Auntie. Our lives seemed calm except for one thing: the long stretches of time without Deddie.

It was in Mozambique that a new family tradition began. Every December, for a month at a time, we went to see my mother's family and then my father's family. I remember those trips as if they were yesterday.

First we would travel by car from Mozambique back to Swaziland to get picked up. At the Swaziland–South African border, we got into a train and took it as far as Durban. There, one of my mother's brothers came to fetch us by car and take us to the Transkei, a homeland area, a town of blacks under black autonomy that was sort of a haven inside South Africa. That was where my mother's family lived.

We'd stay with an uncle for a few days and then an aunt, and they always treated us wonderfully, as though we were somebody very special to them. Then we would prepare to leave the Transkei to visit my father's family. They lived in a section of Port Elizabeth that had been designated for blacks only, a location or homeland—and by law whites couldn't live there, and blacks from other areas had been moved out of their houses and forced to live together in this one area. But, unlike the Transkei, which was black ruled, Port Elizabeth was part of South Africa proper, totally under white rule.

I remember how horrible our reaction was the first time we visited Port Elizabeth. To begin with, there were no lights on the streets or in the houses. People lived in shacks. The streets were dirt roads carved out among the shacks. There was no electricity, no running water.

Then we learned that all my father's relatives lived in one small house. And the house had no toilet inside. We thought, *oh my goodness, it is not only outside, but it doesn't flush.* It wasn't a toilet at all, but a bucket. And there was no running water to wash our hands afterward. We had to wash our hands from a small hand basin of warm water on the stove.

At the same time we felt trapped inside the house because, being black, we were very restricted in our movements. If we wanted to buy a hamburger or fries from the Wimpy, we had to stand at the take-out window. We were not allowed inside, which brought apartheid home to us kids. We just didn't understand why we didn't have the freedom to move around as we wanted to, the way we did in Mozambique.

Still my father's family succeeded in making it fun for us kids. We were taken on outings and shopping trips. Sometimes we'd go to the town proper, and sometimes we'd go to the colored area, Halston, which was safer than the town, where you could so easily be harassed. Port Elizabeth was a port city, east of Capetown, on the southern end of Africa, and had a beach. There was a place called Play Land, with a Ferris wheel, horses, and games, and we really enjoyed that. Despite their lack of means, our relatives spoiled us. They tried so hard to make us happy, but there was always this thing hanging over our heads in Port Elizabeth. This thing that we shouldn't go outside unless in the company of a relative who knew all the crazy laws about where blacks could go and what they could do without provoking a beating from the police or maybe even arrest.

Later on, when we were older, on a visit to my father's relatives, one of our relatives took us with him to his friends' home. They were white and lived in a white area. On the way out, we passed a beach, and there were white police there who stopped us and asked what we were doing in this area. Thankfully, our relative's friend happened to be driving right behind us, going somewhere else, and he got out of his car and said to the police, "This man has come to visit me, to introduce his brothers and sisters who've come to visit him." We were very lucky, saved by the coincidence that our host had set out right after we left his house and was right behind us.

We continued to go on these trips to South Africa, even after it was no longer safe for our mother to come with us. I think they never wanted us to forget that we were South African, that we belonged in South Africa, and that one day, when South Africa was free, we would all go back together to live in a free land as free people.

One of the reasons our parents chose to send us to Mozambique after we left Swaziland was that the new president of Mozambique, Samora Machel, was very supportive of the ANC. Mozambique was the biggest point of sanctuary for the ANC in all of Africa at that time. We had full representation in Mozambique. We had our own political meetings, and there were cultural events. There were always rallies and opportunities to listen to the progress that was being made for the South African people, by the ANC. There were ANC meetings every weekend of one sort or another, and this is where we became ANC pioneers, along with other kids whose parents were also living in exile. It was just a very vibrant political life. And finally we understood what a freedom fighter was, truly understood it.

But I also won't deny that I fell in love with life in Mozambique because it was there that our lives became "normal." Between our wonderful house, the great school, and the complete devotion of our mother, we had a family life of sorts. And one weekend a month or so, Deddie would visit us from Swaziland. I cry just thinking about those visits. Deddie would come in this white Peugeot, which was all beat up but somehow always made the journey. We would run down the walkway through the gate and jump into his arms the moment he stepped out of the car. He still says to me sometimes that he misses that, the way we'd run and jump up on him. He would send word, and Mom would tell us, "Okay, your father is coming this weekend." On that Friday night we would not go to sleep. Instead, we sat up all night, until his car drove up and there he was. And I was always out there in front the moment I heard the car coming.

On Sunday morning, we would all stay in bed with my parents, because we knew Deddie was going back. That's where the pain really started, knowing Deddie had to leave again. It was indescribable, the feeling inside, my heart beating fast, a hollowness. And in the end, I knew it was fear, which came over all of us as we sat there clinging and holding on to him, not wanting him to go, because the possibility was always that he might not come back, that he might be killed by the Boers.

And yet we never felt he loved us less because he had to go. When that moment came, we would walk to the car, all of us, stand around at the gate of the house, and watch Deddie get into his white Peugeot and drive off. We were about five houses from the end of our street. It was a T-junction, and the other side of the junction was the military hospital, and he would drive toward the hospital, turn left, and disappear. There was this huge patch of open land at the corner, and sometimes we would run across it diagonally and try to catch a glimpse of the car, but it would already be gone.

There was a huge hole in all of us after he left. None of us had anything to say. The house became so quiet. During those times, Mama would take us for a long walk to the terraced garden, to walk off the sadness, she'd say. And we walked and walked, surrounded by the tender beauty of flowers and trees and birds. In our garden there was a low wall in front, and sometimes we sat around together after Deddie left, hanging out together, not saying much, lost in our collective sadness, totally miserable. I don't remember that any of us cried often, but there was a sadness surrounding us on the days that Deddie's visit came to an end. His coming and going was really hard to take, something we never got used to.

But through it all, I also understood that the struggle had to be first in my father's life. There were times in conversation with Mama when, for some reason or other, it would come up and I would ask, "Why do we have to do this?" and the answer would be, "For the struggle." We had the sense that this was part of the reason she so loved and respected him— because he was one of those few people who could put the struggle of his people above his own needs and above his own fears.

I also understood that, in going away, my father was making a sacrifice for others and that he was asking us to do the same thing so that another generation of young black South Africans would never go through what he and so many generations before him had already experienced. I do admit that I hated those moments when we had to say good-bye. There were moments when I wished that the struggle did not have to come first, but we lived the struggle every single day. It was like the struggle was the fabric, and our lives were a few threads in it. Whenever things happened to people we knew intimately, their being hurt or even killed, it tore our lives apart, and it was evidence as to why we had to make any sacrifice we could. And for my family, it was Deddie being away from us. I knew that Deddie would never be able to come home and stay with us until it was all over. It was never "When will Deddie leave the struggle so we can all be together?" but instead "When will the struggle be victorious so we can all be together again?"

And so it guided our decisions as a family. When my brothers and I were ready to go to high school and our school in Mozambique ended at eighth grade, we decided amongst ourselves that we wanted to go to high school in Swaziland. First our parents said yes, but later on they decided that the situation in Swaziland might be too dangerous for us. They told us that we would go to boarding school in Kenya instead. My brothers and I sat our parents down and told them that because they had taught us that our family is based on a democracy, we had a right to say we don't want to leave again. We felt we had been moved around enough. We wanted to finish our schooling in one place. We were willing to take the risk, and we would be careful. It was the only time I remember that we were in such stark opposition to our parents' wishes for us.

Finally my parents agreed to a compromise. I would go to boarding school, and my brothers would live with ANC friends and go to another school, but both schools would be in Swaziland. We knew our father would not let us live with him or see him much, because it was too dangerous, but it was comforting to know that he was close by. It was 1982. That same year in February, the ANC leadership decided that my father's life was in imminent danger, and he had to be moved away from Swaziland as soon as possible. Although we didn't know it at the time, he was already totally underground. He didn't live in any one particular place but had what he called "hideouts." He didn't know where he would sleep from one day to the next.

I didn't even know he was leaving until he came to the boarding school to take me out for a weekend. He came on Friday afternoon to pick me up and took me to Mababane for the day. The following day we went to the Wimpy, which was a huge treat. I had a cheeseburger and a bubblegum milkshake, something I'm still stuck on. After we left the Wimpy, Deddie had a bunch of meetings, and I tagged along with him for the rest of the day. It was wonderful being with him. We spent the whole day together and then, sometime that evening, he sat me down. I remember we were in a room with two wooden bunk beds. We were sitting on the bottom bunk, and he started explaining that his life was in danger. There were all sorts of people following him, and it was time for him to leave Swaziland.

If anything happened, he said, we would be looked after by the United Nations High Commission for Refugees. They had our residence permits for safekeeping. So if ever we were challenged, we would be under their protection, so to speak. We were still aliens and not permanent residents, even though we were born in Swaziland. He gave me the names of the people who were going to be looking after us as refugees, and he explained that he would become the chief representative for the ANC in Tanzania and he would see us as much as possible. But, the way my father explained every detail, I knew that he was leaving and that we would not be together again until the struggle was won.

As soon as he dropped me back at school, I walked behind the school dormitory and sat down on a drainpipe and cried. I emptied every vestige of emotion I had. I think that afternoon my childhood ended. And from that point on I hated it there, I felt totally alone in Swaziland.

It didn't help that the culture of the boarding school was such that the bigger girls made you suffer as incoming students and made disparaging remarks about the ANC comrades and the trouble they were causing in Swaziland. I remember one girl who would say to me, "What would you do if I just slapped you?" I don't remember even answering her. I just kept quiet. She never made good on her threat, maybe because she was uncertain of what my silence meant. She became in the end a good friend.

My way of getting back at those girls who tormented me was to be at the top my class consistently every year, every single term. There was an accumulation of marks posted at the end of each year, and I was always number one. I know they resented it, because they resented me for being an outsider and because shortsighted people would tell their children that the movement we were part of made problems for the Swazi people. So there had to be a way for me to be vindicated, so to speak. If my academic life was solid, then it was worth my being in Swaziland. It was a reason to keep going back. And I lived for my studies. I loved my schoolwork, and it was just a bonus that my high grades earned me respect, even a grudging respect from the other girls who resented me.

And the other thing that kept me going were the lessons my parents taught me. When times were tough, when there were ANC cadet funerals, they would sit and talk to us. When there were incidents or bombings or killings, they would explain about the struggle and how we had to be strong and keep fighting and that this was a cause that was worth fighting and dying for. They taught us how to keep going in the face of hardship and pain. It was those lessons that got my brothers and me through our high school years in Swaziland. My brothers and I knew we had to be very strong. And my parents taught us what it took to be strong, by example.

My parents also taught us not to hate, because there was no point in it. We had to correct the wrong that was there. So at the same time that I felt resentful of the treatment I was getting from the other girls in boarding school, I felt this need to explain to them why I was there and why it was important that they support me and not reject me. I remembered how my mother dealt with her frustration, and I followed her lead.

No matter how bad the circumstances we found ourselves in, my mother walked off her anger so that she could concentrate on the important thing—the long-term cause. It was from her that I learned the value of distracting yourself. That's why I guess she so often took us to the beach or to those wonderful terraced gardens in Mozambique. Do something positive for yourself or for others, but don't let the hate get control of you, or the hateful people will have already won.

My father always said to us that the reason for our being in exile, for the difficulty of our lives, was the mis-education of the masses, mis-education of the entire Afrikaner nation. My father was very clear on this point. These people had been indoctrinated very, very wrongly and as a result perpetuated the unjust policies of the apartheid regime. He felt that most white people didn't understand the extent of apartheid and what it meant for black people. And that they needed to be educated and shown how wrong it was. He didn't feel that the average white person in South Africa hated black people or deliberately set out to enforce the ugliness of apartheid. They were just caught up in what the regime told them. And he always told us that we would overcome, sooner or later, not because our guns were better, but because we were on the side of morality and righteousness. We weren't going to win because God was on our side, but because we were on God's side. We were resolved to bring down the regime and its apartheid policies, but when I was visiting South Africa, I didn't walk around the streets hating white people.

One of the most significant lessons my parents taught me was the power of love in marriage. My mother is a bubbly, vivacious, strong person, and she and my dad have a marriage that's very different from what I see with my friends. They have been married for thirty-three years. Each Sunday, when he left her in Mozambique, I remember her sadness. It ran deep, and her way was to be quiet and to walk it off with us. I remember the day my mother's wedding band snapped. The ring consisted of two bands: a plain one and one studded with diamonds. The plain one snapped on a Wednesday. She just fell apart. My strong mother, who I had never seen cry, sat there crying like a little kid who had scraped her knee. Heartbroken, she called my dad in Swaziland to tell him what happened. She didn't stop crying for the entire week. She was in tears every single day.

That Friday, when Deddie came home, he brought with him a new wedding band for her. They went together to have it blessed, and he put it on her finger again. She has it on her finger even now.

The strength of their relationship was also based on an incredible meeting of minds. One of the things my mom missed most when my dad wasn't there was conversation. They talked all the time. And they talked to us all the time as well. And they listened to us and made us feel from the start that our opinion counted and that our ideas had some merit to them. We children felt that if they were willing to listen to us, we must be saying something worth hearing.

They were also very clear on what is okay and what isn't. Fairness was always important. And we could not be cruel. Mother taught us that we could play rough, but never be mean to each other. My brothers and I were all very protective of each other. Our parents taught us to look after each other—something we never forgot when one of us was in trouble—the way they had looked out for us.

There were times in boarding school when I would pray for my parent's safety, I would negotiate with God: "If you look after my parents," I prayed, "I promise I will not do things that will ever make them ashamed of me." And in retrospect, it was like the bargain held. My parents were there for all of us with support and love, through the complete awfulness of apartheid.

They are many things, my parents, but most of all they are warm, loving people. In their family, they are outstanding, and people gather around them. My dad is simple, and my mother has what I call complexities. They let us go in the directions that we wanted to go with some help and guidance, and neither was surprised when I decided to come to America to study.

And then one day, apartheid was over. I was twenty years old; it was 1990. I was terrified. I thought that, because we hadn't taken the country by force, we might still be vulnerable to the Boers. I thought the concessions made and the agreements signed were an indication that we had been only halfway successful and because of this we were all going to have to live in the same neighborhood with the Boers with pistols half-cocked. I was scared. I kept thinking about my father's safety. There had been so many attempts on his life; what would happen now? He had no real protection. His enemies weren't in prison. I feared for his life.

And part of me simply could not believe that apartheid was truly over. In some ways, it didn't feel like it, but there were many things happening around me that said yes, things will be different. And then Nelson Mandela was released from prison. I watched it on television with my family. This man who had been a picture behind jail bars all my life was about to come walking out into freedom. The anticipation was acute; it was as though we were all holding a single collective breath, which we would let out only on the evidence of his actual walking through those prison gates. The first glimpse of his face was an incredible gut-twisting moment. My heart ached. He looked so old. And I thought it was so unfair; thirty years of his life were taken away from him. But Mandela was free!

Would the world finally begin to understand the South African struggle for freedom? Why the struggle had to happen? And why it needed to continue? Perhaps, but it would take time, but for once, time was on our side.

All of us who had been denied freedom, who had sacrificed for the struggle, dreamt, longed and ached for change, now had the hope of a different and new life. We had choices about what to do, where to live, and where to go. When I realized that there was still a great deal of discrimination at the university level in South Africa, I chose to come to America to study architecture at Howard University.

When I arrived in Washington, D.C., I felt as though I had come home. The university environment felt protective, and I developed a very deep bond with African Americans and with their passionate continual uplifting of their people. I made lifelong friends there, people I will never let go of despite the fact that we are now miles apart. And, more than anything, living in America gave me anonymity to live my life the way I please.

My parents are the reason I love South Africa; they are my strongest connection, and I learned from them a freedom to live life the way I desire, the way that makes sense for me. I don't think my growing-up years could have been any happier. I had a great childhood in Mozambique, we were never hungry, we were happy, and everything else was part of the way things were. I wouldn't change a thing, only the many times we had to say good-bye, for we were always saying good-bye.

☲ *Phola Mabiezela is an architect, trained at Howard University in Washington, D.C. She is currently living and working in Pretoria, South Africa, and will be returning to the United States in 2002 to attend graduate school at the University of San Diego.*

My mother with us
in Frankfurt

My family—Frankfurt,
Germany, 1960. (left to
right) Tammy, Daddie,
me, Derrick

Mom and Dad Gordon, 1996

The family—Taiwan, 1965

The Bird Song

I was born during the 1950s in Richmond, Virginia. Just about a hundred years earlier, that same city had been the capital of the Confederacy.

I was named Robert L. Gordon III, after my father, who was named Robert L. Gordon Jr., after his own father, Robert L. Gordon Sr., an Episcopal minister. The first Robert L. Gordon moved from his native Georgia with his family to take over a church in St. Petersburg, Virginia. He was a sturdy, honest, and hardworking man, who believed in being an example to his family. His wife, my grandmother, would die young, shortly after my father, the eldest son, married and became a father himself. During his childhood, my father was a serious young boy. At nine years old, he took on the responsibility of helping to care for his five brothers and sisters. In the mornings, he helped them get ready for school, helped to make their meals, and worked after school to bring in extra money for the family. On Sundays, his place was in the family pew, with his brothers and sisters, instead of playing with his friends, while his father preached his fiery, soul-stirring sermons.

My grandfather believed that education was the key to a better life and was determined that his children would become educated and make something of themselves. So despite the added responsibility fate had put on my father's young shoulders, he went to school every day and was at the top of his class. And when he graduated from high school, he went on to college, where he majored in art. His family was unable to pay for college, so my dad, never one to take no for an answer, joined the ROTC to help pay for school. Once he graduated, my dad found that there were so few jobs for black graduates, and even fewer for those with a degree in art. So, weighing his options, my father accepted a commission as an officer in the U.S. Army, and it became his career. After his retirement, he ended up in city government as a deputy city manager, because helping people was something he liked to do. But during my childhood and teenage years, my father was an officer in the army.

My father stands five feet nine inches and has a medium build, with the Gordon family hook nose, topped with kind, sad eyes. His face exudes confidence and the reserve of a serious man. He smiles to express his agreement or pleasure, but not as much as my mother, who is often smiling and laughing whenever they are together. But maybe my father is so stoical because he had to assume so much responsibility at such a young age. He is very much a pillar of strength and always seems to be in control, no matter what is happening around us and to us as a family. I've seen him very concerned about the many changes that have happened in our life, like moving house, or to another country, or my changing school, or a decision he had to make for us. But, if he was ever afraid, we never got to see it. Thus, it was inevitable we grew up believing that whatever was ahead of us, we would face it together as a family, and my father would think on the situation and then choose a path for us that would make everything all right.

My mother is a petite woman with skin the color of copper, a tiny nose, high cheekbones, and a stand-tall stride, exuding confidence and energy with every step. She was and still is quite beautiful to me. When my mother and father married, she was an elementary schoolteacher. When I was born, early on she started reading to me every chance she got, and I naturally developed a love for books. I also remember all types of games she played with me and my brother and sister when they came along, games that turned out to be exercises that built up our math and spelling skills. In addition to being a teacher she was also the resident hugger, and she'd give me hugs and kisses for no apparent reason except that she wanted to, and I lapped it up because it made me feel wanted and special. School was never a problem for me. All my life, I associated learning with the warmth of my mother's love.

Ours was a small family for the times—father, mother, and three children. I was the firstborn. My sister, Tammie, arrived less than a year later, and my little brother, Derek, was born in between all the moving we did once my father became a commissioned officer.

Both my mother and father would later tell me that the time of my birth was a tumultuous time, not for the family but for the nation. There were race riots and marches and upheavals all across America. Of course, I remember none of that. Nor do I remember my mother's mix of fear and excitement when the army notified her that she and her two children were now authorized to join my father in Germany, where he was stationed. How could I remember? I was just two years old. And yet having heard the story so many times, I can now tell it as if I experienced it last week.

My mother had no idea when she met and married my father that she was buying a tour ticket, destination the world. But she later admitted that that's what she wanted out of life. She had grown up with a sense that there was a wider world that she was missing. You see, my mother, who grew up in Richmond, was very, very close to her parents and, as a result, went to college in a town not too far from them in Petersburg, Virginia.

The farthest her own wanderlust had ever taken her before she met my dad, she once told us, was Pittsburgh, Pennsylvania, for a summer trip. And somewhere inside, she had this need to see the rest of the world.

As far back as I can remember, my mother had a way of making "going somewhere" seem like the most exciting thing we could do together as a family. "I want you to see the world," she would say. "I want you to know how other people live. Go out and explore," she would tell me. Of course, it was a different time then for kids venturing out to explore the outer barriers of their neighborhoods. My mother didn't have the worries that plague today's parents, that someone would kidnap me or hurt me just for the sheer bad of it.

I guess that her great anticipation at finally being on her way across the ocean is what got her and us—my sister and me—through our first great travel adventure, a trip to Germany in the dead of a harsh cold winter.

My maternal grandfather, "Sparky," whose real name was Alex Davis, came to see his only daughter and grandchildren off on the train. My grandfather was a hardworking man. By day, he was a boiler fireman for the American Tobacco Company, where he shoveled coal into a furnace to keep it burning. By night, he drove a taxi. During the war, he worked day and night to provide for his family, eventually owning his own home and sending his only daughter to college. Now he would watch her leave for the first time to go to a place he could not easily visit. I remember his hands and feet the most; they were huge, yet he was one of the gentlest people I have ever known. Later, when I was older, he taught me how to mow lawns in the hot sweltering heat of a Virginia summer, with a push mower whose blades never seemed to be sharp enough to cut through the reedy grass. But Granddaddy Sparky stayed by my side, covering my tiny hands with his large ones as he helped me to push that mower, laughing with me when the mower got stuck for the hundredth time.

Although he was a man of simple means and simple ways, in the wide range of people he knew all counted him a friend. But as gentle as he was, he was a man you would have to answer to if you messed with his daughter. So on the day that we set out for New Jersey, the first leg of our trip to Germany, it was natural that Granddaddy Sparky would be there.

We waited together—my mother, my grandfather, my sister, and I—surrounded by eight big old plaid suitcases filled with our clothes, diapers, bottles, and a toy or two to keep us kids entertained on the long trip ahead. Whenever my mother retold the story of our great journey, she would make sure to include how good she looked, which made my father chuckle whenever he heard it. "You know," she would tell me, "most folks dressed to travel back then, especially when they were going somewhere special. So I put on a two-piece wool suit, hat, and gloves, and a wool coat and shoes that matched my purse, the works." It was her first trip to Europe, and my mother was going in style.

When the train arrived, all of our big suitcases were brought on board by my grandfather, who asked the head porter to look after us. Then, according to my mother, he picked me up over his head to whirl me around and gave me a good-bye squeeze. When the train door closed, I stood in the seat, my mother with my sister in her arms beside me, and we all waved good-bye to Granddaddy Sparky.

In those days, getting a black woman and her kids a berth in a sleeper car to make their long trip more comfortable was not a railroad priority. But, thanks to my grandfather, who knew the head porter, we were able to get a sleeper all the way to New Jersey. Once there, we had to offload all our gear and then take a taxi to McGuire Air Force Base to catch a military plane for the flight to Germany. The kind porter put our bags on the platform and waved as his train pulled away. There my mother stood, looking lonely on that platform with two kids, one in each arm, and eight suitcases.

She had no idea that once we reached our stop in New Jersey there would be not a soul there to help us. Now it's cold, she says, colder than she had ever felt in Virginia; the wind was whipping up and down the train platform, she says, as she tried to hold us and manage the suitcases. And we were on this long platform with stairs so steep she said it took her breath away to just imagine how on earth she would get us and the bags up there. Nobody helped her, and in the end, she had to drag each of those suitcases down that long platform and up the steps to the main station. I was able to walk, she tells me, but I couldn't help her, and she had to carry my sister the entire time.

The saddest part of it all, she recalls, was watching me look at her with those sad Gordon eyes while she struggled to drag the suitcases up the steps, holding my sister in her arms, as I walked beside her holding her skirt. There were people we passed and others who hurried by us, but no one offered help. But my mother didn't care. We were headed for Germany with or without the help of strangers.

It was only when we got to the base that she learned that the military travels at all hours of the day and night and that our flight was scheduled to leave at 3 A.M. that morning. It was not even midnight, which meant we had to wait somewhere until that time. Once again she lugged those suitcases to the taxi—the driver was absolutely no help—and we finally got to the guest quarters, where my mother checked us into a room for a few hours. But in all that carting of luggage she broke her watch and didn't know what time it was. Nor was there a telephone or radio in our room. So she had to go downstairs periodically to check the time.

Finally, at two o'clock in the morning she got us bundled up, called a taxi, which took us back over to the terminal, and then once again had to drag all eight suitcases to the plane. By the time she got there the plane was about to take off. For the first time since we left Richmond, she got help, from an airman, and we boarded the flight.

To this day she believes that she didn't get a lot of help because she was a young black woman traveling alone with lots of suitcases and two babies. The period was one of tumultuous change, a time when segregation and racism in America were being challenged, and there was resistance to those challenges, often with irrational anger and violence. Even the fact that this young black woman and two small children were traveling to be with her husband, who was serving the country in the military, did not earn her any special consideration until she crossed over from the civilian world to the military.

But when I hear her tell that story, it is a tale of victory over circumstances, never a venting of bitterness. What stands out to me is her perseverance. Sure, it wasn't right that no one offered to help her, but she didn't let that stop her. You have to do what you have to do, she tells me all the time. That made a strong impression on me. What happened to my mom really does speak to the times, but some things are timeless. Whenever I find myself in some tough situation—like hailing a cab and then having it pull away without stopping for me; or finding that the best table my early dinner reservations could get for me is a table at the very back of the restaurant near the toilet—when racism imposes itself on my life, I initially get mad, but then I'm reminded of my mother and think, What would she do? Keep your eye on what you want to accomplish and forget about everything except getting it done. In those moments between the train and the plane, my mother knew that if she was going to get to Germany, she couldn't let anything sidetrack her, no matter how tough the situation or embarrassing the circumstances.

Our plane from New Jersey to Germany finally took off in a snowstorm and made its first landing in Newfoundland, where we stayed for three hours. It was like landing in a white tunnel because of the snow, a frightening experience for anyone, but especially for her because she had never been on an airplane before. Our journey continued on to Frankfurt, Germany, where the plane landed on the civilian side of the airport. When we got off the plane, again there was no one to help us. We must have been a sorry sight, Mama all wrinkled and forlorn in her beautiful clothes, standing there with all those bags and two tired kids who had started to cry. After a few minutes of our standing there, not knowing what to do, someone took pity on us and told my mother that our plane had landed on the civilian, rather than the military, side of the airport, and we needed to get over to the military side where my father would be waiting for us. We were instructed to collect our things and get transport to the military side. My mother stood there a long minute, screwing up her courage for one more logistical mountain to climb, when my dad, apparently figuring out what happened, came and found us.

I don't remember how long we spent in Germany, but it couldn't have been long because I have only one clear memory of us there, and it has nothing to do with Germany. But I know it happened in Frankfurt because I remember gray walls, and in all the pictures of our quarters at Frankfurt there are these gray walls.

It is a memory of me dancing. I am dancing alone in the middle of the room, and my parents are watching me. I don't specifically remember them picking me up or anything at first. All I remember is that I am waving my hands from side to side, swaying to the music. I am dancing to a song that I don't even know the name of, but it has loud, wild sounds, with lots of strings that sound like birds singing to each other. Later, when I was old enough to talk, I called it "The Bird Song." That's not its real name. But I call it "The Bird Song" even today. It was dreamy, tropical music, which I will forever associate with my first memory of dancing. Then I remember my mother reaching for my hands and picking me up in her arms, holding me while she danced, twirling me around the room as I waved my hands and swayed with the music. Dancing with her was like flying.

That was the first time I danced to music with my mom who, I would learn, loved all kinds of music. She would rather listen to music than do anything else. All kinds of music—from jazz to big band to country— and all the years of my growing up, I remember her staying up late at night listening to her old favorites: Jack Jones, Johnny Mathis, Glen Campbell, Frank Sinatra. It's because of my mother that I too grew to love listening and dancing to all kinds of music, just as she does. To this day, when I come home to visit her, we stay up into the wee hours of the night, sharing our latest musical discoveries with each other.

By the time I was three or four years old, we were back living in Richmond. As my mother tells it to me, neither one of my parents wanted my father ever again to go on a tour of duty and leave us behind, because we were a family. And I think my parents were determined to prove to us—

and to themselves—that it was not just my father who was in the military but in a sense all of us. We were all in it together. We would survive whatever the military threw at my father because we would all experience the good and the bad together, as a family. And that's how we started our lives in Taiwan.

I had just turned six years old when we moved to a little place called Tien Mou Village in Taiwan. For me, Taiwan was the most exciting place a young kid could ever want to be. We got there not long after General Chiang Kai-shek had established his Republic of China government on Taiwan, after he and his supporters had been driven off the mainland by Mao Tse-Tung's People's Republic of China. This was the period of the two Chinas, each claiming to be the only legitimate government of all China. My father was part of an American military assistance group based in Taiwan to help support the non-Communist Republic of China.

We lived in a house carved into the side of a small mountain in Tien Mou village, very near Taipei, the capital of Taiwan. Our backyard was filled with banana trees, and despite the warnings from my mother not to do so, neither Tammy, Derrick, nor I could resist picking those green bananas and sneaking behind the trees to eat them. And my mother always knew when we had, because like clockwork we each got a bad case of the tummy ache.

The way our house was positioned, from the living room window and the front steps we had a view of a broad expanse of rice paddies and could look down on them as they flooded. I was fascinated as I watched the water running in. When the water finally settled, it looked like an enormous mirror, and the paddies floated on top like little emperors waiting to rule their kingdoms.

Our backyard was fantastic. It led right into a jungle, which was teeming with wild creatures like water buffalo, bamboo snakes, and spiders that made webs so big they spanned the branches of two side-by-side trees. The jungle quickly became my brother Derrick's and my own private playground. Sometimes we wandered it together like pirates or I went with other boys from the neighborhoods—there were always other kids playing in that jungle—and there were days when I left them and Derrick behind and wandered through it alone to the other side. There I found a little village filled with people who walked around carrying baskets on their heads. I sat on the edge of the woods, quietly, never speaking to them, just watching. I'm sure they saw me sitting there, but they never bothered me or shooed me away.

Living in the strange lushness of Taiwan made a deep impression on me, but the most striking thing about living there was the fact that we were one of the very few black families there. We caused such a stir driving around town in our little powder-blue Rambler and were often followed by small crowds. Some people pointed at us, and others even came up to the car and stuck their hands in the window to touch us. It so unnerved my sister that she once retaliated by rolling the window up on a man's hand. I guess they'd never seen anything quite like us, I heard my father tell my mother, and they both laughed about it.

Yet all the attention didn't keep us inside. My mother made sure we were always out in the village or walking with her through the streets of Taipei. It was a city of stark contrasts, with pockets of poverty alongside pockets of plenty. The streets were lined with vendors selling everything from fruits and vegetables to fish and paper animals, like dragons and pigs. There were costumes and shoes, everything you could possibly want. I remember wondering about the sheer number of people I saw on our walks. In addition to the petty cabs, the streets were full of bicycles and people walking and pushing and moving. There were people everywhere, filling the sidewalks, most trying to get wherever they were going in a hurry, and some were squatting motionless in small groups on the sidewalks.

It was so hot and sticky that the heat came off of the earth in waves, making the air feel heavy and thick. The thickness of the air grew worse during the rainy season. And when it rained in Taiwan, you could see it coming, like separate sheets that crossed over the land, drenching each patch of ground as it moved closer and closer, and then passing on.

Our first year there, despite the generally hot climate—the Tropic of Cancer goes right through the island, putting it at about the latitude of Havana—snow came to our beautiful island, the first time in twenty years, my father was told. With the snow came an emerald green mist that rolled down the side of the mountain into our village. And since it was the first time in years that it had snowed, everyone in the village wanted to see it, so there were people everywhere in their cars driving past our house to get to the top of the mountain to see the snow. We all wanted to get a closer look, and my mom and dad packed us into our Rambler station wagon, bundled up against the cold. It was hot inside our box-shaped car as we watched the road, animals, and houses go by on the way up the mountain. As we approached the peak, the road was lined with cars, and we were at the very back of it. It seemed that everyone in the village was already in line ahead of us, trying to get to the top to see the snow on the mountain's peak.

We made progress slowly, traveling on until the traffic came to a halt, which it did frequently. People sat in their cars waiting for the traffic to restart. It seemed that all of a sudden we were noticed, this black American family sitting in their powder-blue bubble car at the end of the line. The people ahead of us started to get out of their cars to get a better look. We sat there watching a growing crowd of people begin walking toward us. They started pointing in our direction, and my father said, "What the . . ." and looked behind us to see what was distinctive enough to have caught their attention. There was nothing, and then it hit him. We were clearly the focus of it all. As the crowd grew and surged toward us, my father made a decision. Without explanation, he threw the car into reverse and steered it back down the mountain.

Later he told us he didn't know why he did it. He didn't know what they were planning, or why they were even walking in our direction. But he just acted on instinct and my mother didn't question him. He had his family with him and he sensed that it might turn ugly. He didn't wait for confirmation. He just saw them coming, and he got us out of there.

I realize now that in Taiwan we were double oddities. First, we were Americans, very unlike the Taiwanese in our style and dress. And then we were black, different in appearance from the other Americans. We received constant attention but were never harmed. None of us, not Tammy, Derrick, or I, ever thought that there was anything wrong with us, only that these people had a driving need to be near us, to examine us. My mother made sure that we were never affected by that attention. She created family activities and took us on trips into all parts of the community, to the museum and on walking tours, and exposed us to every suitable aspect of our surroundings. Now, as I think back on it, perhaps it was also to educate the Taiwanese people a bit about who we were, especially that we meant them no harm. But her first aim was to educate us, to make sure we were comfortable and confident in all of the attention, no matter where we were. If something happened while we were out, something so outside our experience that it could have been alarming to us, or had the potential to demean us, she would take our hands, or make sure that we were all connected by touch, and keep on with the chore at hand, and would respond with, "It's okay, there is nothing wrong with us, these people were just fascinated by a skin color they had never seen before."

But there was another part to her education plan. When we passed beggars in the street, she made sure we understood that they were people with goals and dreams and that they deserved respect too. When somebody in the street looked different from us, my mother always made a point of saying, "See, those people look different from you, but they are neither better nor worse than you. They are just different. Remember that it is not who you are, but what you achieve in life that counts. And you can achieve anything you set your mind on achieving. Don't forget that. You can achieve anything. But you have to set your mind on it."

Even though I was there for just two years, my memories of Taiwan remain vivid. I think it was my mother's sense of wonderment and adventure that made the experience one that I will always hold in my head. Sitting perched on the side of a mountain, looking out into this vast area of rice paddies below me, I had a sense of being in an enclosed community yet felt an almost unlimited potential to explore—and all the time and freedom I needed to explore it.

The life of army children often creates a sense of being rootless, because you are moving all the time, experiencing new things, always having to make new friends, and having to get used to living in new environments. But our parents kept reinforcing the idea that even though we were a military family we were no different than families who weren't in the military. Through attention to detail in our everyday lives and turning as much of our lives as possible into family business—like taking us to school, being at home every day, and helping us with our homework—my mother helped maintain constancy in our daily experiences. And, with this security, we were able to adapt quickly to any changes in our lives and take from our new experiences without losing a sense of self.

My father also played a key role in helping my mother make our lives as "normal" as possible. Even though he worked hard and late, his job was pretty much like other fathers' jobs. He went to work each morning and he came home at night. And the first thing he did when he came home was take off his uniform. Although I was a military son, and ours was a military family, my father never treated us like a military family. We were a normal household. No military stuff in our house; he took off his uniform and was just Dad. He never treated us like he was a drill sergeant and we were the troops. He was just Dad.

There was one time I recall when he wanted a little more discipline in the house. Our rooms were a mess, so much so that my mother put signs on our doors: Rat's Nest for my room and Wolf's Den for my brother's. And although my brother, sister, and I were always clowning around, on this particular day we were especially loud and screaming and running wild, getting into everything. It got so bad that Dad said, "That's it, we're going to get some more discipline in this house. I want everybody to call me sir." None of us minded. It sounded like fun, another family game. Each time we had anything to say it was, "Sir, can we . . . ?" We sir'd him to death so that by the end of the day, he said, "No, never mind. Just forget I said it."

When we finally moved back to the states two years later, he chose to have us live off base in a black community so that we could have a sense of being with people like ourselves, after all those years living as outsiders in cultures other than our own.

In Richmond, my parents bought a home on Griffith Avenue. It was the type of neighborhood where people looked out their windows or sat on their porches watching out for each other's kids and making sure everything was okay. There was a real sense of community, and that supported our family, even when my father worked hard and late into the night and on the weekends.

Although I had fun with my parents, neither ever tried to be my pal or equal. I always knew they were my parents: They set rules we had to follow, like no TV most of the time. My parents didn't want us to spend our lives in front of a TV. They thought it was extremely important to engage us in activities inside the house as well as outside and supported us in any interest that would broaden our thinking. My mother was constantly planning day outings for us, dragging us to museums whether in America or Europe. She also made our house the center of activity for the neighborhood. Although we went to the homes of our friends, all of the cool games and toys were at our house. So the neighborhood kids were often found in our basement playing games, listening to music, and just cutting up. But more than that, whenever other kids came to our house, my mother would become a surrogate mother to them. My friends would confide in her, and she listened to them. She was always empathetic and sympathetic and my friends genuinely liked her. Sometimes I suspected they came just to see her.

That was a very, very important part of our upbringing, feeling so comfortable in our home and with my parents that our friends could come to hang out whenever they wanted to. We were very independent and rarely felt like we had to stay home; when we had to go, we went. But we were always proud and comfortable bringing our friends home.

And then the news came that my father had been posted to Germany once again, and we would all go with him. I was nearly fourteen years old. Just weeks earlier, after a hard-fought campaign, I had been elected president of my junior high school class. Being elected president of my class meant a great deal to me because, several years earlier, when I was nine years old, I had gotten really chubby and the kids had begun picking on me and beating me up. I started weight lifting—in part to lose weight and in part to protect myself—and, as a result, I became a body builder. I never used my newfound strength to pick on anyone else, just to ensure that no one would ever again see me as an easy mark. So being elected school president was further confirmation of my newfound status.

When my parents announced that we were going to Germany, this time the thought of moving made me sad, because we had already moved quite a bit. I associated the move with taking me away from something that felt like a significant achievement—recognition by my peers as a leader. I couldn't talk about it at the time, but when we drove away from school on that last day, as I watched the building and the playground disappear, I felt that the honor of having been singled out by my classmates had been snatched away from me, and I couldn't help but cry.

But once I got to Germany and settled into my school, I knew I would be okay. In fact, the only negative incident I remember from those years in Germany is one involving my dad, not me.

We were in a movie theater watching a film when some of the black soldiers who were fed up with how they were being treated started agitating for some changes. I never really found out what exactly they were upset about, but I know my father had taken me to the movies not knowing what was about to go down. The black soldiers took over the theater while we were there.

My dad was an officer, the deputy post commander. I will never forget what he did that day. He stood up and went to the front and told everyone to calm down. He then turned to the soldiers and said, "Let's talk about this to see if we can come up with a solution." To get the soldiers to open up and talk honestly, he told them he would not give up their names to a higher authority.

Through a series of phone calls with the top brass, the soldiers started negotiations, using my father as the go-between. At one point, command called down—a three-star general who wanted the names of all the soldiers involved. My dad said no. He had promised those soldiers he would not give up their names, he explained, and it was a question of his word. There was a lot of pressure put on him by the top brass, but he never did give up those names. And in the end the soldiers got some relief and many of the changes they were protesting for.

It was only when my father had to go to Vietnam that we were separated. We could not go with him.

It was night, I remember, and we were getting ready to go to bed. My mother sat us down to break the news to us. She was crying, with my father by her side. I remember distinctly that he didn't cry, but rather sat next to my mom, holding her hand, letting her explain to us what was happening. His doe eyes reflected no fear, only concern that we might be upset about it. He held her hand while she said what she wanted to say to us and then added, "I don't want you guys to worry, because everything will be all right. We are a family, and we've been in this together since the beginning. Everything will be okay." Then my mother led us in a prayer:

"Our father who art in heaven, hallowed be thy name. Thy kingdom come, thy will be done on earth as it is in heaven. Give us this day our daily bread and forgive us our trespasses as we forgive those who trespass against us. Lead us not into temptation but deliver us from evil. For thine is the kingdom, the power, and the glory forever and ever. Amen."

When my mother had finished, it was deathly quiet, we were surrounded by the silence, and I kept praying in my head . . . *And God bless Mommy and Daddy and me and Derrick and Tammy and please let this be the last overseas tour that Daddy goes on without us. Amen.*

My father was the keystone in our family structure, and suddenly he was being taken away and nobody could tell us for how long. I had heard Mom and Dad talking before, that we were a family and wherever he was posted, we'd go with him, or follow as soon as he arranged a place for us to stay. But, quite clearly, we were not going to Vietnam. This was one tour he'd have to make without us. I cried for him and for us, but mostly for myself because I didn't really understand why he had to go alone and what that would be like for him and for us.

My mother drove the day he left. Much of it is a blur. I remember we sat in the backseat, the three of us, Tammy, Derrick, and me. We were still and silent. We dropped Daddy off to catch the plane. I still don't remember the good-bye kiss and hug, the last touch of him, or even if we waited until the plane took off. It was all so hard, and none of us wanted him to go. But my father had a sense of duty, and he never deviated from that. The model he provided for us was that fidelity to duty was not a corny thing but tied up with the very essence of a man's honor.

The whole period while he was gone was in soft focus, like I was sleepwalking. His coming back was another matter. Mom told us to get in the car one day and just said we were going for a little drive. She didn't tell us where we were going, and suddenly there he was. He just appeared. We screamed, "Dad, what are you doing here?" We were screaming, crying, and laughing. It was just great. If you can imagine having too much joy in you bursting to get out, then you can imagine how I felt. It was a moment where our family had come almost full circle, together and safe again.

I ended up going into the military myself, but not because my father pressured me to follow in his footsteps. I'm sure both my parents would have been happy with any career that made me happy.

In high school I wanted to be an astronomer. Since an early age, the stars and the heavens have fascinated me, and still do. If I had tried that, I'm sure both my parents would have supported my choice, but other things attracted me. Before the end of high school, I gravitated toward politics. But once I was in the latter part of my high school years, the naval academy started to recruit me, and eventually I got appointments to three academies, including West Point. My father looked over my shoulder at all the brochures I had spread out, and he was there to answer questions for me, but he didn't try to influence my decision. He just said, "Look at everything you have in front of you and make the best decision for yourself." So I buried myself in all those brochures, and only after I had made my decision on West Point did he take me out in the backyard and show me how to execute a snappy right face, left face, and about-face. And a little bit about close-order drill. Just so that in my first week at the academy I wouldn't stand out as a greenhorn who had wandered in an open gate, someone who knew nothing at all about that stuff. In a way, I was just that. You know, even though he was army and we were a military family, I was never brought up as a military son. I cannot remember even one moment when I felt any pressure to follow in my father's footsteps.

One of the best things I remember about my father is that on any score he never really told me what to do. Look at the facts, he'd always say, and make your decisions based on the facts. I learned from his example that a decision made after you considered all aspects rationally was going to turn out a better decision than one you came to emotionally. And he always let me know that he trusted my intelligence to figure out the best course of action.

Now, years later, after the academy and being commissioned as an army officer myself, and then becoming a lieutenant colonel myself, I am proud that I've had a military career and have in essence followed in my father's footsteps. Some people will look at you skeptically if you say your father was army but you were never pressured to go that route yourself. But for me, that is the unvarnished truth. He would have been proud of me no matter what path I had chosen. Of that I was always sure.

I've had a very good career. The military has been good to me in terms of education and providing me with an opportunity for leadership and an exposure to a diverse group of people; I've gotten to command people from different races, religions, and socioeconomic groups. I've been fortunate. I worked for General Colin Powell at a very early stage in my career, as his aide de camp. Knowing a black officer who had achieved so much, coupled with the knowledge that my father had done well in the military, gave me a positive perspective on what I might achieve in my own career. The lesson was clear: No matter what may have gone down in the old days, it was now possible for black officers to make a difference and to be recognized for their contributions. Even though racism was pervasive in the military, it was never an option to use it as an excuse not to succeed. Thus, it was not easy, but it was now clearly possible to be recognized for excellence. Teaching at West Point, I've had an opportunity to help cadets, black and white, build more productive military careers.

My father's experience was different. He was an officer when there were two officers clubs, two restrooms. But that meant he was on the scene to participate in the integration of the army, which must have been a dramatic, frustrating, as well as satisfying time for African Americans in the military.

I want to make clear that it wasn't just in my military ambitions that my parents supported me. As a kid, I was the dinosaur king and attracted a crowd of kids whenever I drew dinosaurs on my sketch pad. I could draw a brontosaurus or tyrannosaurus on request. During my service as an aide de camp to General Powell, who at the time was the assistant division commander to operations and training, I had an interesting experience. One day General Powell wanted to stay in the office for lunch, and since I was his aide I didn't go to lunch either. I sat there and opened a magazine called the *Armed Forces Journal*. Paging through it, I saw an interesting face. I picked up a piece of paper and pencil and drew it, really drew it, not just a photolike copy of it but a stylized rendition. Another staff person walked into the office, looked down at my picture, and said, "My gosh, you really have a talent."

I then took the picture home to my parents, who had encouraged me on and off to start drawing again because I hadn't been doing much with the art since high school. When they saw the picture, they really liked it and the next day went out and bought me all of these art supplies. This was their grown-up son, already established in a career, but if he had a talent they were going to support that talent. That got me started again and, amazing as it must sound, within a short time I had a picture in a gallery. My gift for drawing seems to be for portraiture, but I love doing landscapes too. I did a pastel of West Point, which was shown in a number of galleries. There were so many requests for it that finally it was made into a print and is one of my best-selling pieces.

People often jump to the conclusion that I inherited my interest in the military from my father and my talent for art from my mother. But it was my father who was an art major in college. My mother is more left brain, with a primary interest in language, especially precision in language. She sees the rules of language not as oppression but as protection against ambiguity and consequent misunderstanding. But just to show that these things are never as simple as they seem, my mother picked up painting later on and sold some of her work as well. My house is full of her paintings. I don't have nearly enough free time to paint right now, because I'm finishing my Ph.D. at Princeton and teaching at the military academy. It is a busy life. I used to be a White House fellow and worked with national services, so I chose to do my Ph.D. on National Service Reform.

I was able to survive living in so many different places, all those childhood dislocations, because my parents never failed to support me. They were always there. My mother spent every family outing we had teaching us about the culture of the place, the people, and the environment. But, in retrospect, I think what she was really doing was teaching us about ourselves. Each time someone tried to use race to demean us, she would nip it out right away and remind me that it was okay, constantly reinforcing the idea that I am black and should be proud of that because that's an important part of who I am. Often, she'd play twenty questions with us. She'd pull me onto her lap, and my brother and sister would sit on the floor at her feet.

"What does it mean being black?" she'd ask. "Does it mean you don't have two eyes?" "I have two eyes," my sister would say. "What about your nose, or your mouth," Mom would say, "or your hair? Does being black mean you don't have hair?" And when she said that, she played with my hair, tickling my head, making me laugh. "Do you think being black means that there is something different about you from the other kids?" she'd say, holding me, her face next to mine. "What do you think, Robbie?" I said nothing, but sat thoughtfully in her arms listening to her breath against the side of my face, holding her hands as she held me. "Being black means that you are as much a human child as any other kid in your class," she said. "Being black is who you are, and you have to be proud of that."

It was through my mother's constant reinforcement of my self-assuredness that I came to believe in my most private thoughts that I was okay, regardless of what people might say about my black heritage.

I think because the travel exposed us to so many different races that I am comfortable in any environment, with diversity and with myself. I was fortunate and didn't have a lot of those issues that sometimes plague children who grow up in the inner city.

In retrospect, when I was a teenager going through the rough years with my face breaking out, being a little bit gangly, and trying to connect with other teenagers and people, my parents always had the time to listen. They were hard times for me, but my parents encouraged me in that awkward phase of growing from an adolescent into a man. My parents were there to help me through. No matter what I did in my life, they both made me feel like I could take the chance and step out, and they would love me no matter what.

⌇ *Lieutenant Colonel Robert L. Gordon III is an Academy Professor and Director of American Politics at West Point. Formerly, he was the aide de camp to General Colin Powell.*

My first year
of college

My paternal grand-
father, Ulysses S.
Kilgore Sr., and
my mother.

Ulysses S. Kilgore III, in
uniform as a cub scout

Like Breathing Air

I dream I am back on Provine Street. A recurring dream, a half dream maybe—one of those dreams you have in the halfway zone between awake and asleep. Memory has stored it all, everything in place. I am no more than six years old, walking slowly through the alleyway that runs alongside our apartment building. I can smell the honeysuckle that grows on the overhang, draping down the metal fence, its scent so strong that as I inhale I feel its sweetness in my nose, tickling the little hairs inside. I see the buildings, the alleyway, and my mother with me, holding my hand.

We are on our way to kindergarten. My mother is talking to me as we walk, telling me something about Mizz Bernard, the woman who owns the grocery store. But she is not just talking to her little boy. She is asking me what I think she should buy my father for his birthday, and do I think my father would like a new sweater, and other grown-up stuff. Asking my opinion of things, as if I were an adult, is a habit of hers.

It started—her asking my opinion on things—when I was very young, when I used to spend the hour before supper in the kitchen with her. She would talk to me even before I could answer back, as I sat at the kitchen table watching her, her arms covered in flour as she made gingerbread. By the time I was five years old, I had the job of pouring molasses into a cup and spooning sugar into the bowl as she sifted the flour. I was so proud that she asked me what I thought of various things going on in our lives, and treated me like a grown-up, even though I was still just a child.

My mother was a woman of great beauty, face and figure. Even as I watched her grow old through her later years, her beauty never diminished for me. She was something to look at—skin the color of light caramel, black, black hair, her sweet face topped by little bangs. Her hips were her crowning glory, and I remember well how magnificent her figure looked in those old-fashioned dresses she used to wear. Her eyes and her voice stirred something deep within me whenever she called my name. She often called me her "loving son" or, at times when she wanted to be serious, "Bookie." I'm not sure why I got the name, but to her and to everyone who lived there on Provine Street, I was Bookie.

Provine Street, that long, windy street lined with the apartment buildings and stores, nooks and crannies where we played house in cardboard boxes and made mud pies to pretend that we knew something about cooking, holds the most treasured memories of my early childhood. On the corner of Provine Street was the grocery store owned by Mizz Bernard, who was the kind of store owner who fussed and carried on about people paying their bills on time. But when anyone really needed a hand or some extra time to settle their account, she invariably gave it. Especially to those with children, so that no one would go hungry. Up the street from her store was Anderson's candy store, where there lived a parrot that talked. It quickly became the neighborhood hangout. Next to Anderson's was Potts Kindergarten, where I went to school nearly every day. Diagonally across the street was a store where

Mr. Claude raised chickens and sold them wholesale. My father knew him and often bought our chickens from him. We called his place the chicken store, because it sold only fresh chickens, and no other meats.

The Provine Street of my twilight-sleep dream is fifty years old now. I have been back to the real street as an adult and my eyes, my senses, report that it is no longer my street, that other people live there now, people I don't know, and that Provine is their street now. But something pulls me back night after night, not like a bad dream, but rather like a soothing bedtime story I repeat to myself again and again, very slowly so I don't get to the end before I fall asleep. And then I realize what it is, what I am after, longing for, what it is I am trying to re-create. Suddenly, it is so clear: that sense of belonging and the certainty of my youth.

Provine Street, and the streets around it, the world where I grew up, the only world I understood until I was much older, is an all-black world. All the children, all the aunts and cousins and mothers and fathers, all the store owners, including the woman who owns and runs my kindergarten, are black. And I remember this with pleasure and delight, as well as with a sense of pride, because it was the most nurturing world any parent could want for a child. Not because we thought of it as a black world, but that it was indeed a world where every person who lived, worked, played, or connected with my life in any way, was black like me. The strange thing is that our community of black people, where our neighbors always seemed like family, was never questioned—it was just accepted. We knew there was a "white" world, but it didn't impinge on our world. I was unaware of racism as it exists today, not because it didn't exist but because I hadn't named it anything; nor did those immediately around me call it anything or talk about it. I was just aware that there were two different worlds. It was not anything that I questioned, because everything I needed to make my life complete was right here, all around me.

No matter where your mother or father might be, you were never alone or lonely on Provine Street. If I was hungry or caught in a rainstorm or even just wanted to talk to someone about my day at school, and my mother wasn't home, I could go into anybody's house, any time, and get food and shelter and company. No door was ever closed. It was as though you were an extension of every adult's family. They would often talk to you about improving yourself. Even people who hadn't gone to school would often stop you and ask you how school was going for you, remind you about staying in school and making something of yourself.

We were raised differently back then. Community counted. Grandmas and aunts sat in rocking chairs on the little porches of their houses or at the window of their apartment buildings, their bottom lips bulging with a pinch of snuff. And you didn't walk by without waving or saying, "Good afternoon." Politeness was a way of life for us, and if we didn't "act right," my mother would know it before nightfall. There was a certain way of doing things. If a group of boys were cursing or talking about something that was unacceptable and an older person came around, they just knew to stop or lower their voices. Not out of fear of some punishment, but out of respect. Some days after school my friends and I could be wrestling on the ground and an adult passing by would stop and check it out to make sure it was all in fun. And if it looked too mean, that adult—usually Mizz Mary or Mizz Dorothy—would just stop and say, "What you boys up to down there, you aren't fighting now are you? Ya'll know better than that, now, don't you?" And we'd say, "Yes ma'am, we're not fighting, we're just playing." Even now, because of how I was raised, I can't step into an elevator without speaking to whoever might be in that elevator with me. I have to say something just to acknowledge that other person's importance, their humanity.

Of all our neighbors, it was perhaps Mizz B that made the strongest and most lasting impression on me. Mizz B was something else. Her name was Beatrice and she was light-complexioned and had naturally red curly hair. She was a heavy smoker and liked to drink. She lived next door to us, and most afternoons she sat on her porch, listening to the music of Big Joe Turner—she loved Big Joe Turner—and watching the children walk by on their way home from school. She used to tell me I was one of her favorite children. I never knew why, except perhaps because my mother allowed me to run errands for her, and there were days when my mother would come and sit and talk and laugh with Mizz B. Whenever Mizz B wanted cigarettes, she sent me to the store. One afternoon, she sent me to the store to buy cigarettes and when I came back she had a Coca-Cola waiting for me. She asked me to sit on the porch with her for a bit, while she smoked and listened to Big Joe Turner. To the hauntingly strong sounds of Big Joe, Mizz B sipped her own drink, and in between sips, with her hand on my shoulders, she would say, "You're gonna be something some day, Bookie. You're gonna be something." Her words— as well as those of my family and everyone on Provine Street who knew me—became a part of me without my realizing it. Whenever I got into a difficult situation, their words of encouragement and support would come to me.

As I look back on it now, I wonder why everyone was so optimistic. After all, the opportunities for a black boy growing up in Memphis, Tennessee, in the 1940s were very limited. Maybe you could become a preacher or a teacher or an undertaker, as long as you restricted your professional work to other blacks. But there was no Horatio Alger future for us. Work hard and pay your dues and keep your nose clean would not open up new vistas for a black kid. Yet, somehow that didn't matter. We were supposed to make ourselves better. And not just for us. Whenever we made ourselves better, we did something for our community, and for the race.

I grew up in a large family, ten sisters and brothers all together. From early on, there was always an emphasis on education, and we dutifully woke up each morning, took our baths, brushed our teeth, and got ready for school without much fuss, especially with there being so many of us. When we got older, my mother expected us to get ourselves together and get ready for school on our own, and we did, ironing our clothes and going through our morning ritual, sometimes getting to school barely on time.

Even when I was a little kid, my mother recognized me as a real person, an individual beneath the skin of being her son. Between us, an easy closeness developed that exceeded anything a child had a right to expect from a harried mother of ten. I was someone she would choose to talk to, choose to share her thoughts and feelings with, and who would, in turn, receive with trusting innocence all she had to give. Although I loved both my parents growing up, and they both contributed heavily to shaping my ideas and the way I learned to manage the world around me, I was clearly closer to my mom because of the long hours we spent together during those early years.

Although my mother usually handed down a decision to us children, my father had a say about everything that had to do with raising us. My father was a gentle man, and he never raised his voice to us. Instead, he would give us the logical reasons for why he felt the way he did, expecting us to understand him and agree with what he had to say without question. He was a hardworking man and had a steady job in a restaurant located in a white neighborhood. A sign out front said ALL ARE WELCOME, but months would pass, my father said, without a black person coming in to eat there. He worked almost every day of the week, every week of the year, and was off one day a year. Despite this lack of leisure time, he was a happy man and often came home to us laughing as my brothers and sisters and I ran to greet him. Maybe because he was a man of few words, maybe because his smile said so much more than he could have put into words, that smile is forever etched into my memory. That smile told us how much he loved us.

Every day after work he would stop to pick up some treat for us—candies, cake, or ice cream. If he ever missed a day I don't recall it. During the winter, if we weren't out on the street to see him coming, as soon as he reached our door he would make a tap, tap, tap noise on our mailbox to tell us he was home. And whenever we heard that tapping, all ten of us ran to greet him. Because there was never enough room to fit all of us into his arms, we grabbed any free part of his body—I usually got a leg—and were carried along like dangling tentacles from an octopus. He did a comic struggle to walk with us, all the time laughing hysterically.

When he came home from work in the summer, we were able to spot him walking down the sidewalk as he approached our house. When we saw him, that was our cue to take off racing each other to be the first to meet him. Whoever reached him first was swept up into a bear hug and tossed into the air, while the rest of us children scrambled to grab what we could of him, knowing that we'd each get our chance to be tossed into the air in his strong arms. Through it all, he laughed with us. After he divided up the treats, he'd sit on the steps and watch us eat, holding one or two of us on his lap and listening to us go on about our day. I remember looking up from the cake I was eating, my mouth covered in crumbs and stray morsels of frosting, as he watched me stuff the last bit into my mouth, smiling at me, for no reason except that it gave him pleasure to see me enjoying my cake. That my father was a happy man in those moments when he came home to us carrying treats for his children stands out in my mind.

Although my father worked every day of the week, he earned very little money for his long hours—something I wouldn't learn until many years later. It goes without saying that we lacked for nothing in terms of our emotional well-being, but I will never understand how my mother and father used such limited resources to make sure we were housed, clothed, and had all the food that ten growing children could eat. We never heard them complain to each other, nor was there ever any indication that we had to worry about anything that we needed.

The harshness of the outside world that rarely intruded on ours when I was little boy was one that I could not fully escape as I matured into manhood, and it was only natural that the protected life they had built around us would require lessons designed to arm us against it. One such lesson was taught to me by Mizz English, the woman who sold us our newspaper.

Mizz English was very close to my family. She ate dinner with us often, and each time she saw me she had a newspaper in her hand and would take time to teach me a new word or show me the sports scores. She and I were especially close, and both of my parents treated her like she was family. Which is why I didn't question it when my mother asked me one morning to dress in my Sunday suit because Mizz English was

going to take me somewhere. My mother didn't say where we were going, and I didn't ask, because I trusted her. I got dressed and thought
nothing more about it.

Mizz English arrived early that morning to pick me up. We walked
everywhere in those days because it was very expensive to have a car. As
we left, I waved good-bye to my mother and excitedly turned to Mizz
English to ask where we were going. She didn't say anything for a few
moments, and then she said, "We're going to a wake, Bookie."

I had never gone to a wake and didn't really know what a wake was,
and I asked her, "What's a wake?"

"You will see once we get there," and she said nothing more for the
length of the short trip. We finally stopped in front of a big old house
with a gate. There was a driveway where people were standing and
milling around. Once we reached the porch I saw a sign that said THAYES
FUNERAL HOME. The doorway was clogged with even more people.
Nearly all of them were dressed in black and looked as though they were
ready for a church service.

Mizz English took me by the hand, and we walked up the steps to join
the collection of people entering what looked like the biggest living room
I had ever seen. In the middle of the room were rows and rows of chairs,
most of them occupied. Still, a big crowd of people stood behind the
chairs, murmuring quietly to each other. We were at the back of the
crowd as men dressed in black wearing white gloves, led those ahead of
us to empty seats. When we sat down, I heard noises that sounded like
someone was crying. As the rows began to fill with people of all shapes
and sizes, my eyes followed the men dressed in black as they seated
people in different rows, some in the front, some in the middle, and some
in the back. As I watched them seat, in the very front row, a group of
women, all dressed in black and wearing hats, and a little boy and a girl
who were holding each other's hand, it was then that I noticed the big,
black, shiny box that was sitting at the front of the room. It had gold han-
dles, and the top of it was open. As I allowed my eyes to slide down the
length of its long lines, I noticed that only half of the top was open, and

there inside lay a black man. He looked like he was sleeping. It was then that Mizz English spoke to me, even before I could say the words myself. "Bookie," she said, "that is a dead man lying in that casket. He is not sleeping." I looked up at her, and she continued, "That man died because he was shocked to death with electric wires, because he was accused of hurting a white woman. It was her word against his."

I didn't know what questions to ask because I didn't understand what she was telling me. I had never seen a dead man before, and as we filed past the casket she took my hand and held it tight. "Just keep walking" she told me, as the line moved slowly past the casket.

I felt many emotions that day, and the one thing that didn't make sense to me was how a person could be accused of something bad and then be killed because of it. If one of my friends told my mother that I did something wrong, she always gave me a chance to explain. Even at my age, I had an idea about the special finality of death. I just didn't understand why it had happened to this man and his family, and I had no way to deal with what seemed like an arbitrary punishment, and an extreme one. So I didn't say anything to Mizz English. I don't remember much more about the funeral, not even the walk back to Provine Street with Mizz English. Maybe she talked about what more had happened to that man and his family, but I don't remember. I just thought of that man's black face and the sniffling and crying of the children sitting on the front row with a full view of their dead father. I was thinking of their faces wet with tears and covered in grief as Mizz English walked me to the door of my home. I was really glad to be back.

My mother held the door open for me. "Thank you Mizz English," she said, casually, as if I had been taken for an ice cream. "We appreciate you taking time with Bookie."

"He was a nicely behaved young man," replied Mizz English, as she turned to go.

My mother and I sat down in the kitchen. "How was it, Bookie?" she asked me. I was quiet for a moment, remembering everything I had seen. She asked once more, placing her hand on my shoulder as she did so, and

I finally said, looking into her face, "I saw a dead black man, Mama. He had been shocked to death because a white woman said he had hurt her."

Looking into my eyes, my mother took my hand, and then she began to explain to me, slowly, patiently, the details of this poor man's circumstance, which had been reported in the newspaper. "Bookie," she said, "it is a common thing in this part of the world for black men to be killed for something like this, even when they are innocent of doing anything wrong. That's why it's important for you to listen to your father and me, and carry yourself in a way where you won't get that kind of attention or be in a spot where somebody points a finger at you and says, 'That black boy, he's the one that done it.' That's why I always tell you to pay attention in school and do your homework, finish your education. That's why you have to be careful who your friends are, where you go, what you do, and how you talk to people. Especially people who may be able to say you did something that you didn't do."

The whole time she talked to me, I looked at her and just listened, thinking about that man lying in his casket and the sorrowful sounds his children made as they sat there watching us pay our final respects to their father. I knew my mother wasn't trying to scare me, and I wasn't really scared, but I felt sad and something else. It's hard to describe what I felt. I was certainly relieved to be back home and happy to be in the kitchen with my mother, away from the dead body and all those crying people. But the other things I felt inside were hard to put into words.

I didn't know what to do with the experience. At the time, it seemed to have little to do with my life. We were not around white people except for the few times we went into town. Even then, there were separate water fountains and bathrooms, and my contact with white people was very limited. Because it wasn't something we talked about, I didn't give much thought to them or their lives. I never once envied them or wished to be anything except the son of my mother and father and living with my brothers and sisters in our house in our neighborhood. Our lives, the way we lived, it wasn't something we discussed; we didn't have a name for this situation where whites lived in one world and blacks in another. It's just the way things were. It was just like . . . like breathing air. White people had nothing to do with me and nothing to do with my life on Provine Street.

My mother never said why she asked Mizz English to take me to that funeral. And although it was an experience that eventually slipped to the back of my memory, it nevertheless left a deep impression—one that would come back to me more than once as I became a young man and learned more of the world and the ways of people who lived in it.

When I was nearly seven years old, we left Provine Street behind, moving to the William Foote Housing Complex. At the time, I thought we had moved into a middle-class community. The building we moved into was all red brick, and our new house had three bedrooms, one bathroom, a big living room downstairs, a kitchen, and both a front and back yard. All the people living in that community took pride in their surroundings and planted flowers everywhere.

My sister Christina loved to decorate windows. She decorated ours with Priscilla curtains and ironed those little crocheted scarves that were starched so stiff they could stand on their own. The coffee table was covered with a glass top, and beneath the glass were our family pictures, laid out for all to see. In that house we also had a little blue-and-white plaque that said "God lives in this house." I learned many years later that our new home, as beautiful, nice, and safe as it was, was a housing project.

Once we moved in, the time I spent with my mother became less. On top of taking care of the house and the ten of us, she also had a part-time cleaning job at the Malco Theater, one of the local movie houses. Blacks were only allowed to sit in the balcony, which actually turned out to be the best seats in the house.

Although she never stopped working, I cannot remember a time when my mother complained about being tired. Work was the tradition in which she tried to raise us. There was another tradition she was determined to keep up as well. She called it "making a way for our family." She encouraged me in whatever I wanted to do in my life, whether it was going to camp or joining the Boy Scouts, even when doing so meant she and my father had to work extra hours to get money to make it happen. During those times, I would tell her, "Mother, don't worry about getting that for me, I don't need it." But she would respond, "Bookie, sometimes it isn't necessary to forego something in life just because it doesn't seem immediately reachable. You have to put your effort into it, and a way will be made to help you get there."

No matter what my brothers and sisters or I wanted to do, she always supported us or found a way to make it happen. She often said that you have to reach beyond your immediate grasp for whatever it was, and if you can put your energy into it, you can set other subtle forces in motion to complement what you are trying to do.

The only time I ever saw my mother's confidence in her belief that "a way would be made" threatened was also the only time I saw my father's smile disappear. By then, we had been living in our new house about two years. I had learned that my Cub Scout pack would be marching in the Cotton Carnival Parade. From the time I saw my first parade, as a very young boy standing beside my mother, mesmerized by the colorful floats and costumes as they rolled by us, I developed a deep love of parades. I used to think that parades never ended but rather passed by your spot on the sidewalk and just kept on going. My mother, who was my best source of information on everything, never actually informed me to the contrary. So, when I learned that my scout pack was going to march in the Cotton Carnival Parade, my first concern was for my feet. Fortunately, on the day of the parade, our cubmaster filled us in on the facts of parade life: where the marchers gathered to start the parade, which streets it would march on, and where it would end. I was excited and looking forward to marching in my very first parade, and even more looking forward to the Cotton Carnival that my father promised me we would all go to after the parade had finished.

The Cotton Carnival was held in south Memphis right off of Beale Street. There were actually two Cotton Carnivals in town (and two parades), one for blacks and one for whites. The parade for blacks marched down Beale Street and was the official opening of the Cotton Carnival. When the day of the parade came, I couldn't wait for it to get started.

Marching in that parade with my Cub Scout pack made for one of the proudest moments of my parents' lives. They stood on the side of the street watching, as we marched by in our gold-striped uniforms. I wore the grin of a Cheshire cat on my face. They waved as I passed by, and at that moment, with them watching me, I felt so much love from their beaming faces. The parade ended just before sundown. It had been one of those summer days when the sky was a clear cobalt blue, with puffy white clouds drifting across the blue background, and a breeze that left cool in its wake accompanied the evening sun. In the hubbub of the parade's end I met my parents, and we went off to the carnival.

By the time we set out, the sun had gone down and the lightning bugs were out. There were smells of barbecued pork and cotton candy in the air, and my mouth watered just thinking about how they would taste on my tongue. Inside the carnival, there were booths with food, performers, and all kinds of different wares to buy. All the booths and the major elements of the carnival were run by whites, and only a few of the performers were black.

When we got to the carnival site, there was a mass of people at the entrance waiting to get in. We got caught up in the crowd, and in the excitement someone pushed my father into one of the booths. The owner of the booth, a white man, said to my father, "Look, don't push against my booth." My father didn't say anything, because in those days, blacks did not openly talk back to whites.

The crowd surged forward, and again my father was pushed against the booth, and the owner got upset and said to my father, "I told you not to push against my booth." My father, who I had never seen angry in my whole life, turned around, balled up his fists, stuck them into the air in front of himself, and said, "Look mister, I'm not pushing on your booth, it's the damn crowd. I can't hold the crowd back behind me; they are pushing me into your booth." That white man saw only this black man mouthing off at him with his fists balled up, and his face turned into a snarl, its color bloodred.

My mother suddenly cried out: "Bill, no Bill, Bill, please don't, Bill!" But my father continued to stand his ground, as did the white man, who perhaps was shocked and angry that a black man dare get in his face that way. My mother just called my father's name, "Bill, Bill, no Bill, please, don't Bill," because what he was doing was something you just didn't do. It was one of those moments when a man does what he thinks a man has to do but his wife knows that in this moment their lives could be turned upside down, inside out.

Fortunately, the crowd suddenly thrust us through the gate and away from that man, his booth, and the whole awful situation. Maybe we were lucky and caught a white man more concerned about the money he could make that night than putting an uppity black man in his place, but he didn't follow us or call the police or report my father to those night riders who kept the social order in many Southern towns.

Once we had passed the entrance, my mother just grabbed my father by the arm and held onto him. I saw the relief in her face as she said, "Oh my God, Bill. What were you thinking?" I learned from that situation how important it is to think before you act, but also that every man, even the most rational, has a breaking point past which reason doesn't rule. Despite the fact that my father was one of the gentlest and calmest people I have ever known, that night showed me a side of him that I had never seen before. I never realized that he could summon that type of rage or that he lived his life with a tight throttle on it. How it must have torn him up inside to live his life that way.

Looking back on it now, I see that experience, more than the wake that Mizz English took me to, as the beginning of my awakening to the racial dynamics of the times. I was in my world and whites lived in theirs, but we did come together on occasion, and when we did there was a palpable tension that could easily explode into a deadly situation. That night at the carnival, I realized that although I didn't quite understand what was happening, I knew my father was in trouble, and I saw the tension and felt the danger. And although I was a skinny little kid, I loved my father and knew I would do what I had to do to defend him.

There were no black lawyers with any kind of power and no black judges who could have helped us if my father had gotten into trouble. Chances are justice would not have been served if my father had been shot down in cold blood by that booth owner or dragged from our home in the middle of the night and lynched. I understood my mother's over-whelming fear—that in the bat of an eye, she could lose the man she loved, the father of her children, the man she had chosen to make her life with. It was never a question of fairness when it was black versus white.

When I was thirteen, my mother bought me a suit for Easter and had the pants altered at the store where she bought them. But because she wanted to surprise me, she had them hemmed in my absence and they were hemmed too short. She told me to take them back and politely tell the store manager they were too short. I remember the exact words I used. "Good afternoon, sir," I said. "I want to speak to someone about my suit. The pants were hemmed too short, and I want them to be re-done."

The man I spoke with said, "They look all right to me." And I said, "No, I'm telling you, look at them, they are too short." I held them in front of me, showing him that they fell just above my ankles. But he just said, "You watch how you talk to me or I'll have you arrested." I was shocked at his answer and quickly left the store. I didn't realize that I wasn't even supposed to challenge him. I didn't realize that I couldn't even criticize the work that this white man had done on my pants, infe-rior that it was. If I had, I would have risked suffering the wrath of a per-son who seemed to have authority and power over my life without any right to have it.

In retrospect, I can see that this is what segregation did to people: It convinced some that they were better than others; that no matter how shabby their own lives, they were always better than some folks—namely, blacks.

But the way my parents raised us, and the way they lived their own lives, spared us this knowledge until we were old enough to handle it. Growing up, I had no idea we were anything except fortunate to have my mom and my dad. I had no idea we were poor. Why would I? There was always food on the table, we were always neat and clean, and my father always seemed to have enough money to meet his family's needs. I certainly had no idea how much hatred some whites had for blacks. To the contrary, I learned from my parents that there were white folks who were very comfortable dealing with black folks and black folks who were very comfortable dealing with them. Both my grandparents had good relationships with whites because they both owned property in Memphis and had everyday dealings with whites.

Even later, when I was sixteen and had gotten a job at the UPS in Memphis, I had still not locked onto the system, still lacked a full awareness of its rules and regulations. One evening, during my supper break, I decided to take a stroll with a co-worker. We headed toward Front Street. That week happened to be the week of the Cotton Carnival, and the white Cotton Carnival was on the periphery of Front Street. As we walked down Front Street, a policeman stopped us and told us, "You have to turn around. You can't walk down Front Street." And we said to each other, "What is this, we can't walk down the street? We're not trying to do anything except walk a ways down a public street!"

We turned around and walked back to our office and passed our break in another way, but that incident brought back the memory of the funeral Mizz English took me to years ago, and then the incident with my father at my first carnival, and finally the incident with the pants. Over time, all of these events became part of the awakening in me that there were things that black people just couldn't do outside of their world. I was mature enough at the time to appreciate the absurdity of it, but I was still unable to think through the reasons why things were the way they were. It seemed that my grasping the magnitude of this issue was something that was gradual, a gradual awakening.

Maybe part of the reason I couldn't comprehend racial inequality was because at home everyone was telling me that I could be something, do anything I wanted to. Nobody told me "You're a black boy and that will keep you down." Instead, there was Mizz B sitting on her porch telling me, "Ulysses, you are going to be great," and my father who never took no for an answer or allowed anything to stand in the way of my progress. Every opportunity they had, my parents, my neighbors, my teachers, they would tell me I was going to be something special, and after a while you say to yourself, "That's me they are talking about and they know me. They know what I can do," and you start to believe it. The adults around a child are the mirrors in which the child sees himself.

Later, when I became a community advocate, I took with me the lessons of my own childhood. I learned that you have to be so careful when dealing with children, your own or anybody else's, because as you see them, they come to see themselves.

Perhaps that's why the one time I made a big mistake it changed my life so dramatically. When I was eighteen, I fell in love with a beautiful girl named Margaret. A natural part of love is wanting to be intimate, and unfortunately I didn't listen to my father about birth control. There was an older guy in Memphis who was a good friend of mine. He had a girlfriend and she told me that you can't get a girl pregnant the second time around and I believed her. That became my method of birth control. My father always told me to be careful to always use rubbers to assume responsibility. Unfortunately, I didn't listen to my father. I was still a teenager when this happened, and I guess our bodies mature faster than our minds.

I was shocked when Margaret told me that she was going to have a baby. I thought about my father and what he would say. I thought about my mother, who had so much confidence in me doing the right thing in any situation. But at the same time, I'm ashamed to say, I was also a little proud. When I told my friends, they congratulated me, called me a man. To an adolescent mind, it was a mark of masculinity. So much for the value of peer influence versus adult influence.

My sister Rita found out about the pregnancy from Margaret's best friend, and she told my mother before I even got home and had a chance

to tell her myself. When I walked into the house, I was numb from thinking about what had happened, what was happening to me and to this girl
I thought I loved. I went to the kitchen. My mother was there waiting for
me. She had her head down when I walked in and then she looked at me,
and I knew that she knew. All she asked was, "Is Margaret okay?"

I said, "She's all right."

"Are you sure Margaret is okay?" she said, and I said, "Yes."

Then she said, "Is Margaret pregnant?" and I stammered, "I heard
that she was. She told me she thought she was."

"Is she or is she not?" my mother asked.

Finally I said, "I think she is, she thinks she is, and I guess because of
that, I guess she is pregnant."

She then called Margaret on the telephone and talked to Margaret's
mother. When that telephone call ended, it was confirmed that Margaret
was pregnant. I left the house and went for a walk to the park. When I
came back home that evening, my father was there. He said, "I heard
Margaret is going to have a baby." I said, "Yes," and he said, "Are you
going to college?" I said, "Yes," and he said, "Are you going to take care
of the baby?" I said, "Yes," and he said, "Okay."

I married Margaret and we stayed together for two years. Early on, we
realized we were still young, mentally and emotionally, and we didn't
even understand what being married really meant. Being a husband and
a father is more than just calling yourself those things. We acted it out as
we went along, but marriage and parenthood were roles we were trying to
master. We didn't know how to do it. I was so immature at that time.

There was very little holding Margaret and me together besides the
baby, and eventually I went off to college and Margaret stayed home. We
very quickly grew apart.

I hurt many people in that moment of teenage irresponsibility that
had set two lives spinning wildly. I hurt Margaret, a beautiful lady. I
went to college and she didn't. And I eventually married a woman I met
in college. But Margaret isn't the only one I hurt. I hurt my child, providing her much less of an ideal setting, certainly less than my parents

provided for me. And twenty years later, I learned just how much I had hurt my mother.

After I became an adult and had more practice being a father and finally understood what it meant to be a father, my mother came to see me for a weekend visit. It was only then that she told me that she and my father had not been married the first time she got pregnant.

My mother and father met in college. He was a math major, and she majored in chemistry. They fell in love.

Both came from prominent and accomplished families. My mother was the daughter of a Methodist minister/carpenter, who worked most of his life raising money from rich whites to build his churches. After he raised the money for the materials, he took out his carpenter tools and, together with other members of the congregation, built the churches.

My father's family was better off financially. They owned a lot of property in Memphis, and they were part owners in the only cotton gin for miles around. Even white folks brought their cotton to this gin. The family was wealthy enough that my father drove a model T Ford when he was sixteen years old.

My father's father, Granddaddy Ulysses, was not only the first black postal worker in town but also the first black man to own a restaurant. Well, actually, today, we'd call it a diner. When the crowd at his diner got rowdy, my granddaddy would shoot his gun into the floor. I never saw him do it, but if family reports are to be believed, his restaurant became a legend in its time whenever he released a shot and brought the house to order.

Shortly after they started dating, my mother became pregnant. She told her father, who took her down to the restaurant of the man who would one day be my granddaddy Ulysses. He wanted to have a little chat with the man. My mother said that she and her father walked proudly into that restaurant and sat down at the counter. Reverend Royal said to Ulysses Sr., "Can I have an important word with you?"

As my mother told me the story, he came over and her father, Reverend Royal, told him what he needed to know. "My daughter," he said, "is pregnant with your son's child."

Granddaddy Ulysses thought a minute and then responded, "My son will continue to go to college."

Reverend Royal said, "No, I don't want you to disrupt your son's going to college. I'm bringing my daughter here only so that you and your son will know, because this will be your grandchild. You don't have to do anything for my daughter's child. This is my daughter and I will take care of her and her child." He nodded at Ulysses Sr., who was left speechless. Granddaddy Royal and my mother rose and left the restaurant, in pain, but with their dignity intact.

As it turned out, of course, they did marry, or there would be no narrator to this story. But only now, when she knew I would understand, did she feel she could tell me of the pain she was in as she and her father left the restaurant that day. As a child, all I had been told was that my mother and father married and had ten children and that Granddaddy Ulysses and Granddaddy Royal soon became the best of friends.

But the thing that got to me as I was listening to her tell me this story was my grandfather's cold reaction to the news. I felt my mother's loneliness as a young girl, alone with her father. A young girl of her time who had missed her period, with the bottom falling out of her world. And her father saying to her boyfriend's family that they didn't have to do anything for her and her child, saying that my father didn't have to marry her, that the man who had made her pregnant didn't have to accept this burden. That she would be forced to bear and raise her child alone and unmarried, forever dependent on the kindness of her parents. More than I had ever understood, my mother had known and felt Margaret's worst fear when she discovered she was pregnant. It affected me in such a way that I made a vow that I would never cause any more tears in the life of any woman, no more pain and suffering ever again.

My own father's reaction to Margaret's pregnancy was to ask if I was still resolved to finish college, but included as well concern that I not abandon her. Sadly, my father died before I graduated from college. He died unnecessarily at the age of forty-five, cheated out of getting to witness the fruits of his devoted fatherhood. He was coming home from work one night and stopped by the drugstore to pick up treats for those of my brothers and sisters still at home. At the drugstore he became ill. Somehow, the police showed up and, finding this black man wobbly on his feet, gasping for breath and maybe less than fully coherent, decided to take him to jail rather than to the hospital. It was at the jail, when my father was lying there and struggling to breathe, that another man in the cell with him called one of the guards and said this man is sick, really sick. So finally they took him to the hospital where he was declared dead on arrival. The doctors said he died of a cerebral hemorrhage.

He died right before Christmas break. No one called me. I drove home from college with some friends who lived in the same town. When I was getting out of the car, my mother came out the back door of the house. She was crying. "Oh Bookie," she said. My first thought at hearing her use my nickname was that she was overcome with emotion at seeing me. But then taking a closer look at her, I saw grief in her face, and she answered the question in my eyes. "Daddy is dead," she said. "Daddy is dead!" It was as if somebody had pulled a shade down over my face.

After the funeral was over, I asked my mother, "How could this have happened?" and when she told me, I went to see a reporter and asked him to investigate. He was a white reporter who worked for the *Memphis Commercial Appeal*. He wrote an article in the paper about my father, about what had happened to him, how he was taken to the jail instead of a hospital, and what a terrible injustice had been done to a man whose only crime was getting sick in a public place.

No one in the black community believed that a white newspaper, which had never before printed anything kind about black people—and within its pages had referred to black women only by their first names, never using any titles, Miss or Mrs.—would ever print an article about an injustice done to a black person. But this white reporter wrote my father's story.

Shortly after the article was out, I went to see a lawyer. He thought we might have a lawsuit, but he wanted money, a retainer, that we didn't have. The prospects of a black man's family winning a judgment against the city were apparently so slim in those days that the lawyer would not take the case on a contingency basis, as most such cases are taken. I talked to the men who had been in jail with my father and they told me the whole story—how he had been struggling to breathe, how long it took the police to take him to the hospital. And as I heard them tell me, I wondered how much pain my father had been in, if he was afraid in his last moments of life, and I wished I could have been there to help him as he had helped me all those years.

In reflecting on my father's death, I remember that both he and my mother taught us that no matter what predicament you are in, there is always a way out if you stay rational and don't give up on yourself. My father bequeathed us each a piece of himself, what we needed to continue to move forward as a family, and we have always had a strong sense of that whenever we have come together as a family.

Now, each year at Christmas, my brothers, sisters, and I gather in Memphis to remember our parents and the legacy of love, strength, and courage they gave to us. My father died in 1955 and my mother in 1987, but both died in December. Our gathering together at Christmastime is a small way in which we can acknowledge the twin gifts of life and love that they gave to us.

ᴄᴛᴏ *Ulysses S. Kilgore III is the president and CEO of the Bedford Stuyvesant Family Health Center, a community health facility providing quality medical care and health information to help people better manage their own health. Ulysses and his siblings continue to pursue their lifelong commitment of honoring the memory of their parents.*

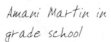
Amani Martin in
grade school

Nathaniel Martin
(my dad) and me
at eighth-grade
graduation

Me and Mom celebrating
little league victory

When Things Come Together

c⁀ɔ

M y parents are dreamers, and that is part of what I love about them. It is because of their dreams for me that I was able to have a chance at a better life than they had—although there were some bumps along the way. But their love, acceptance, and willingness to let me make my own choices cushioned those bumps.

It all started when my mother, Thelma, met my father, Nathaniel. She was from Jamaica, fairly middle class, and he was born and bred and still lives in what used to be known as the ultimate cliché of urban decay, the South Bronx.

My father had a talent for many things, including playing stand-up bass for a local jazz group. But his first love was helping people solve their problems, and early on he chose to do so by becoming a neighborhood activist. Being a neighborhood activist is rewarding, in that everyone in the neighborhood knows you and comes to appreciate what you do for them. Unfortunately, it's not the best way for a young man to provide anything more than a modest living for his family.

Although the Bronx my father was raised in was by many standards an environment that limited possibilities, the home in which he had been raised was one where education was very important, where he and his siblings were pushed to achieve in their studies and in music. As a result, my father grew to love books and learning and to treasure scholastic achievement. And that was part of what made him attractive to my mother.

Married to my father, my mother found herself, for the first time in her life, living just above the poverty level. When I was born we lived in a tiny apartment on Southern Boulevard, which was barely big enough for two, let alone the three of us by the time I came along, and it lacked a terrace and was a far cry from the turquoise waters and honey-colored sand of my mother's native Jamaica. Although my parents lived by the rule that cleanliness is next to godliness, our neighbors did not always do so, which became evident when my mother spotted several large bugs of the inner-city variety crawling around my crib. Without raising her voice, revealing no panic but only sure resolution, she said, "That's it. You're going to your grandmother's." What she herself was willing to endure for love, she was not willing to subject her son to.

It took time and money, but once my parents were able to move to a nicer place, and my mother had developed a little more confidence in her ability to manage the urban scene, she came to my grandmother's to get me. Whenever she tells me the story, she describes how my grandmother is holding me in her arms, and then she arrives and with one motion plucks me from my grandmother's arms and hugs me so tightly that I start to cry, and then she starts crying. It was, she tells me later, the one way she knew how to express her excitement that we were together again as a family, just to hold me as though she would never let me out of her sight again. And that's how I will always remember her, as always show-ing me that she loved me, without hesitation or qualification.

Once we moved back to the Bronx, we lived in an apartment where I shared a bedroom with an older half brother, Noonie, my father's son from a marriage before he met my mom. I'm sure my life could not have been a ball, growing up in hard times and a tough world. After all, the Bronx was still the Bronx. But I do remember a childhood of joy and humor and love. There were memorable moments from my childhood that still cause me to laugh out loud, because they come out of the joy-filled character of our life together as a family.

Most important, I recall that my parents' relationship was a positive focal point in our lives. They were physically affectionate in front of us and openly talked about loving each other.

Early on in my life, my mother was the center of my world. Since my first awareness of her, I have always been very proud to be her son. She married young and so is just twenty years older than I am. To me she is my young mom. When I was in second and third grade, she often came to school. She came to see about my progress, to see if I was behaving myself, and to talk with the teachers, to make sure they knew her son had a mother who cared what happened to him day by day. Each of her visits to school was a surprise. She never told me what day she would come but would just arrive. She was tall, five-foot-nine, and slender, with skin the color of café au lait, and she wore her hair in a big Afro, like Angela Davis. While she seemed strict about certain things, like coming home directly after school and finishing my homework before I could watch television, she always had a ready smile for me. She would take me on special trips to the zoo or bring along my favorite flavored cupcake whenever she came to visit my school. She was a fun mom in that she liked to laugh and she liked to see me happy.

On those special trips to school, I could always expect her to look great. She wore beautiful colorful dresses with matching shoes and handbags. Whatever she wore, she made it look beautiful, and I do not remember once when she didn't look every bit as pretty as my friends often told me she did. She often brought a snack for my whole class—yellow cupcakes with chocolate icing. When she arrived, the other kids in my class would say, "Hey, it's Amani's mom," and they seemed just as excited that she had come.

Her visits would provoke me to show off, and I did the stupidest things to get attention, like stick my foot out in front of my desk when one of my classmates walked by. No one was ever seriously hurt, although several of my friends purposely tripped over my foot and then told the teacher, which resulted in my punishment, usually a short sentence sitting in the corner. It seemed that my teacher had an uncanny sense of timing—the end of my punishment always seemed to coincide with the serving of the cupcakes, when all was forgotten in the melee of my classmates' little hands grabbing cupcakes and smearing icing all over their faces, with crumbs and paper cupcake wrappers dropping to the classroom floor. Of all the kids in my class, I was one of the few whose mom visited regularly. I was at that age when showing off in front of my friends was where I was coming from, and my mom was something to show off about.

My mother and father were together nine years before they broke up the first time. One thing that contributed to the breakup was the fact that Noonie recognized that my mother was not really his mom. I saw him struggling with the issue of living with my mother and not knowing who his own mother was. The nicer my mother tried to be toward him, the more it raised the question, "Where is my own mom in all this?"

But I'm getting ahead of my story.

The way my parents raised me, it was understood that I would go to school, study hard, and go to college. I never questioned any of it, because it was always assumed that I would do better in life than they had, and sharing their dreams about what they wanted me to accomplish early on gave me something to strive for.

We lived not that far from an exclusive New York City suburb, near the border of Connecticut. Sometimes on weekends, my mother would take us for drives through different neighborhoods and admire the houses. She would say, "I'm getting a house like that one someday, with the split levels, arched windows, and a huge garden." And she would pick bits and pieces off different houses as we drove by them. "I like the windows and the roof on this one and the circular driveway on that one," until finally she had a picture in her mind of what our new home would look like. And it actually happened when I went to college.

My mother, who had middle-class roots and came from a family that believed in finishing what they started, had dropped out of college after she married my father and then became pregnant with me. Once her kids needed less from her, she went back to college and completed her degree in psychology. "I always knew I would go back and get my degree," she told me when we were standing together at her graduation. But she had always loved real estate, and once she finished what she had started twenty years before, she went in a different direction. She became a successful mortgage broker and eventually bought the house of her dreams.

My dad grew up working class, raised by his mother. After an older brother died of leukemia when my father was only ten years old, he became the oldest of six brothers and sisters. His own father, my grandfather, took off one day and didn't come back until many years later, leaving the family to take care of itself when it needed him most. Which left my father, Nathaniel, a surrogate dad for his brothers and sisters. From that point on, he started working to bring in sorely needed money, becoming essentially the caretaker for his whole family while still a child himself. He saw it like putting on a new pair of shoes that were too big. "It was okay," he used to say. "I grew into the responsibility." Despite their poverty, his mother made him go to school every single day, no matter what the family needed. She would repeat to him again and again, "Nothing is going to get in the way of your education."

In fact, both my parents were taught that education mattered, and that expectation also became a big part of my life. At the dinner table, my father would often ask my opinion on current political and foreign affairs, or quiz me on bits and pieces of my homework that he knew I had been struggling with. He wanted us to know more than just events and dates. He wanted us to understand history as an ongoing play or movie, with a sometimes crazy cast of characters and an even crazier plot.

My father knew something about everything. The only sadness I re-call as a child is that I never had enough time with him, because there was always something he had to do for someone else, and he was often out solving other people's problems. "It's my work," he'd say, grabbing his coat on the way out to go deal with somebody else's problem that had been dumped in his lap.

I became more conscious of my father and his work whenever I was out with him running errands in the community. I noticed the way other people acted around him. They addressed him as "Mr." and asked his opinion on pretty much anything. It seemed that my dad was larger than life for so many people in our community. He was active on the school board, contributed his expertise and community contacts to ongoing elections for various offices, and ran for the assembly seat for his district. He is very easy to talk to and is a very good speaker when he is trying to make a point, and I learned as his son that he can be very persuasive. I felt very protected by him, because he had a way of easily taking charge of a situation. Whenever my brother or I had problems with other kids in the neighborhood, bullies picking on us or threatening to beat us up, my dad went out to look for them and dealt with the situation. We knew he took care of it, because we didn't have problems after that.

There was one time when I had to go to the hospital for a bad ear in-fection. My parents were still living together, and my dad took me. It was a typical New York hospital ER scene, with a packed waiting room, and we had to wait and wait for what seemed like hours and hours. Compared to an auto accident or a bullet or knife wound, an earache looks tame on paper. But my father knew the pain I was in. At first he comforted me and told me to be patient, but finally he saw that I was in agony and went and sought out somebody from administration. "Somebody needs to see my son soon," he told him. "He's in pain, and we've been waiting here far too long." I ended up seeing a doctor shortly after that. And that created a powerful image of my father taking care of me and making sure I got fair treatment.

There were moments in our life as a family when my father seemed too focused on the external view of who we were. He harped on things like eating with the right fork, speaking with other adults in the right way, and making a good impression, and because of that, it was sometimes hard to be completely relaxed around him. I was always watching my manners. My mother, who is strict but easygoing, just let me be myself.

My father started early to teach me about the fact that I had come from a proud race of people. He wanted me to be aware of racism and that things might happen to me that would not happen to boys who weren't black, and that at times I would be treated differently. He started taking me to rallies when I was very young. My first was in support of the victims of the violent suppression of the Attica rebellion by the state police. I don't remember how old I was. I don't even remember if I could talk, but the crowds of people, the excitement from the humming of voices, made me feel like an activist too. By taking me to that event and others like it, my father exposed me to the reality that in many respects we lived in a racist society, and there would be times when we needed to stand up against that. He was fascinated with the concept of power and what it meant. Every chance he got, he talked to me about the nature of power and how it fit into our lives, and he always stressed that education was one of the keys to power.

We settled in the Bronx because it was where my father had his roots. When he became a community activist, we were completely tied to the community, for better or worse. When I was born, my dad was studying for his master's in organizational management and was also busy learning firsthand how the system worked and how to change what cried out for change. Over time he would become very good at his job, but it did take him time. Which meant that when I was growing up, especially in the beginning, he struggled to support our family.

Our neighborhood was working class and filled with Jews, blacks, Hispanics, and some Italians. All the kids on my block played together. I always had white friends growing up. But these were working-class kids, not the sons of the elite white kids I'd meet later in prep school.

But my best friend growing up was my half brother, Noonie. He is six years older than I am. I admired him and followed him everywhere, and the way I saw him was no different from the way a lot of younger brothers see their older brothers—someone to look up to. He was smart, and he was interested in animals. He used to say he wanted to be a vet, and he kept snapping turtles as pets. Noonie let me help him take care of them until one of them took a bite out of my hand. He could be very affectionate with me, very protective. I think he loved me. I trailed after him, like an unwanted tail, the way most little brothers do. One day I was playing with two kids on our block. One of them was my age and the other was Noonie's age. They lived two doors down from us, and they were white. The older of the two hit me, really hit me, and my brother went after him. I was proud to be his brother that day, and after that I looked up to him even more.

The problem between us was his discovery that my mother was not his mother. It wasn't a secret that my parents kept from us, but it was never discussed. As a child I couldn't understand why Noonie needed to know more about his birth mom, because when we were all together with Mom, she treated him no differently than she did me. She held both our hands, hugged him, and punished him just like she did me. I never saw a difference in how she treated him from how she treated me. Now, as an adult, I better understand that all human needs are not rationally expressed.

I guess there was some level of disappointment and sadness building up in him, and one day he let it out. He just got really mad and screamed he didn't want to play with me anymore. When I asked why, he didn't answer any of my questions. He was so angry with me, and I hadn't done anything. One day, I referred to "Mom," and he screamed, "She's not really my mother," and ran off. I felt so sad for him—and for me. He was my brother, and I felt like I was losing him.

No matter how hard I tried to act like everything was okay, eventually it became a sore spot between us. So much so that during the night, if I rolled into his space, he would hit me, or pinch me, or kick me to chase me back to my side of the bed. Often, in the middle of the night I would wake up crying. My mom intervened when she heard us fussing, and my father would just tell him, "Leave your brother alone."

Over time, being together with him didn't feel the same. It felt like I was often in his way, because without warning, he would give me a push or a shove. He was much bigger than I, and whenever he hit me, although I got mad at him, I was more scared and confused than angry. I felt powerless, but I mostly missed the way we had been together. A lot of it must have been just kid stuff, the way older brothers tease younger brothers, but it was relentless with him because what was causing the anger would not go away.

I didn't understand the complexities of our relationship as a family; I only knew that there were so many times when Noonie and I were happy together. Happy to play together, to run in the street together, making a united front as the brothers we were when one of the other kids threatened one of us. There were days when our closeness was tangible, as thick as thieves, and then there were days when there was that wall of resentment between us.

One afternoon, Noonie and I were playing in our room and he pushed me really hard into the dresser. I hit the edge of it, cutting my head. My mother walked into the room and saw me sitting on the floor at the foot of the dresser, crying, with blood on my forehead. She asked what happened, but I was crying so bad, I couldn't tell her. She picked me up into her arms and took me to the bathroom, where she washed my cut.

Later that evening, long after Mom had put Noonie and me to bed, I heard her and Dad talking. It started off as a low murmur; it was hard to hear them. Then their voices got louder and louder. Next thing I heard, Mom yelled at Dad, "That's it. I can't stay in this house. I can't jeopardize my son any longer!" And then there was silence. Shortly after that night, we left. The tension between my brother and me was part of it, but I would learn years later that there were also things happening between my parents.

My mother, who had always worked part-time, didn't have a fulltime job and needed to save money and make preparations for us to live on our own. For those next few months we moved in with my Aunt Laura and Uncle Tony in Queens to give Mom time to find a job and a new place for us to live.

I didn't understand what had happened. All kinds of thoughts went through my head, and I didn't know how to talk about them. My mom and I never talked about it, and I didn't know what to think. All I knew was that I missed my father and playing the games that Noonie and I used to play. Living with my aunt and uncle helped because my uncle took time to do fun things with me, like fishing and working on his house. He was renovating his house and let me be his helper. He was always giving me projects and showing me how to do different things with wood and bricks. Each time I did something with him, he told me I did a good job, and sometimes took me for a treat, which made me feel good that he cared so much. It was something I came to miss when we finally left nine months later.

My mother found us an apartment in the Bronx, not too far from where my father lived. It had been several months during which I rarely saw him, and I missed him, and Noonie too, even though we had fought a lot.

My mother got herself a full-time job, and worked hard at it. Because she was busy trying to sort out our lives, whenever Mom was home she was doing something—paying the bills, cleaning the house, never just sitting around. Sometimes she asked me to help her out in the afternoons and taught me how to wash clothes and do dishes and to take care of the house until she came home from work.

Early on, she would say, "I want you to be responsible, to learn how to take care of yourself. You're not always going to have someone do it for you." Part of the reason she paid special attention to teaching me responsibility at a young age was that in West Indian culture, men tend to be very spoiled by their mothers, sisters, wives, and girlfriends. My mother was especially sensitive to the fact that her brother—successful and smart as she was—was also spoiled, because he had been waited on so much by his mother. She didn't want that for me.

I was in sixth grade when we separated from my father. It affected everything. I didn't do my homework. I stopped participating in class. It got so bad that I was threatened with repeating a grade. Up to that point, I had always been a good student, good enough to be considered for skipping ahead to fourth grade early on in my third-grade year. But in sixth grade, I spent a lot of time in punishment. I spent at least three months of that year grounded. When I was tested, my scores were really high, so my parents and the teachers knew I could do the work. My mother and father must have recognized the problem and guessed that part of it was that I wasn't seeing my dad often enough, because things changed. One day, my mom came home and said to me, "You're going to see more of your father." And I started having visits with him on a regular basis.

Dad owned a plant store next to Yankee Stadium, and the day of our first visit she packed me into the car and dropped me off there. Once she'd gone, I stood in front of my father, who got busy talking the moment my mother left. I don't remember what he talked about, only that he did a lot of talking. I said very little, mostly because I didn't know what to say. Instead, I watched him and listened. Maybe I was nervous, and being nervous made me shy and afraid to say anything that might change the moment.

I didn't see Noonie on that visit, because Noonie was now in a special boarding school. My father explained to me that our fighting at home had been just the beginning. Noonie also had problems with other kids at school, which I didn't know about then, and my father had been called in to talk to the principal many times. In the end, he felt that what Noonie needed was more attention. My father found a private school attached to a naval academy and scholarships to pay for Noonie to go. When Mom came to get me that evening, I couldn't help but think about Noonie. I didn't talk to her about it, but I thought a lot about him. It had been months since I'd seen him, but I still remembered in vivid detail many of the fun things we used to do together and those times he stood up for me, and that I loved him. I wondered how he felt being alone in that boarding school.

That visit rekindled my relationship with my dad. Sometimes he came to take me to get ice cream, or to go to the movies, or just to hang out together. I loved those times we just hung out together the best, and I wanted to see him as often as I could.

Once my dad came back into our lives, school became easier. I didn't have to repeat a grade and moved on to seventh, where I started to apply myself and get good grades again. That same year my father enrolled me in a weekend academic program that prepared inner-city kids to go to private school. My father knew the guy who ran the program and was able to get me in. From the get-go I saw the difference between the other kids and me. Although we were all from the Bronx, they lived in the South Bronx, a much tougher part of the borough, and I lived in the North Bronx. I had to commute to the program by bus.

Most of the other kids in the program were also a little older, and I was shy with them. When we went on school trips I sat in the front of the bus, while many of the other kids sat in the back of the bus, making noise and doing crazy stuff, like making out. They talked about rough stuff and bragged about how they hung out in the street, and because I wasn't allowed to do that, I had very little to add to their conversation and often felt out of place with them. I had been in the program for a month when I tried to convince my dad that I didn't need to stay in it. But he wouldn't let me out. "You have to be ready to go to private school," he used to say to me. "I want you to have a chance to finish up in a good private school so that you can go to any college you want." "I'm not interested in doing that," I said to him one Saturday morning when I didn't want to go. But he made me go anyway.

I tried everything possible to get out of the program. One day I came home and told him that I had been mugged on the way to school. When I came into the house I looked bad—my shirt was ripped, my face was smudged with tears, my eyes were red. He looked me up and down, and I could tell that he didn't know if he should believe my story. My dad is a smart man, especially street smart, so he put me in the car and we went back to the neighborhood to find the guys who jumped me. As we drove through the streets, I described to him what the guys looked like. And as I finished describing them, just my luck, right in front of us walked two guys who fit the description that I had made up. "Amani, is that them?" he asked excitedly. Feeling sick inside, I said, "Ah no, that's not them, they looked like that though, but that's not them." But my little scheme worked. Even if he didn't believe me about being mugged, he apparently saw the lengths I'd go to just to get out of that program. I didn't have to go back after that.

By the end of the seventh grade, my grades were so much better, and in the eighth I seemed to hit my stride and regained the ground I had lost in sixth grade. It just seemed that things had come together.

In the middle of eighth grade we were given a test for high school. My scores were very good, and I got a choice of two of the best schools in the city, Bronx Science or Stuyvesant. Knowing that I had been accepted at two of the city's premier high schools gave me a lot of confidence. But on my visits to my dad, he had been talking more often about prep school and how important it was for me to try to go, and it was starting to get to me. Dad believed the keys to the kingdom were in who your school friends were. Although I was happy where I was, I was also restless for a new environment and new experiences. My school didn't have good facilities. I loved sports and played a really good game of tennis, but there was no decent tennis court at my school. In fact, there was no physical education program to speak of, and it made me think about what possibilities might exist with this boarding school thing that my dad was constantly talking about.

It gave me something else to talk about with my dad, to seek his advice on, and gave us a connection. Even though my father had come back into my life, he still did not live with us.

Mom worked hard to make our new place a home. My father, who had never made a lot of money working so hard most of his life, contributed what he could to help us, but it didn't make up for everything we didn't have. Each month I'd overhear my mother fretting about how she had to choose to pay one bill over another. As I watched her trying to stretch a fixed amount of money over too many bills, it became clear to me that our financial situation was not very strong. She wouldn't talk about it to me, but on some nights, when I was supposed to be asleep, I heard my mom talking on the phone to my dad about how she could barely make ends meet and that she was tired of it. Whatever money he was giving her was not enough.

There were times when Mom gave me money for things that I needed for school, and I knew there wasn't a lot more of it. There were also times when she couldn't give me more because she didn't have it. I remember once wanting a new pair of pants for school, but there wasn't enough money. "You have to wait," she said gently, not in anger.

There were times when life was tough without my dad, and I felt if he loved me, why wasn't he there all the time?

I knew my brother and me not getting along was part of the problem. But it wasn't until I did something that shook Mom's faith in me, causing her to compare my behavior with my father's, that I learned there was something deep-seated in their relationship she couldn't deal with.

It all started with my love for baseball. It was my favorite sport, and I was in Little League as soon as I could pick up and hold a bat steady. In junior high school, I was on a team, and we played to win.

Well, one afternoon, I sneaked away from school to be with my friends. In my eagerness to escape, I stupidly walked by the window of my elementary school principal. When she saw me, she called my junior high and told the principal that I was playing hooky.

That night, when I got home, my mother was waiting for me. She waited until I was in the kitchen before telling me that I was grounded for one month and couldn't play in Little League until that month was over. I tried to defend myself, but she wouldn't hear it. I was busted.

For one month I went to school every day and came home right after school to do my homework. I did my best to follow every rule my mother laid down, hoping somehow that she would let me out of punishment early. My hope lasted until the end of the second week, when it was clear to me that Mom had no intention of cutting my month-long punishment short. And I took it in stride and did just fine coming home on time after school. Until the last week, when my team had to play one of the toughest teams in the league. They needed eight players to take the field, and with me grounded, they only had seven. The game would be forfeited without me, and it was my fault. It was all I could think about on the way home from school the day of the game. Just as I got home the phone rang. It was my coach, Fat Nick, who knew that I had punishment, but I had told him there was a chance that my mom would let me out to play, and I hadn't seen him since I said that. So when I picked up the phone and heard Fat Nick's voice, I just listened. "Amani, we need you," he said. "Are you still in punishment?" I wanted to say yes, I can't come, but it was my team, they needed me, and it was my fault that they were in this jam anyway. So after listening to him talk about how important this game was, I finally said, "No, I'm out of punishment just for this game and my mom isn't home right now, but it's okay for me to come." "Are you sure?" he asked me. I lied to him and said, "Yeah, I'm sure." "When can you get here?" he asked. "Right away," I told him, and quickly hung up the phone in case he heard the hesitation in my voice.

Rushing, I put on my uniform under my clothes. When Fat Nick saw me, he asked me, "Why are you dressed like that?" because everyone else had shown up in uniform. I said, "Oh, it's no problem, I'm okay, I'm not in punishment." So he let me play, and we won the game.

When I got home that evening, my mother was waiting. When she saw me she asked me the usual questions, "How are you? Where have you been?" There was a pause. "Don't lie to me now," she said, "because I see your uniform sticking out from under your jacket. So either you were playing baseball or doing something else that I should know about."

I didn't know what to say. There was nothing but silence from me. I hung my head, and finally she said, "Okay, get your case." "What?" I asked in confusion. "Get your suitcase," she said, "because you are leaving. I want you to pack your clothes right now." I was still confused, but the look on her face was that don't-you-even-try-to-argue-with-me look. So I dragged my butt to my room, pulled out my suitcase, and started to pack.

What is going on, I thought, what is she doing? I don't know what I packed, I just pulled things out of the drawers and threw them into the bag. When I was just about finished, I went to the kitchen to get my oatmeal.

Quaker oatmeal was my favorite food. No matter what time of the day, I could eat it. Mom was standing at the counter, and as I reached into the cabinet to get the box of oatmeal, she said, "No way, put it back. That oatmeal stays here. You are taking only your clothes out of this house." And at that moment, I realized she was serious. I left the kitchen with my head hung even lower than it had been before. I went to my room and waited for my mom to come and get me. It wasn't too long before she came to my room and said, "Go to the car." "Where are you taking me?" I asked. "I'm taking you to your father. I can't trust either of you, and I think you both need to be together right now." In the car, we were surrounded by silence. I couldn't believe this was my mom, my always happy, always supportive mom acting like this. I didn't say anything during the ride to my dad's.

She dropped me off at my father's plant shop. My dad was waiting for us on the sidewalk. "You keep him" was all I could hear as she drove off. I was really upset and crying as I watched her drive away. My dad came up behind me and put his arm around me, not saying much, which was unusual for him.

After a few moments of my sniffling, he said, "Let's go for a walk." He took me through the neighborhood, with his arm still around my shoulder. We walked down the street away from the shop and away from the direction my mom had driven in, just the two of us, in silence. He finally said, "You know how your mother is about honesty. Even the tiniest hint of dishonesty makes her crazy. But you know she loves you." I wiped my eyes and didn't say much. "Women are sometimes hard to understand," he went on, as we continued on down the street. I felt good that he was trying his best to make the situation better. I couldn't believe my mom had done this, taken me out of Little League, punished me for a month, kicking me out of the house, and even denying me my oatmeal. I didn't understand why she had done that. I had just wanted to help my team, and she hadn't even given me a chance to explain that. I told my dad the whole story and he stopped us in the street, put his hand on my shoulder, and said, "Amani, it's better to be honest, even if people don't want to listen to what you have to tell them." He talked about the many times when we were living together as a family that he had told Mom he would be coming home for dinner at 7:00 P.M. but wouldn't get there before 10:00 P.M. And by then, we were all in bed, which meant he had missed dinnertime with his family. He told me she finally got fed up with his saying one thing and doing another, and that was part of the reason why they weren't together anymore. "Never tell your mother you will do one thing and end up doing another," he said. "Always tell her the truth." It really helped to hear this from my father, and I was glad that we were together, talking and walking down the street. While I was confused about what Mom had done, he led me to believe everything would be okay, very soon.

About an hour later, my mother called and asked to speak to me. We talked it out. I got a chance to tell her the whole story, about how it had been my fault that my team was in trouble, and I had felt obligated to help them. She let me talk until I had finished and then said simply, "You have to tell the truth, all the time, that is the most important thing." Although she understood why I went to help out my team, it was in the end unacceptable to lie. She said my dad would drop me off at Uncle Tony's house, and she would pick me up. That very same day Dad dropped me off, but he didn't leave before my mom came. He waited with me until she got there. When she came, she gave me a big hug and asked if I would get her something from the kitchen while she talked with my father. It was that incident that restarted the conversation between my parents and in the end led to their getting back together.

For the entire time Mom and Dad were separated, I dreamed of the day they would get back together. Then, it happened. Although my parents were fantastic as parents and they seemed to love each other, they found living together, accomodating each other's needs and schedules, very difficult. My father was even more committed to his work. There seemed to be an endless line of people in our neighborhood who needed my father, and even more meetings that he had to go to. It was hard for us to have regular family time because of his schedule, and even though we were all back together again, his absences made it seem at times like we weren't. I rarely saw Noonie, because once my parents got back together, he didn't come to visit us regularly. My dad went to see him. Even though my mom often asked Noonie to come and be with us for holidays, he rarely did. And when he did, we had very little to talk about and both found it hard to be together now that so much time had passed.

I was nearly thirteen when we all started living together again, and being back together as a family allowed my father to push me more into the idea of prep school. I had to choose a high school, and all along my dad had encouraged me to aim high. I had scored well enough to get into the two best public schools in the city, but I started to interview at prep schools. I interviewed at several of the best in Manhattan. They were expensive and we knew it, but first I had to decide where I wanted to go; then I had to get in; then we'd let Dad see if he could get us a little help with the tuition. While I was interviewing, my cousin Hope, who is older and at times more like an aunt figure to me than a cousin, suggested that if Dad was going to pay so much money for me to go to school, why didn't I think about boarding school. Also, my best friend, Jeff, who was a year older, had gone away to prep school the year before. He talked about how great boarding school was and how different it had been from our school in the Bronx: the opportunities to play different kinds of sports, to travel to other places, to live away from home. He told me all of the fun things he did and that I had to try it. The fact that my best friend was away at boarding school and the way he described the great times he was having was the additional push I needed to think seriously about what I had to do to get in.

I did my research and learned all I could about various schools. By the time I finished reading everything, I had a good idea which ones I wanted to go to. There was a big chance that I wouldn't get a full scholarship and my parents would have to pay, which would be a hardship for us. I couldn't even imagine where we would get that kind of money, and I became pretty discouraged just thinking about it.

One day, shortly after that conversation with my aunt, the principal of my school, Mr. Himes, the same principal in whose office I spent nearly three months straight while I was having problems in the sixth grade, called me in. Our relationship had improved since those days, and he had followed my academic progress for the past two years. He called me into his office to let me know that I had been selected to participate in a program called "A Better Chance," or "ABC." It was a program that provided help to inner-city kids who had good grades and needed a little tutoring and guidance to help them get ready for prep school. The program also helped kids who got into prep school get a full scholarship. Mr. Himes said my chances were very good, and I should just apply. He gave me the paperwork, which I filled out with help from my father. My dad was the kind of person who knew exactly what kind of references I would need and who he had to ask for them.

Once my application was done, I had no sense of how it was going to work. I didn't get to choose which school I wanted to go to but was excited about what might happen. I sent my application off and that was it.

In the early spring of eighth grade, I checked the mailbox nearly every day. One afternoon, I opened it and there was a package addressed to me. It was from the Taft School in Connecticut. I remembered from my research about all of the prep schools that Taft seemed like an interesting place. When I read the envelope I thought, *"yeah!"* and ripped it open to find a catalog that described the school. I remember looking at the pictures and thinking, *Wow, this is where I want to be.* The grounds looked so lush and green, and the pictures of the kids made it look like they were having so much fun. It didn't matter what they were shown doing, from sitting on the steps of a main building to running across one of their expansive sports fields. What mattered was that it was very different from my school in the Bronx. The catalog pictures captured the idea of everything I thought prep school might be. It was beautiful. As I closed the catalog, I saw the letter inside the back cover. It read, "Congratulations! You have been awarded a full scholarship to Taft."

It was on that day, at that moment, when I realized that my life had changed. I realized I had possibilities. I was exhilarated and very proud. My mom and dad were ecstatic.

I was ready to go. There were so many things I wanted to do, and I knew that I couldn't do them where I was. I wanted a new environment. Although I went to a solid academic junior high school, I wanted a different challenge, and everything I had researched about prep school made me believe that I could find that challenge there. The day I received my letter from Taft, I felt that all the experiences I had gone through— Mom and Dad splitting up, the struggle to live after that in a new place, not doing too well in school—were behind me. I was ready for a new adventure.

In prep school everything was different. There were really smart kids at the school, and the school itself was spacious, clean, and just beautiful. Although I saw the beauty in my surroundings, at the same time I was scared. There were very few black kids, and everyone else seemed very wealthy. The work was challenging. Some of the kids already had a couple of years of a foreign language, with a summer or two to practice it on vacation in Europe. Some had taken calculus before I took geometry. But even though I felt out of place, externally I made sure I presented a picture of a kid at ease. In the end, my dad thought I could do it and so did my mom; nobody knew me the way they did. So I reasoned that if they believed in me, I could make it. I had grown up in a mixed neighborhood, and I knew I could make it in an environment that wasn't all black.

What stays with me most about my prep school days was my parents' desire for me to fit in but not lose my cultural identity, which would be easy to do in a place like Taft. Every chance he got, my father talked to me about the nature of power and how it fit into our lives. The two-and-a-half-hour drive from my house to Taft was a long one and offered the perfect opportunity for him to give me his usual speech. He'd say to me, "Amani, I want you to have every opportunity to learn everything you can while you're at Taft." He instructed me on what courses to take, what not to take, how to make the best of my free time, how much time to spend in the library reading books on black history. He understood more about the prep school experience than I did, although he had never been enrolled in one. My dad has an uncanny knack for understanding experiences he's never had, and he was nearly always right.

But we didn't just talk about what I should be doing. He also talked to me about himself and what was going in the old neighborhood, who was doing what, and his chances of running for the assembly. I liked listening to him talk about his thoughts on life, but I also felt that he didn't give me credit for having learned some of these things from him already. After all, he had been talking to me, teaching me about life and the injustices of society, since my first rally.

During those drives, there were certain things that my father would say to me that I would think about afterward, when I was alone, that didn't strike me as completely true. Like that "the establishment" will always think of you as an outsider, as the black boy. I never thought this was true. As I look back now, I realize that he wanted me to be aware that some people will use race to put you down. He didn't want me blindsided when I came up against that kind of racism, which I inevitably would. But he also taught me that in the end I had to make my own choices, and it couldn't matter what others thought of me. I had to have a sense of my own self, defined for me from inside, and that this was more important than what others might call me or say about me behind my back. I realized that some people might think of me as a black boy, but the ones who mattered to me knew me as more than that. More important, it didn't matter what anybody thought as long as I knew I was doing the right thing. My sense of myself was what mattered the most, and my father had given me enough confidence so I didn't need anyone else to tell me what I was worth.

Once I finished prep school, I decided to stay in Connecticut for college and chose Trinity College. As soon as I arrived at Trinity I saw that it wasn't very different from Taft. There were many of the same assets and deficits—very few black people, lots of rich kids, and many of the same opportunities that Taft had offered me. I knew that I needed to and wanted to grow in a different way, because I had already been there and had the white-dominant cultural experience that Trinity was offering. I eventually chose to spend some of my time in college abroad, in order to broaden my perspective.

My years at Trinity made me realize that I loved my cultural heritage—the music, the food, the ease of showing emotion, rather than hiding what you're feeling, not pretending to be anything but yourself. When I went home for the summer, I needed one or two weeks of transition time to shift from school mind-sets, but it wasn't bad; I was pleased to be home. What was strange was when I would go from my apartment in the Bronx to the summer homes and neighborhoods of my extraordinarily wealthy friends from Trinity. The transition from school to home was easier than the transition from my home to the homes of my friends.

My parents were a united front through the entire time at prep school and through college. If my father didn't come to my school functions, my mother came. They were proud of me and made that clear by supporting me in everything, from coming to school on parent's day and sitting through those awful baseball games (our team sucked), to driving me the distance back to school after weekends at home. They always made it clear that they were proud of me, and they knew and expected me to do well in school and in my life.

Everything changed for me when I moved to D.C. after college. I went there because I wanted to be in a black environment. There I met a group of friends who were just like me: They were black and had gone to elite schools and universities. My new friends and I bonded in our shared experiences, and it was the first time in a long time that any of us had this extended group of black friends. Living in D.C. and hanging out with my new friends made me realize that there were certain levels of comfort I had not experienced in years. Just being among people who were like me, where I didn't have to explain the subtle nuances of things that were part of my culture, made me feel complete.

———

They say a child doesn't really grow up until he has to face the inevitability of the aging process and death. I was living in Brooklyn, and one day I got a call that my grandfather had passed away. Before we gathered together to go to the funeral, Mom had called me to ask if I would give the eulogy because my dad was too nervous to do so. I said sure, it's okay.

After the service, my dad came up to me. It had been months since I had seen him. He had always been a hard worker, and that day he wore it on his face. His eyes were red, and he looked thinner than I had ever seen him. I was quiet, ready to listen to whatever he had to say.

"Son," he said. "I realized today that I have nothing else to teach you. Everything that I could have wanted to pass on to you, I've done so. You've shown me that by the way you've handled the eulogy." When he finished telling me how proud he was of me, I said, "Dad, does that mean you're not going to talk to me anymore?" And we both laughed, as he slapped me on the back and reached his arms around me to give me a hug. His hug even felt weaker than I was used to. Pulling away from him, I gazed into his face. He looked like he had been ill, and finally I said, "Are you okay?" "Yes, I'm fine," he said. "I'm just fine."

By the time we received our condolences, and I had gotten one or both of my cheeks kissed by every lady in the church who knew my grandfather or my dad, my mother was ready to leave. As we walked toward the door, I saw Mom looking at my father, who was standing across the room, and she said, "Your dad looks sick." "Oh, he's fine," I said, "just working a bit harder than usual." We both watched him cock his head as he listened intently to the conversation of the person before him.

After the service that day, we all went our separate ways, and it would be another two months before I received a telephone call from my grandmother telling me, "Your father is in the hospital, and he wants you to call him."

When I heard her words, my heart felt like it skipped a few beats. Ours was the kind of family that, no matter what differences existed between us, when a crisis happened or when someone was born or died, our differences were set aside so that we could be united as a family to get through it. "What's wrong?" I asked. "He fell off the bus," she said. "He fell off the bus?" I repeated. It didn't make sense to me. My dad was a pretty athletic guy and wasn't in the habit of falling off anything. I called the hospital right away to talk to him. My dad has a really strong, clear, forceful voice, but as I listened to him explain what was wrong, I could hardly understand a word he said. I promised to come as soon as I could. I was scared.

I was working in Manhattan, and he was in a hospital in a Westchester suburb about an hour away. I immediately took off from work that afternoon and took the train to the hospital to see him. It was a calming ride, and on the way there I thought about the one time my father and I hadn't talked for two years. I had just graduated from college. He always loved hearing from me, but I was the one who usually called. At one point I decided not to call, to see when he would call me. One month passed, two, three, four, five, six months, and I thought, *He isn't going to call me.* This went on for two years. It sounds ridiculous as I look back on it. This was the man who had driven me back to prep school all those times, teaching me about the relationship of the world to myself on those long rides, and I hadn't called him nor he me, not even on holidays or birthdays. I had just thought that if he couldn't pick up the phone and call his son, then I wouldn't call him either. He was my father, I had reasoned, and that was his responsibility. He had probably thought just the opposite. It had been difficult not to call, but I had decided to just forget it, and so I hadn't.

Finally, when I came home to see my mother for Thanksgiving, I thought, *You know what, it's Thanksgiving and it's been two years since I've talked to my father. I will call him.* When we finally connected by telephone, he acted as if nothing had happened. He just started talking like no time had elapsed since we last spoke. "Hey, how are you? What's happening?" he asked, and I felt sad and disgusted that he didn't say anything about our silence.

After that, I didn't call him again for another long stretch of time. I thought the onus was on him. More months passed, and I finally decided to move back to New York. When I moved back, I called him to let him know that I had returned. We never addressed the long silence, and I decided that I was in the same city where my father lived and I wanted to have a relationship with him. I had moved back to New York because I wanted to have a career in television. When I was ready to look for a job, he used his connections to help get me some interviews. I was uncomfortable about it, but he insisted. And it was then that I realized this is how my father really wants to parent. He wants to be able to give me something, to help me, to say this is what I did for my son. He had spent his entire life helping other people through his connections and his knowledge of how to make the system work. And finally, it just clicked in my head, that his understanding of parenting comes from a very tangible perspective of helping me out. He wanted to be able to give me something, to help me in his way, to say to himself, "Hey, I did right by my son." What I needed had to be a need that he could respond to in his own way.

And that was the beginning of understanding my father. Providing for me made him a better dad than his father had been to him, because even though he and Mom didn't stay together as a couple, they both contributed as parents, each as he or she was able. He never stopped telling me how proud he was of what I had accomplished. When he wasn't with me physically, living in the same house, he didn't understand how important it was for me to hear from him. But when I needed him to come through, like needing money for school or whatever, he came through. And now, something had happened to him. He was in the hospital and needed help, and it was my turn to come through for him.

My dad is a big guy and usually weighed 190 pounds. But that day, seeing him lying in that hospital bed, he must have weighed only 135 pounds. He was emaciated, and my first thought was, *Is my dad going to die?* He could talk, but he was weak. He said he had fallen off of the bus because he had been sick and was weak in his legs and arms. When he fell off the bus, he hit his head and they rushed him to the hospital. Once he was in the hospital, the doctors ran a series of tests and discovered that he had an auto-immune disease similar to lupus. It affected his appetite and he couldn't swallow very well, and, whatever he ate, he couldn't keep down, and then he was tired all the time. His doctor was really guarded when I asked for a prognosis. In fact, he didn't give me one. He just said your father is very sick.

Standing there that day looking at him, I didn't know what to do. I just felt incredibly helpless. One of the things I learned from my father is that when there is a problem, you try to fix it and talk about it afterward. I wanted to cry, but I thought, *I can't react that way, he needs me, and I have to handle this.* I started to research the illness and made connections and talked to specialists. I found the national expert on the disease, who happened to work in New York. I wrote him a long letter and asked him if he would go see my father. And he did. After this guy went to see Dad we all felt better. He told us that my father was getting good care, and he would be okay. The doctors treating him were on the right track, and he would be fine eventually. We were all relieved.

Although he got better, it was a gradual process, and he stayed in the hospital for quite some time. I went to the hospital right after work, from Manhattan to Westchester and back home to Brooklyn, every night. It was a really long ride, but I made the trip nearly every day, until he got stronger and was finally discharged from the hospital. That experience was a turning point in my relationship with my dad. He had always been the strong father, and now he had to defer to me. He hadn't taken the magnitude of his illness very seriously, and when he fell flat on his back, he finally had to rely on someone else, and I was that someone else. I was the person to tell him what to do, how to eat right, get his rest, assuring him if he stayed with the program everything would turn out fine, much the same speech he had given me time and again when I was a little boy. I wanted the doctors and other caregivers to know that this man's son was looking out for him. Even though I trusted the medical personnel, I still felt like there had to be a presence there for my dad, just as my parents always wanted my teachers and administrators to know that there would be someone they'd have to answer to if anything went wrong with me.

When he was finally well, he said, "You did it son, you brought me through it. You took good care of me and I love you for that. You did an incredible job."

There may be some argument about how well a boy can grow into manhood without a father, but I do believe that when a boy has a father, the father's role is to be someone to emulate, to be someone your child can define himself against, someone he can grow into, and, yes, sometimes grow past. That is how I was able to forge my own personal identity. To this day, some of the things I like best about myself I got from my dad. He was always the kind of guy to talk to people, to help them understand their problems, and then to help them through their difficulties in any way he could. He has a history of service to other people. If I am at all like my father in those ways, I'd be very happy.

I also admire the way my mother has been, her stability, her spirituality, and her constancy. As much as my mother endured, she taught me to live a life of integrity and responsibility, to have the character to accept fully the consequences of my actions and to be willing to make sacrifices for what I believe in. Her lessons were as important spiritually as my father's were practically.

One of the most difficult tasks for a black parent is to instill a sense of confidence in a child growing up in a society that in a thousand ways tells the child he is second-rate. My parents tried to insulate me in certain ways from that pernicious influence of racism by stressing education and by providing me with all those opportunities to grow that would give me the successes I needed, which in turn gave me the confidence to reach for my star, whichever star it turned out to be.

ᘓ *Amani Martin is a television producer for HBO sports. He divides his time between New York and Los Angeles.*

The Cunningham women
(left to right) me,
Dorothy, and Debbie

Dorothy and
Calvin Cunningham

Dad receiving honorary
title from the American
Board of Diplomats in
Pharmacy, 1969

As the Night Follows Day

It was the summer of 1979, between my junior and senior years of college, when my grandmother heard the news on the radio. Mind you, the news report didn't mention anyone's name. Not my name, not anyone's. It just said that nine college students appeared to be occupying the offices of the Bureau of Alcohol, Tobacco, and Firearms.

I don't know how she knew I was one of them, but she did. Maybe it came out that those nine college students were from Harvard. Maybe my parents were already talking to her about their concern that I was showing some signs of ideological infection and getting involved with some radical political groups on campus. But she picked up the phone and called my parents. "Do you know that your daughter is occupying a government office?"

I had made the decision to occupy the New York offices of the Bureau of Alcohol, Tobacco, and Firearms because earlier that year five people—members of the Communist Workers Party—had been killed while organizing in a public housing development in Greensboro, North Carolina. The Klan had gunned them down.

Just before the Klan arrived, the police, who should have been there protecting the organizers, had all conveniently gone to lunch. You know, a working man is entitled to a lunch break. The Klan was so busy murdering these people, they didn't see a cameraman, who happened to be there and who had skipped his own lunch, taking footage of the whole thing as it was happening.

I had seen the tape. The Klansmen came up, totally cool, cigarettes hanging out of their mouths. They never once looked behind them to see if anybody was there, because they knew they had been given a green light.

At a trial that followed, it came out that a federal agent from the Bureau of Alcohol, Tobacco, and Firearms had actually told the Klan whom to kill. The agent was never charged and never appeared at the state murder trial or federal civil rights prosecution. In the end, he seemed to have disappeared and was never heard from again. That's why nine of us decided to take over a government office in the World Trade Center. Our goal was a coordinated effort directed at national newspaper and television attention to publicize the fact that the government had been a player in the killings.

The actual seizure didn't turn out as any of us expected, not that we had any idea what to expect. Then again, none of us were experienced office occupiers. One of the BATF agents said he would shoot us right between the eyes if we didn't surrender ourselves, just like they had shot Sandy Smith, one of the five people killed in Greensboro in 1979. I don't know about the others, but I was terrified. Even thinking about it now gives me the shakes. We had no weapons, no means of defense, just a bullhorn and nine of us who weren't quite sure what we were doing.

It took a long time before we were all booked and released that night, so by the time I got to the door of my father's house—my parents were separated by then—it was already pretty late. But my father was waiting for me, ready to explode. I mean, he was on fire! He laid into me, intoning in a state of barely restrained rage that I had done something that was not respectable, that I had broken the law. And, when he learned that I had been charged with a felony, my father, who is a doctor and the model of respectability, went into meltdown, telling me that after all I had worked for, after all he had worked for, here I had gone out and in one dumb moment blown any chance I might have had to become a doctor or a lawyer, which were his twin dreams for me. When it seemed he had said everything he could think of, he then informed me that he was throwing me out of the house. Unbelievable, I thought, as I found myself standing at the door to my mother's house. It was unbelievable at the time, and even now, that he would do such a thing.

My mother, who is a psychologist, was outwardly calmer. I say outwardly, because inside she was on fire also. She just showed it differently. "I raised you better than to do something so stupid," she said and then went into therapy mode. "This is acting out and you don't need to." That's when I learned that she and my father had concluded that my revolutionary act was really an expression of my rage about the fact that my parents had recently separated. Even before I got home, they had already come to a decision that the whole family had to go into therapy.

What really got to both my parents was the fact that I was also charged with assault. When we announced, "We're taking this office over, we're sitting in, you all should leave," this one woman started flailing all over the place. To steady her, I grabbed her arm because I thought she was going to fall, and that's why I was later charged with assault. I don't remember what the investigators said exactly, except that I had been charged with a felony. That's all my father had to hear. He was convinced that if I were convicted, my life would be ruined. And he made sure to remind me of that at every opportunity. As it turned out, the charges were immediately lowered, even before we got to court.

As angry as they were with me—and this went on for days and days, if not months, afterward—my parents came to my every court appearance. The trial itself ran about five days, which is a long trial for such a minor thing. Each day they sat right in the front benches to show everyone that this crazy kid had parents, and they supported me, even though they didn't agree with what I had chosen to do. In the end, I was convicted of a misdemeanor, but because I came under the youthful offender act, my record was later expunged.

It was the summer before my senior year in college, and for the rest of that summer, even after my arrest and trial, I continued to participate in radical politics. Each morning, my father and I would argue all during breakfast about what I was doing. (By then he had decided I could come back into his home.) He'd say, "How can you do this? Black people never won anything this way. You know this isn't the way. Communists are crazy, look what they did in Russia. You're gonna get yourself killed for nothing, for a cause that has no prospects for success."

He tried other tacks as well. "I've paid so much for your education. You could do so much with your life. This is throwing your life away. What do these people stand for anyway? Why do you think this makes sense?" Then I would tell my side of the story, and he'd listen.

We argued through breakfast, and we argued in the car as he drove me to the train station. Although these arguments were highly adversarial, as I look back on them now, I realize there was a lot of love evident in them. When we reached my train stop, I would give him a big hug and kiss good-bye and he would just burst into tears and say, "You are going to get yourself killed. I am so worried about you." Then I would go over to my girlfriend's house, and her father would be waiting at the door and I'd have to hear the whole thing over again. And I'd say, "All right Uncle Russell. Thank you for sharing, but we've got to go. We're really late for our rally, good-bye. Don't worry. Yes we will be careful."

And then back at my mother's house, we'd return to the same topic once again. She had her own way of approaching it. First she'd say, "I like these people. I think they are basically good people, but I think they are going about it the wrong way." Then we got down to brass tacks. "I just think you're being really dumb about it. You are a very righteous and selfless person, but you better start thinking about yourself or you could get screwed. You need to look and see what is making you do this. I think it is some deep unrequited stuff from your childhood." And when I said, "No, it's not. It's just politics," she said, "Politics is never just politics."

How do I remember exactly what she said that day? Because my mother was always so good at knowing what to say in a crucial moment, at finding the words that wouldn't antagonize you or make you want to defend your position more but would instead cause you to stop and think.

Still, when we finally started to get a lot of TV coverage for what we were doing, whenever it came on the air, my mother would call me over and say, "Quick, come, your people are on TV again." My mother was such a good friend to me. Through the trial, the charges, and all the changes in my life at that time, she was often my best friend.

When I returned to school, I continued to be involved in radical politics. And even though both my parents had no use for this kind of talk and told me so, I kept inviting them to various events and political rallies and discussions and meetings. And they came. They argued with me that what I was doing was wrong, wrong, wrong, but they came to every event I invited them to. They said they were there to show support for me. And that meant everything to me.

Years later I asked them why they really came. They said, "Because we didn't know what you would do next." And so they tried to weather the storm and to have whatever moderating influence they might have on me, because the other choice was just to let me go my own way totally, and they were even more afraid of that. Whatever madness they thought I had embarked upon, they wanted to continue to be involved in my life. They went to my rallies, and they encouraged me to bring my friends/comrades home to meet them. They argued with them, sometimes into the night. But they always treated these friends with respect. They went out of their way to tell them and me that they respected our commitment and convictions.

Looking back on those days, I am still proud of what I did. I still think the cause was just, although now I would probably use different tactics to achieve my ends. But when I look back on how my parents handled it, I have to give both of them tremendous credit, because I'm not sure I would have been able to handle such a situation as well as they did. Through it all—the stress on my family, the fear, the fright and turmoil, the fact that there was another child in the family who was affected by this whole thing—both my parents were there for me. They never said to me, "Lose that crowd, they are ruining your life. You cannot see them. Don't ever bring them to my house." Instead, they said, "You are ruining your life, but bring your friends over for dinner, so that I can talk to them some more."

My earliest memory of my father is actually two very vivid memories. One was learning how to cook salami and eggs with him when I was about three or four years old. My mother wasn't home, and my dad dragged two chairs up to the stove, one for me and one for my sister. I knew if my mother came home she would kill him for having these young babies at the stove flipping and spattering greasy salami and eggs all over the place. But that's what we were doing, having a ball cooking breakfast with my dad.

When my father makes a meal, he doesn't just make it. He has to describe every part of the meal to you as if it is a work of art in progress. I remember how he began, excitedly telling us, "I am going to fix you the best meal in the world for breakfast, the best meal you've ever had. There is no better breakfast. It is salami and eggs. Now, first you have to get some salami, but you can't get any kind of salami, you have to get this special Genoa salami. It has to be pink and glossy." And then he held up a slice and said, "See, look at this. Perfect. Next you've got to heat the pan and wait until you are sure it's hot enough. Now listen to the sizzle; don't you love it? Now smell it. Oh goodness, doesn't that smell good? Mmm, mmm, now smell it again." He narrated every sensation.

My father grew up during the Depression when, he says, there was never enough money to buy the amount of salami and eggs that he wanted to eat. He vowed that when he got older he was going to make enough money so that he would be able to feed his children salami and eggs whenever they wanted it. Of course, first he had to instill in us a love of salami and eggs. That was no problem for him, because my father is such a great storyteller that he can describe salami and eggs to a group of strict macrobiotic vegetarians in such a way that would make everyone's mouth water. So we learned to love salami and eggs.

My other memory of him is his "man on the street" interview with my sister and me, something he did whenever we went on a trip with my mom to shop or to visit a museum. The one I remember most clearly was when my mother took my sister and me out shopping and bought us new shoes. We went to a shop filled with all kinds and colors of shoes, and Mom took us to a section just for little girls and told us we could pick whatever pair we wanted. We were so excited. Mine were red patent leather and my sister's were blue. When we got back home, we took the shoes out of their big fancy boxes and showed them to our father. That's when he took out a tape recorder and said, "Ms. Cunningham, I see you have a new pair of shoes. Can you describe these shoes to me? What color are they?" And I said, "My shoes are red." "Why did you choose this color?" he asked. "Because Carol has them," I said. "And who is Carol?" he asked. "She is my best friend." My father was always like that, picking out ways to make my sister and me express ourselves, and find comfort in saying what we felt and how we thought about things. I remember him as a very present person in our family. Intellectually, verbally, he has tremendous charisma. If he is in a room with a crowd, he will be the center of attention.

My father is nearly six feet tall. But with an ease that belied his size, he could sit on the floor playing with my sister and me. He showed affection toward us in public by picking us up, hugging and kissing us, and swatting us on the butt, while being supportive in every other way as well. When I was very little, my father's lap was like the universe. I just remember spending so much time on his expansive lap. I must have really been tiny, because I have this image of his lap like a world, my legs stretched out and still not reaching his knees.

As I grew older and started to participate in school performances, my father, who was often late, always came to see me. Each time, his arrival was preceded by a small disturbance in the audience, as he found his way to a seat. If I were backstage waiting and peering through the little peek hole in the curtain or standing in the wings waiting to go on, without a doubt whenever the rustling started I knew my father had arrived. At the end of the performance, there would be lots of clapping, and my father seemed to clap louder and longer than any other parent. It was a recognizable clap, the way he cupped his hands, bringing them together powerfully and rhythmically, making a distinctively resonant clapping, and I knew that was my father.

My first memory of my mother is of her sitting on the edge of my bed reading me to sleep with a story. But if you ask me what I think of when I think of my mother, it is the sheer amount of energy she poured into us. Especially when it came to getting us to see the world visually. You see, before my mother trained to become a psychologist she was an artist. She couldn't pass a tree without noticing its structure, the way it branched and how the leaves grew, or the colors of flowers and how their petals blossomed in perfect symmetry. And she wanted to share that visual world with us.

Once, when I was nearly five years old, I sat on the floor with her, surrounded by paper and crayons and colored pencils and markers, coloring and drawing, with her pointing out and asking me about shapes and shadows and colors. Even when I was barely able to use scissors, she brought things home for me to make with her. And we watched her do things around the house, especially my father's favorite house, the one that he bought in a middle-class, nearly all-white neighborhood, with lilac trees in the front yard and back garden, and bay windows. My father was so proud of that house, and he loved tending the lilac trees.

The house was really just a standard ranch house, but it was special to my father. He fell in love with the bay windows that let in enormous amounts of sunlight, even in winter, and the lilac trees that showed themselves to us in our first spring living there. When we moved in, they looked like dead trees, but my father was reluctant to cut them down, so they stayed. When spring came, the trees blossomed profusely and gave off that sweet purple aroma, which we all saw as a thank-you gift to him for having spared them.

In a way, that house was validation to my father. But, to my mother, it was a chance to revel in her skills as an artist. When we moved in, the kitchen was salmon pink with that boomerang Formica. My mother took one look around and went into action. She redid that entire kitchen and turned it into an old-fashioned country kitchen with oak plank floors, church pews, and rustic stuff. It was beautiful. She made everything she touched beautiful. Including my sister and me.

But what comes to mind most was how the kitchen was a central part of our lives together. After school and while my mother made dinner, she would call us in to come and sit at the table with our storybooks. Whatever I was reading, she used to say, "Why don't you read that out loud to me?" Nearly every book I owned I read aloud to her. Sometimes she was fussing around the kitchen making complicated meals, and I'd look up and ask: "Mom, were you really listening to my story?" Somehow she always convinced me that she had heard every word of it.

On the weekends she took us to museums and drove us around the fancy neighborhoods and talked to us about the houses and how they were built. "Do you see that house over there?" she'd ask. "That's French provincial." And she explained to us what made it French provincial and how to identify the type.

There were loads of space in the basement of our house, and because my mother was learning how to sculpt and paint, she filled the basement with these incredible sculptures, along with brushes, paints, clay, and every kind of art supply we wanted. It was really her space, and she worked hard at her art, sitting at her little table working while she let my sister and me paint beside her. When she entered her sculpture in a local contest and won a prestigious Silvermine award, we wanted to learn how to make sculpture too.

But although that studio was her special space to work, she made sure we understood that everything in that studio—and she meant everything—was for us to use as well. She never said to us: "Don't touch that or don't use that." Instead she said, "Would you like to use this? Can I show you how to use that?"

Growing up, my sister and I felt so unequivocally, intensely loved by Mom and Dad. Everyday it seemed they wanted to show us something or take us somewhere. My father brought home microscopes and petri dishes and showed us how to do experiments. He often took us on long walks, which he liked to do most after it rained. During those walks he'd point out things like spiderwebs that had caught drops of rain water and discuss with us the lifecycle of such bugs that had gotten caught up in the webs. But it was always my sister and me with my father. I don't remember my mother ever really joining us, and there were times when I wondered why not. Nor do I remember my father ever playing man in the street with my mother after she bought something, the way he did with us. But I just brushed it aside, figuring it was because my mother was so busy herself.

You see, in addition to raising us and doing her artwork, there were often large groups of people surrounding my mother in the living room—black people and white people—usually talking, but sometimes they were listening to someone addressing the group. I often ran through the living room while such groups were there and heard snippets of their conversations. It had something to do with bussing. "Being bussed in" was a term they often used. In the town where we lived, most blacks lived on one side of town and whites on another. And I knew, because my mom took us to school each day, that we were the only black family that didn't get bussed in, and those people came to our house to talk to my mom about it. She was, we'd later learn, the person who brought people together, the facilitator, and it was something that she was very good at. This is the same mom, mind you, who later wondered where I got my political genes from!

But I will always have this picture of my mother in that roomful of people. A room that she had created to allow this group from diverse backgrounds to find a space to air their ideas. Making people feel welcomed in our home was something she liked to do, expressed most often by the time and effort she put into making sure there was enough food for everyone when they came over. I watched her make our house a place of welcome, a space that was filled with lovely flowers and food that she had prepared. Watching her put everything together made me think that perhaps she was getting ready for a discussion between friends rather than a discussion between two adversaries. My mother believed in working through a situation rather than letting it sit and fester. I have many memories of her sitting at the telephone, a pad of paper on the kitchen table, calling people and setting up a time and place for meetings. And taking special care with the cleaning up and decorating and cooking, doing everything that might help the people who were coming feel comfortable and cared for. Whenever I asked her what she was doing, she would say, "I'm setting up for my group meeting."

There were weekends too when Dad and Mom would either have people over at the house, with more long discussions that would go on late into the night, or they would go out, telling us they were going to dinner at someone else's house or to a party. What I remember very clearly about that time, however, was what my mother looked like when she got dressed up to go out.

My mother was beautiful to me. She had pretty red lips with a smile to go with it. When she was younger, before she met my dad, she was a model. Whenever I spent the night at my best friend's house, and the next morning my mom came to get me, I never hid from her or pretended that I didn't want to go home. No, not me. Whenever I heard that my mother was at the door, all I could think about were her bright-red lips and that smile that I couldn't wait to see coming to get me. She had an uncommon way of making me feel as if I were the most amazing child in the world. And her eyes! She had these big warm eyes. I just remember her being "really, wow."

She had a way of always making me feel that everything was okay. Whenever she was around, everything seemed to fall into place. My mother communicated warmth with her smile and love through her touch. It wasn't so much what she said to me but rather the sense of calm that settled around me whenever my mother was present. My dad is very insightful about the world but does not have the patience it takes to read people's moods and emotions. You would never talk to him about your friends or boyfriends. But my mother is hugely insightful about people. When I was growing up, I used to believe that my mother had this great laser-beam judgment of people. It was almost magical, her ability to size up a person.

I think that was part of the reason why my mother and father didn't go totally crazy when I got arrested. My mother understood and respected the people I was involved with and knew that they were motivated by something deep and were not just flakes. And my father trusted my mother's instincts about people.

Strangely, although my parents didn't stay married and didn't believe in public displays of affection, they always showed an enormous amount of respect for each other as people and particularly as parents. I do not remember one fight they ever had over how to raise us. Even when my mother had to tell my father that she thought it was time we moved out of his suburban dream house in the middle-class, virtually lily-white neighborhood. She wanted us to be part of a black community, where there were other kids we could go out with, with a social life that we could be a part of, and he listened to her.

Changing to a new neighborhood came about when my sister and I started junior high school. Despite all the other things he talked to us about—I mean every intellectual issue under the sun—my father had this idea that he didn't want to raise us with a chip on our shoulder. So he didn't talk directly to us all that much about race and race relations, or if he did, he didn't talk about the subject as if it had something special to say about our lives. Instead, when he brought up the topic, it was often in the most general of terms, suggesting that sometimes some people could be mean to other people because of their skin color. My father wanted us to be "nonracial," to be accepted for our intellect, what we brought to the table. But as things turned out, we couldn't be. The world wasn't yet ready for the children my father would deliver to it.

We weren't the only black kids in the junior high school; the school was maybe ten to fifteen percent black. But both the black and white students treated my sister and me as though we had no right to be there. Because we didn't live in the black part of the school district, we didn't have to ride the school bus and didn't have that built-in chance of meeting new people and making friends. Because of not being bussed in, we weren't invited to the social events that come along with making friends at school. By the time we were teens, the white kids didn't invite us to parties either and showed no interest in hanging out with us. And it was clear from the disinterest by both groups that neither the black boys our age nor the white ones were asking us out.

At first, when white boys didn't want to date me, I thought something was wrong with me. My mother often assured me, "Nothing is wrong with you, honey. You are beautiful." I really had no idea it had anything to do with race. But I didn't fully believe my mother when she assured me I was beautiful. With everyone pairing up and no boys interested in me, there had to be some element of appeal I lacked. I couldn't understand why boys would reject me just because of my race. It had to be something about me physically.

As part of my parents' plan to expose us more directly to our own heritage, we started spending summers on Martha's Vineyard, at the beach called the Inkwell. Once we started to go there, our circle of black friends grew larger, and we developed a larger community social network. I still had a huge self-confidence problem, but now it had less to do with racial rejection and more to do with my image of myself.

In my mind, the Cunningham women are really beautiful, and I thought of myself as an ugly duckling in comparison to my mother and sister. I had short-cropped hair and wore braces. At times I was mistaken for a boy, which added to my awkwardness. It was horrifying. I was just very, very homely as a child. My sister never seemed to go through an awkward phase. She went from cute child to stunning young woman. My hair seemed nappy and dusty colored, while hers was curly and a dark rich mahogany color. She had a big Afro, but my hair wouldn't grow. And people would say things like "At least you're smart." Or they would say things like, "Was Debbie always the pretty one and you always the smart one?" And it was an insult to both of us. Debbie, who was also a good student, felt as awful as I did hearing those kinds of remarks.

Even during college I still believed I was an ugly duckling, despite the fact that by then boys showed interest in me. What turned things around for me was my experience the summer I got arrested. As protesters we had to use the bullhorn on the street. We had to do it over and over again, until it was like nothing to approach total strangers and ask them for their support. And by the time I was done, being rejected and having to go on anyway, to convince people of the justice of our cause, I toughened up so much that it became easier for me to deal with rejection without losing confidence in other areas of my life as well. And during that process I finally understood something my parents had tried to teach me all along— not to let others judge your worth, not to let them validate you, to believe in yourself when others didn't.

The night before I went to college, both my parents sat me down for a talk. My father started quoting from Shakespeare's Polonius speech— the "To thine own self be true" speech. He got so caught up in Polonius's advice that he got out his *Hamlet* and read the whole damn thing. I didn't understand why my getting into Harvard meant so much to him, but now that I have my own children, I can understand it. At any rate, that night the other thing he did after that whole Polonius routine was to give me "some practical father-to-daughter advice," he said, "about boys."

"Boys are the enemy," he began. "They are dangerous, violent animals," he went on. "I know, because I was one." Then he said he was going to tell me "the routine." "Don't ever bring a boy to your room. If you do, make sure you're not alone. If you're alone, stand up the whole time. If you don't stand up, sit down, but only on a chair. If you sit down on the bed, keep the light on. If you turn the light off, never lie down. If you lie down, keep your legs closed. Never let a man pay for anything for you on a date. It's always a quid pro quo—if he pays for you, he wants something."

He sounded as though he would never end. I was wishing he'd go, back to the Polonius monologue. Finally, I cut him off. "Okay, Dad. Enough!" By that time I already had a serious boyfriend, whom my mom knew about but my father didn't. That's the problem with these father-daughter lectures. If they are early enough to do some good, the girl doesn't know what the heck her dad is talking about. And if she knows what he is talking about, it's already too late.

An hour later, my mother came into the room and said, "College is a time of great experimentation and great freedom, and you should use it to explore the kind of relationships you want to have with people and with men. It's a time of great sexual opportunity, and you should really take advantage of it. Whatever you do, don't marry a man without sleeping with him. It's like buying a car without test-driving it."

My parents were very different from each other. They met at a party. My father was a medical student and at the time my mother was a nurse. It was nearly love at first sight, they told me. Her friends called my mother the café au lait Elizabeth Taylor. My dad was a tall, dark, and handsome medical student. My parents were considered two beautiful up-and-coming poster kids for their community, a generation that would achieve far more than their parents had. Everyone thought they were perfect for each other, Dorothy and Calvin. I think they married because everyone thought they were the perfect couple, and it would have been letting down their friends if they hadn't. I think they each loved the idea of the other, and they had all these dreams of themselves as a famous doctor/nurse team that would go and save a little piece of the world together. But they never really got to know each other before they married and had kids.

I think that's why my mother was always there to talk to us, even when we didn't know we needed to talk to someone. I talked to my mother so much in high school that she became my best friend and remained my best friend all through college. We talked about everything, including our relationships. I talked about the silly mishaps my boyfriends and I had, and we laughed together. And at times she talked about my father, how they had met, how intelligent he was, what a good doctor he had become, and then, once in a while, how dense he could be about personal matters, like feelings. And then one day she just announced that she and Dad had been talking and that she had decided they should part, go their separate ways. That there were some things she wanted to explore that were separate from being a wife and a mother and were more about her own development as a person. I felt terrible, because as little as I understood about what was driving them apart, I knew that I loved them both, and I loved them together, not apart.

Years later, after I got arrested, my father took me on a vacation, just the two of us. He had concluded that he had messed up my life by having his marriage fail and that that's why I did what I did. He felt very guilty about it, blurting out something about it, and he said, "You've been angry with me since the day your mother left." And I said, "I am angry, but that isn't why I occupied that building." And he said, "That was the lowest point in my life. Nothing ever hurt me as much as seeing your face the day Mom packed her things and left our house."

I would never judge my father harshly. I owe him too much. I just accepted that my mother and father couldn't give to each other what they gave to us. And that instead, they both filled up their lives with their work and with making sure that our lives growing up were as good as they could make them. My father is the most dedicated and intelligent doctor I have ever met. There is no one who can think through a problem like he can. My mother has an unbelievably full life. In addition to raising us, working in the community, doing her art, she decided to become a psychologist, and that meant getting her Ph.D. Both of them gave us a model of productive lives. Neither one ever spoke badly of the other or made us feel that the other was deficient in any way. They just sort of left it to us to figure out what had happened for ourselves. In that regard they were not only outstanding parents but also outstanding people.

Looking at it now, I think the reason my parents' marriage didn't work is that my father is essentially reserved. Deep down inside, he is very cautious, living through his head and not his heart, which is my character also, unlike my mom, who really lives through her heart.

My mother sometimes has these completely out-of-the-blue ideas that very few people would come up with, but she makes them work. And it's clear that she put a great deal of thought into them. She is smart, but it wasn't brains alone that made them work. It was also how much of her heart she was prepared to pour into something she believed in.

For example, after working as a school psychologist for a number of years, she decided to open a private practice. But she would only do so if she could open it across the street from where she lived. So she joined with a group of like-minded professionals, and they rented the building across the street from her house. It wasn't an easy endeavor, putting such a project together. A lot of people had to sign on, each with his or her own agenda, each with ideas about how it should be done. But it did come together, and the neighborhood now has a service facility it didn't have before, a whole building of psychologists and other care providers. If her heart tells her to do something, she does it, and it usually works for her.

When I graduated from college, after some thought I decided to go to law school. At that point, my parents were still not sure that I wouldn't be a Communist all my life, so when I said lawyer, they were ecstatic and said to each other, "Quick, we better take it." They really wanted me to be a successful corporate lawyer, and I became one and worked for a corporate law firm for two years. But at the end of two years, I wanted more and decided to go to work for the NAACP Legal Defense Fund. When my father heard, he was horrified. He said, "I didn't pay all of that money for you to end up at the LDF, messing around with those people for no money. What's wrong with you? This is not what black people struggled for, so that their brightest stars can take a big salary cut." It was a loss of prestige for him. But I knew he would come around, because what he wanted even more than prestige was for his daughters to be happy with the contributions they were making in their lives.

After working there a while, I sent him a clipping file about the LDF. They weren't cases that I was working on per se, but about the organization overall. He totally changed his tune. And then when he called me, he'd ask, "Honey, what case are you working on now?" He became okay with it.

What he didn't know is that even here so much of my success was based on the values he gave me. Whenever I was in litigation, I knew almost instantly when the other side was not well prepared. I had this feeling of "Gotcha!" But I also sat up and paid attention when the other side started to ask these pointed questions that told me they really knew my case. Whenever I came across those well-prepared lawyers, they always reminded me of my father. He made sure he was always well prepared and knew his stuff.

Several years ago, my father had a heart attack. Of course he was a horrible patient and insisted on knowing everything that was going on in his case. He had a couple of setbacks during the process of getting well, and he knew he was having these setbacks, but watching him during that process, I realized that he was the kind of doctor who was a great problem-solver, was smart, and really applied himself. Confidentiality kept me from knowing how he was dealing with his patients' illnesses, but when I saw my dad in the hospital dealing with his own case, I realized that he was the kind of doctor I would respect if I were a doctor. That's the kind of lawyer I wanted to be. One that other lawyers respected because they knew that I had done the necessary preparation and knew the case extremely well.

I worked on many interesting cases at the Legal Defense Fund, but one really formative case occurred while I was still a law school student. It was a voter fraud case and took place in Selma, Alabama. Just going there was a transforming experience.

Selma, Alabama, is a movement city. You drive into Selma from

Montgomery over the Edmond Petis Bridge. If you know the story of Bloody Sunday, you know that during the Civil Rights movement, black people were marching from Selma to Montgomery over the Edmond Petis Bridge. The bridge is steeply inclined, and it's impossible to see over its high point to the other side. So when people were marching from Selma to Montgomery climbing up one end of the bridge, they didn't know what was waiting for them over the crest of the bridge—a phalanx of state troopers and deputized civilians carrying guns.

Now I was in Selma helping to defend LDF clients, who had been Dr. King's deputies in that part of the state, against charges of voter fraud. The courtroom was packed everyday. It was a movement trial, and it was very, very exciting to be a part of it. And that is when I decided one day I would be doing voting rights litigation at the Legal Defense Fund, and if I couldn't do that, I didn't want to be a lawyer.

And I think my father understood that because he realized where my need to do socially important work came from. When all is said and done, my parents, both of them, are really principled people. Which means for me that they charted their lives based on guiding principles, not on what they wanted in the moment. That doesn't mean they never succumbed to temptation or let character flaws determine behavior, but only that they were forever trying to get it right. Like most people, they were fallible, and I saw it in the life we lived together. And like most kids, I found it painful to learn my parents weren't perfect people. But with all their flaws there was a grandeur about them. They made their mistakes, but when they did, they never pretended that they hadn't. They made me a decent person by who they were, and through it all they gave me an incomparable life.

⟢ *Danya Cunningham is a voting rights attorney and an associate director of the Working Communities Division of the Rockefeller Foundation. She was formerly a defense attorney for the NAACP Legal Defense Fund.*

Edith McClean,
my mother

Me on a return trip
to Jamaica

A Certain Measure of Grace

❧

I grew up in a little place on the north coast of Jamaica, called Lime Hall. It was eight miles from Ocho Rios. Lime Hall was a place where doors were never locked at night and children ran from one house to another to play, without their parents worrying. The day-to-day simplicity of our lives was reflected in our small colorful houses, with little curtains on the windows. It was a place where neighbors came over to share in the joy of a young woman giving birth and the sadness that surrounded an old man dying.

But, of course, it is not only the old that die, and it was my father's unexpected death that became the before-and-after moment of my life. Our neighbors in little Lime Hall came running early that morning when my mother cried out after finding my father, a man in the prime of life, lying on the ground, nearly paralyzed by what the doctor later called a stroke.

They helped my mother lift and carry him from the ground to the bed. And they were there during my father's final few days, crowded into his bedroom praying loudly for God to be with him, while they murmured more quietly for God to protect and bless us, his family, if it was God's will to take him. And as they came, they stayed for a last meal with my beloved father. They ate where they sat. Some on the floor, others on benches and chairs that had been pulled into the room and gathered around the bed and along the wall, so that Dada could see their faces and our faces, filled with love and sadness, and in the case of his children, with uncertainty, but beside him to the end.

Despite the grim prognosis given us by the doctor, his death, barely a month before my ninth birthday, came unexpectedly. Now that I'm older, I realize all family deaths come that way, no matter how sick your loved one might be. It is human nature to believe there is still hope until the last breath. And so, none of us were prepared when it happened, not my mother or my brothers and sister nor I. Before my father's death, our lives together were marked by days of pleasure with each other and the life we lived together. After his death, a tornado of new responsibility hit my life, laying on me things that I had never before had to consider, having to be more than a sister to my siblings and more than a daughter to my mother.

My father's name was James Uriah, but I called him Dada most of the time. Calling him Dada made him mine alone, and it seemed to fit him, because he was the kind of person who, with a touch, a hug, or by rubbing my head, said everything is okay. When Dada was alive he was the giver and I was the receiver. When he died, I became a giver as well as a receiver.

My mother's name was Edith. She was a woman who believed that things should be done a certain way, always speaking perfect English at home, and sitting us down to eat properly rather than on the run, as we all wanted to do when our friends beckoned to us at times after school. Deviating from the correct way of doing things—her way—only asked for trouble. She was short in stature with coffee-colored skin. On her head she often wore a headscarf that wrapped around her head twice and knotted in the front. Sometimes she wore men's pants around the house; I'm not sure if they belonged to Dada or if she made them especially for herself. She loved to cook and take care of the house and our needs, constantly making sure that our clothes were washed and freshly pressed. With limited time and resources, she managed to do so much for us. As I grew up I learned that she was a proud woman of great complexity.

I still recall that the way she cared for us had been one of the things my father loved most about her. On our walks home together from school, he often talked about "what an amazing cook your mother is, and look at how she keeps our house so very clean, and us in order." Then he would casually mention that I should never complain when mother asked me to do something to help out, and I never did. Except once, just before he died.

My mother loved gardening and prided herself on being a good gardener. She could make any plant come to life, even if it was brown and shriveled up at the root. In her garden were grapefruit trees, pimentos, roses, daisies, and other exotic flowers. Her garden was one of the most envied in our little town. I watched her pull the weeds and dig the trenches, arranging the shrubs and bulbs in patterns that didn't make sense at the time. But once those flowers bloomed, the profusion of color and the harmony of patterns that the different types of flowers created were more than pleasing to the eye. Mother poured a great deal of attention and love into those bushes, so that soon thereafter, they appeared in every corner of the garden, lined in rows, with alternating colors—deep red, yellow, pink, and white flowers. She was so good at growing roses that people from all over the village knew about her roses and would come to our gate and ask for a clipping. She often allowed strangers from surrounding towns to come into the garden and cut what they wanted. No matter how many flowers people took, there always seemed to be plenty left in the garden for us. And perhaps those flowers grew so abundantly because my mother gave them away so often. Hadn't she studied gardening? some of these people would ask. She would thank them and, smiling her sweetest smile, reply, "No, I taught myself." At dinner with us after they had gone, she would beam with pride when telling us how many people came to ask for her flowers that day and about the compliments she had received on the structure of the garden.

My mother had a certain special grace about her. This was often reflected in the way she stood and listened, showing real interest in whatever we children had to say. Having her rapt attention when I spoke to her made me feel important and as if she cared about what I was feeling and thinking.

Most evenings we ate a family dinner, and Mother was always seated at the head of the table next to Dada, watching us eat the food she had cooked, holding a ladle overflowing with greens or plaintains over our plates whenever she thought one of us was ready for seconds.

Every day when she helped me get ready for school, she made sure that each part of my school uniform—the stiffly starched white shirt and pleated skirt—was ironed to perfection. The shirt was so white that it was almost blinding in its brightness. I was so afraid to get it dirty before leaving for school that I often ate breakfast in my underwear, so that any drops of food that fell from my fork or mouth wouldn't land on my precious white blouse, marring its perfection.

Once dressed, my mother would smooth down the collar of my blouse to make sure it wasn't wrinkled before I left the house. She would also check my hands for telltale signs that I hadn't scrubbed my nails as she had instructed, taking both my hands in the warmth of her own, which smelled like whatever she had cooked for our breakfast. I love the memory of her checking my hands, inspecting each of my fingers individually, pretending she had found some dirt, saying, "Now what's that?" and when I said, "What?" and bent my head down to look, she would playfully pinch my nose. Her hands were strong and rough to the touch yet gentle. Satisfied with her inspection, she'd kiss me and usher me out the door, often repeating a string of commands as she did so: "Don't forget to wait for Daddy after school, remember to lift your skirt when you go to the bathroom, and watch out for. . . ." The only one I heard and remembered as the door slammed on her voice was "Don't be late. I will have something nice for you when you come home this afternoon."

After I had my own children, what I had thought at the time was my mother's strictness I now understood to be an expression of her caring for us. She wanted us to be good children, behaving when we were supposed to, learning our lessons and heeding her when she tried to guide us. Of course, many of her ways would seem so old-fashioned today. For instance, she believed that a child should be spoken to first, before addressing a grown-up. However, there were times when she made exceptions. Prim and proper is the description that best fits the way my mother strove to raise us. She was always fixing my clothes and smoothing my hair in place before sending me off to school because she abhorred the idea that someone might sneer at me if everything wasn't perfect.

As prim and proper as my mother was, my dad was relaxed and easygoing. In retrospect, they were a good match for each other. "Let them be themselves," he would say to her when she corrected our English.

"I don't like them speaking that dialect," she'd say. "Proper English is to be spoken in this house."

"They are doing okay," Dada would say. "Let them be themselves."

I was the firstborn of the four children in our family. From the time I could walk and talk, Dada lavished attention on me. He knew I loved sugarcane, and often when he came to get me from school we'd stop and sit next to the stream on the way home. As the water bubbled over the rocks and I found the perfect place to sit, he'd pull out a piece of sugarcane and peel it for me. I watched him peel the tough outside off and cut the inside into tiny bite-size pieces that he handed to me on the tip of his pocketknife. "Careful now," he'd say as I lifted the bits off the knife.

When I bit down on the little chunks of cane, light-brown juice squirted out of my mouth and landed on Dada's shirt. He often laughed at the way I greedily stuffed all the pieces into my mouth. "Careful now, you don't have to eat that too fast you know," he cautioned me. "Remember what your mother would say with you eating that fast." As we sat there, he would ask me, "What did you do today, Sister?" I don't remember exactly when Dada started to call me Sister, a name he used only for me, but he rarely called me by my christened name, Joyce. When he called me Sister, it made me feel special and grown-up. When I finished chewing my cane, he'd ask, "You've had enough?" When I nodded yes to him, still chewing a bit, he'd reach out his hand to take mine and we'd walk home together.

Often on those after-school talks, sitting and eating cane, Dada had a habit of looking into my eyes, brown, bright, and friendly, just like his own, I'm often told. He never looked down or away when he talked to me, always into my eyes. When I asked him why he looked at my eyes all the time, he said doing so told him what was happening inside me. "Can I see inside you too?" I asked.

"When you get bigger," he said.

"How?" I asked him.

"You will just know," he said.

I didn't understand what he meant, but when I played with my friends or with my brothers and sisters, I tried to mimic just how Dada held his head, and I looked at them, without saying what I was up to. And they would ask me, "What are you looking for?" Embarrassed, I never answered.

Those moments we spent together, talking and eating sugarcane, were some of the happiest of my growing-up years. We talked about everything, what had happened at school, what I was learning, the fact that I had walked outside without my shoes to be with my new friend who didn't have any shoes. "Better not tell your mother," he'd say, which made us both laugh. I was full and happy at those times, not so much because of the cane he always had for me, but rather because I was spending time with my father.

We could always count on Mother being in the kitchen when we got home, surrounded by the smells of the indescribably delicious dishes she had made for our dinner. As we came through the door, we were often met with "I hope you two are hungry." And Dada, who was never one to miss a chance, walked up to Mother and lightly smacked her on the bottom or playfully pulled at her hair and kissed her on the cheek, shooing me away playfully with one hand while he held Mother close to him with the other.

The summer of the year before Dada got sick, Mother insisted that I spend time with the cousins at Aunt Dora's. After the first two days, I used to think, "Please, can I go home now?" I wanted to see Dada and to eat Mom's cooking. But I was afraid to tell my aunt because she would tell Dada, and he thought I was a big girl now, although I didn't feel like one, especially here without my parents. I missed everything—our house, Dada, Mom, my brothers and sisters, and the things we did together. But whenever I tried to tell my mother that I didn't want to go to Aunt Dora's, she would say, "They are family. You need to get to know them." They lived near the sea, and she knew how much I liked being by the ocean. But I missed my life with my family more than I wanted to be at the sea.

Also, at my aunt's I never got the nice things that my mother gave me at home. One day, in the middle of my stay, Dada came to visit, and we went for a walk with my cousins on the beach. He brought one of Mother's spice buns with him. We all thought she made the best spice buns in all of Lime Hall. They were studded with plump juicy raisins and pieces of dried citron, and lots of ginger and other spices. Her buns were always dark brown, like chocolate, dark, soft and moist, never too sweet. When I saw the bun in Dada's hand, I jumped up and down and said, "You brought me a bun!" I threw myself on him with excitement. I said, "Dada, you know the last one you brought? I never tasted it." At that moment, he took out the bun, sliced it, and handed the slice to me, which I immediately popped into my mouth, savoring its richness. After a few slices he asked, "Have you had enough?" Taking one tiny piece more, I smiled and nodded yes, thanking him with a mouthful of bun. He handed my cousins the rest and said to them, "I want her to be happy." We had been walking on the beach and when we reached the house, Dada looked at me and said he had to go. My heart said, "Don't leave. I want to go with you." But I was nearly eight years old and a big girl, so I watched him leave and felt sad all in my bones. Later that evening he came back to take me home. I can't explain what I felt when I saw Dada in the door of my aunt's house telling her he'd come to take me home early. Although school would start soon, it felt like my summer vacation had just begun as Dada drove us home.

One of the best days in our little house was Sunday. There was time to sit down for each meal of the day, with a properly set table for breakfast, lunch, and dinner. We children went to church with Mother, while Dada fixed something in the yard, or the house, or with the plumbing. The busyness that guided our day-to-day existence was absent on Sunday. There was time for everything, and we lived properly as a family on that day, as Mother liked it to be.

Each meal was special, but breakfast was the best, with eggs and fried dumplings, salted codfish with achee, and all kinds of good Jamaican delicacies. Before any eating took place, Dada read the Bible and then he led a prayer to God, giving thanks and asking forgiveness and blessings over us, the food, and what we had. Mother and Dada always sat close to each other at the table. Whenever any of us children tried to sit next to them or wedge in between them for attention, we were gathered into their arms. For that one day, everything else was forgotten and we were together. The freedom of those days was easy and left an indelible mark on me, and I am grateful to my parents, and especially my mother, that she never hid anything that happened in our lives, especially when Dada got sick.

His sickness came early one morning just after my eighth birthday. It was a time of harvest for those who farmed and a season of hard work for Dada who was a plumber. Dada was a tall, lean man, with a sturdy build. He had dark mahogany skin, short, very soft hair, and a smile that came easily to his face. He liked to help anyone and would sometimes bring home stray cats and dogs if he saw them on the road. He was always working in someone's home or office, fixing their pipes, as he called it. The morning he fell, all of us children were asleep in our beds. Dada had the habit of getting out of bed at five o'clock every morning to prepare for work. That morning he left the house to go out back, and because she kept him company in the morning, Mother was in the kitchen making coffee for them to share before the house awakened.

They knew each other's habits so well that when Dada didn't come back, Mother went to look for him. When she found him, he was lying on the ground on his back, not too far from the back door of the house. She cried out his name so loud that it woke all of us.

I know I was startled at the sound of Dada's named being yelled in the quiet morning. So much so, that I jumped out of my bed and ran outside in the direction of Mother's cry. By the time I got there, she was calling us to help her. She screamed, "Children, come! Somebody, please come and help me with James!" When I saw my father flat on his back like that, his eyes closed, my heart felt like it twisted in my chest. I fell on my knees next to him. I couldn't do anything more than hold his hand and frantically call his name: "Dada, do you hear me? Dada, open your eyes! Dada, open your eyes!" By this time, my oldest brother Jack was there, and all the other children in the house were now up, and the next-door neighbors, who had probably been aroused by Mother's cries and the noise that we were all making, had come too. I heard people asking, "What's happened?" And my mother told my brother Jack to get the doctor. Later, he told us that he ran the entire way to the doctor's house. It was over two miles.

I knelt by my father, holding his hand and rubbing his face. I kept talking to him, calling his name as I knelt there. "Answer me," I begged. "Dada, I want you to answer me, I want you to answer me." My mother ran into the house to get a blanket to cover him and a pillow to put under his head. By the time Mother got back with the blanket, Dada had opened his eyes, and I felt he had heard me calling him. He stared at me but didn't say anything.

When the doctor finally arrived, it was already late morning. We were all waiting in Dada's room, where the neighbors had helped to carry him. After the doctor examined my father, he announced that he had had a stroke. We watched quietly as the doctor gave my mother instructions on what to do to take care of my father. I remember the doctor coming and going several times that day to check on my father. Dada's eyes were open, but he lay quite still on his bed.

And that was the beginning of our lives changing irrevocably. It is difficult to forget the last days that Dada was alive. Although he was sick, his spirit never dimmed. In the beginning I thought, as a child does, that he would get better. He had to get better, he just had to. It never occurred to me that my strong father would not get out of that bed one day and be himself, doing the things that we had always done together. But, as I watched him stay in bed more than he had ever stayed in bed before, it finally became clear that everything had changed. He who had always been strong, working and helping all of us, now got out of bed only to drag himself to the bathroom. I don't remember how long the first part of his illness went on, only that just as I was hoping he might be getting better, he had a heart attack and was taken to the hospital.

It all passed in a blur, the time in the hospital, how long he was gone. There was a silent hardness to the quiet that engulfed our home. Mother was there but always busy, going back and forth to the hospital, cooking for us. She didn't say much to us, just worked to make sure our surroundings and habits stayed as close as possible to what they had been before Dada's accident. She was like a little machine. I don't remember how long Dada was in the hospital. I just remember him coming back home. In those days, the late 1950s, you didn't stay in the hospital for a long time if there was no hope. Although none of us was told it at the time, I think Mother knew that Dada had been sent home to die.

It seemed to go on for some time, perhaps because I was young, and when you are young time seems to stretch and extend itself much more than it does when age catches up with you. In retrospect, looking back over those days, it happened fairly quickly.

It's Sunday now, and many months and weeks have passed since my father's stroke. I am in my father's room with my mother and Dada. She is heavy because she is going to have another baby. Dada is in bed. He has been there for what seems like forever now. "Honey," says Dada to my mother, "cut the flowers to give away, but this time don't give them all away because I will be needing some." My mother makes a small sound, but says nothing.

"Honey," he calls to my mother later that same day. "Please get Mr. Trevor to come and shave me today." It had been a while now that Dada couldn't lift his hand to touch his face.

"Are you sure?" she asks.

"Yes, I'm sure," he manages to say, as they exchange knowing looks.

The week Mr. Trevor came to shave Dada strange things happened. In the past, my mother was the disciplinarian; Dada never spanked me. But one day toward the end of the week, Dada was sitting in a chair in the kitchen in his bathrobe, his cane leaning on his knee. Mother asked me to do something, and I said, "But Mom," and my father heard and called me to him. Before I reached his chair, he took his cane, and with the hook end, he grabbed me by the neck and pulled me to him. I was surprised because Dada had never done anything like that to me before. He pulled me across his lap and slapped me. Not hard, but it was an act that stunned me. "What's that for?" I asked. "Don't you ever talk back to your mother that way, because I will not be here to correct you," he said. I felt embarrassed and ashamed. My father had never hit me before, ever; his hand had only touched me with tenderness. "What does this mean?" I thought.

And then it came to me. Oh my goodness, he thinks he is going to die. He can't die; he's going to be here. He has to be here, to see me grow up. That evening, I couldn't sleep, thinking about Dada and everything that was happening around us, and to us. I heard my father talking with my mother. "You have to name the baby," he said to her. "It's going to be a boy, and you will have to name him yourself." Up to this point they had named each of us children together. I didn't hear my mother say anything, and the silence settled empty around us like the darkness of the night.

The week passed, and everything that happened around me felt strange. Many of Dada's good friends came over to our home. That Sunday they crowded into his bedroom to sing and pray for him. I kept telling myself, "He is going to be here, he's not going anywhere, he is going to be here." Dinnertime came, and Dada was propped up on his many pillows while we all gathered around him to eat dinner together. Although he asked for certain things that night, he didn't eat much. My mom cooked what he wanted. There were chairs and benches, and whoever couldn't find a chair sat on the floor, and we all had dinner. It was the first Sunday of April.

After dinner, people left just as dusk came. It was about five or six o'clock, early still. For whatever reason, we were exhausted that night and went to bed earlier than usual. On Monday morning, my brother Jack usually went up the street for milk. Every Monday, we bought fresh milk from people who lived up there, but on this particular morning Jack didn't want to go. He didn't give a reason; he just didn't want to go. My mother said to him, "Go get the milk. Your father will need to drink it." And my dad said, "You know, when he comes back with that milk I don't think I'll be able to drink it." Jack brought back the milk and my mother scalded it, preparing it the way my father liked to drink it. My mother set the glass of warm milk on the table next to his bed; it stayed there for the rest of the day, untouched.

Jack and I went to the stream behind the house to play together. We ended up in the exact spot that Dada and I often sat in after school. While we were down there, fooling around, a neighbor ran and called us. "Your father wants all of you to come now!" We both ran to get back to the house, and I was the first one to get there.

Something had happened in the short time since I last saw him. His mouth was now crooked to the right and his voice was kind of guttural. But he could talk and seemed to have all of his senses. He called each one of us into his bedroom, one at a time.

He took my hand as I stood next to his bed. Without words, he pulled me to sit next to him. I could see him straining to speak, and when he did, his voice came out strong. I looked at his face, and into his eyes. They were brown like they had always been, but not so bright anymore. "Sister," he called me. "Yes," I whispered. "I know you're gonna be a good girl, and you won't give your mom any problems. You must look out for the younger ones and take care of your mom." He rested a moment and then continued, "I love you so much and you will not be seeing me, but I will always be with you."

Because he was unable to really sit up, I leaned across him on the bed, placing my head on his chest. I held his hand tight, feeling the little scars from cuts those times he had cut cane for me and nipped himself as well. I lay there listening to him breathe, feeling his chest rise and fall. He sounded tired to me, and I moved my head beneath his chin and felt his lips on my forehead, warm and slightly moist. He kissed me again. And I lay there feeling his warmth as he murmured, "Good-bye my sister, good-bye." "Where are you going?" I asked. He said, "I am going where I'm called." And this time I understood.

"Do you remember your grandmother?" he asked. I did. Grandmother died when I was four. The memory of her lying in the coffin, not moving, had always been a stark one for me. Her very long hair had been braided and neatly laid down the front of her body. "Do you remember your grandmother? Well, that's what's going to happen to me too." Silence rested between us. "No matter what, I will always be with you and you will always remember me," he said. I felt his heart beating beneath my ear, and the reality was that he was with me right there at that moment, he hasn't gone away, he is still with me.

After he had said his good-bye to each of us children, we stood in the bedroom doorway, watching, confused, not sure what to do, and looking at Dada and my mother, who had come in to sit next to him on the bed. Dada used to sleep on three pillows, and Mother moved two of them to the side of the bed so that they supported him as he lay on his side. He was trying to talk to my mother, who moved from the bed to her knees beside him. Her elbows rested on the covers as her face nearly touched his. They were whispering to each other. A neighbor woman said, "Let us get out of the room and leave them together for a while. They have to say their good-byes." I left the room, went down to the stream, sat on our rock where we had sat together so many times before, and cried. It was about noontime on Monday. Dada never spoke to me again.

The night came, and at 7:15 P.M. Dada passed away. I was out on the veranda, and the neighbor woman who had called us from the stream came and said he was gone. I looked up at the moon and said, "No more Dada. No more Dada." That was one month before my ninth birthday.

After his death, my mother gave birth to my little brother, Maxi, and went to work shortly thereafter. She, who had never worked a day that I could remember while my father was alive, now became the breadwinner of our family. I became a mother to my little brother Maxi. To my mother, I became a surrogate partner. To my sister and two other brothers, I became the person they looked up to when our mother wasn't at home.

By day, my mother was silent and moving through her new responsibility of working to take care of us. At night I heard her crying behind her bedroom door. I went to my father's grave to talk to him because I felt my mother had too many burdens to bear and couldn't hear mine.

Time passed. My mother remarried several years later, and when I was sixteen, I left my family in Lime Hall to go live with friends in Kingston—friends my mother knew very little about. I began to work for my friends, taking care of their children, and a year later met and married a man my father would not have approved of. He was seventeen years older than I and had a drinking problem, which didn't reveal itself until after we were married. He was a good provider, and in the beginning I thought we were well suited as marriages go. In fact, he was a factory owner and there was always plenty of money, and houses for me and my siblings when they came. But he lacked the one thing that my father would have wanted for me: He was a begrudging giver. But I had chosen him because I wanted stability and certainty, which I had not known since Dada.

Eventually my husband and I had four children, whom I love dearly. When they came, I finally understood the depth of love and responsibility that a mother feels for her children, even if she never speaks about it.

My husband and I tried everything to save our marriage, but the drinking got worse the longer we were together, and the sad part is that it didn't seem to be connected to anything that was on the surface of our lives. He never talked to me about it the way my parents used to talk out their problems, and over time the drinking came between us in a way that threatened my children and me. Leaving my husband was the hardest thing I had ever done as a woman.

My mother, who had not approved of my husband but accepted my choice, was there for all of it. For my marriage, she made the cake, arranged for my dress, and did everything necessary to make my wedding a success. For the birth of my children, Mother dropped everything and was there when I needed her, and even when I didn't ask. She had overcome many obstacles after my father died. She found the means to get out and find a job and held our family together through those hard days and months after Dada had passed. And now, after marriage and children, my mother had come to hold me together too.

Then out of the blue everything changed. I was offered an opportunity to come to the United States. My marriage had ended, and I needed to make a new life for my children. I was offered a job in America, to clean house for a wealthy American couple. I didn't even have a passport, so I scrambled and arranged everything quickly without knowing what lay ahead.

The decision to leave my children with my mother was bittersweet and tough. But I was determined to make a better life for them and for myself. Going to America was my best chance to overcome the mistake of my marriage and to make a fresh start for my children. I was prepared to go only with my mother's blessing, and she gave it without forethought. She would mother my children for the time I needed to get back on my feet, she said. And it was at that point in our lives as mother and daughter that I fully understood how my mother and I were part of one whole and that her life and her ways flowed into my life and my ways.

After my marriage ended she said to me, "There were times when you thought I didn't love you, after Dada passed, but I loved you so much and counted on you to help us make it through. You were my support, and I didn't know how to tell you except to do things for you. I will take your children," she said.

In retrospect, I recognize the astonishing courage my mother possessed to hold us together as a family after Dada's death. I realized that her silence held love, which she passed on to me, just as my father had done so openly. But, for Mother, it had to be different because she was different from Dada. And her strength and courage were not diminished, because she kept them inside and shared them when I needed them the most. From my mother I learned I could do anything, and her example of strength and courage kept me going, a lesson that I would use to raise my own daughter. My mother gave me the gifts of strength and courage, and my father taught me how to receive them.

ᏗᏌᎧ *Joyce Hunt has been the proud owner of a successful cleaning business for the past twenty-five years. She plans to retire in late 2001, after she turns sixty-five years old. Although she lost her father when she was very young, she drew on the lessons he taught her as she became a woman and a pillar of strength for her mother. She passed these lessons and her love on to her daughter Donna, whose story follows this one.*

Me, in front
of our new
home in
Connecticut

Me, at the
typewriter

It's Crying Time Again

My mother's name is Joyce Eliose and to me, she is very beautiful—her skin, her hair, the way she wore those lovely floral dresses of bright, happy colors, yellow, red, sky blue, and green. When she met and married my father, she was in her twenties, and my dad was in his forties. My dad was tall and dark-skinned, a big man who had many moods, most of which I never got to see because we left him before I was six years old. I am dark like him and inherited his big brown eyes, wide mouth, and short thick hair, but I got my mother's hips, which are round and wide and womanly.

In my memory I am about five years old, and one of the things that stands out the most about that year of my life is that my father had two houses, one in the city and one in the country. He also had a factory where black iron furniture and big red clay pots were made. The factory was very close to our house in Kingston, on a street called Bass Drive, where I was born and lived until I was nearly six years old. There were four of us children. Tommy and Mark were my two older brothers, whom my father sent off to boarding school, so I saw them only on school holidays and at Christmas. They were both big and tall like my father, their skin different shades of chocolate brown. And then there was my little brother Lance, who looked more like my mother and trailed along after me around the house, just as I trailed along after my mother. Whatever time my mother wasn't working in the factory with my father, she spent at home with Lance and me and Tensie, our housekeeper. Our lives seemed normal, but the day came when everything would change almost without warning.

Before I started to go to school regularly, my mother sometimes took Lance and me to the factory, where we sat at her feet playing with rust-colored clay, making a whole village of houses and people while she worked with her papers. We were surrounded by big clay pots as big as my father and empty black iron chairs like those we had at home on our veranda. There were people everywhere in the factory, lifting pots and moving furniture. When I asked Momma what they were doing in my father's place, she told me they worked for him. Even though I didn't think of it the way I can now, I was impressed with my father's factory and that all those people worked for him.

Before I could even button my own dresses I remember my mother as a constantly moving force of energy. With her five-foot-six frame and smooth, toast-colored skin, she had a ripe mouth with lips shaped like slices of peach. She never wore makeup, or at least I never saw her use it. Looking at her now, I can tell that she must have been a real fox when she was younger. She has a shape like one of those little Coca-Cola bottles, that says "Bam, I'm here!" But she is more than her shape. She is in charge of herself, and it shows in the way she carries herself and in everything she does.

There are moments from those early years when we were all together as a family that deserve to be brought out, tenderly dusted off and remembered at special times in my life. For example, the way Momma used to pick me up and let my short little legs wrap themselves around her waist as best they could, so that I could hang off of her, like she was a tree trunk and I a branch extending from it, as she carried me from one room to the next. No matter how tired she was or how often I raised my arms to her, she never denied me. It seemed at the time that we were connected by something invisible that kept us close, no matter how often we were separated by her work or other circumstances. The knowledge that she was often closeby provided a comfort and stability to my life. Momma used to tell me that when my father came home from work and found me hanging off her, he would say, "Joyce, if you don't put that girl down she will never walk and will expect to be carried through life." My mother answered him with a shy laugh and said, "She's my only daughter; what am I suppose to do?" When she eventually stopped carrying me, I crawled and then walked behind her, getting dirt all over my clothes, especially those afternoons we spent in the garden. I was just very curious and didn't want to miss anything.

Even when I did something bad, or went against her wishes in some small way and Momma punished me, she made me feel like it wasn't the end of the world and everything would be just fine. Her way of letting me know that I mattered was there in the attention to detail that defined everything she did with me: the way she held my hands and guided them as we planted bulbs together in the garden; or how she placed her knee on the chair to stop it from moving, while I stood on it and watched her peel vegetables for our dinner. And how she carefully wrapped her hands around my head after she had braided my hair, patting and pressing it tenderly and saying that I looked even prettier than when she last did it.

When finally I started to go to school, the first week was a hard one. I was scared to go to the bathroom, so I wet myself nearly every day. The toilet had a tank on top with a long chain that dangled down with a wooden handle. It was so big that it looked like a monster to me. I was ashamed to tell my teacher that I was scared, especially because the other girls didn't seem to have a problem. So I just waited in my seat, legs squeezed tightly together, until I couldn't squeeze anymore. So for those first few days, I peed on myself and had to be taken home before the schoolday ended. In the beginning, I didn't tell Momma what the problem was, and everyone wanted to know what was wrong with me. It also was a time when my brothers Mark and Tommy were home from boarding school. Each day that first week, one of them walked me to school, and on the days I peed on myself, they heard about it first, because they played with some of their friends near my school and came and got me and took me home. Momma never made me feel bad but instead took me by the hand to the bathroom, cleaned me up, and said that I had to start going to the bathroom the regular way instead of waiting until it was too late. Then I told her about the toilet monster, and the next day she took me to school and to the bathroom and showed me how the toilet worked and made me understand that it was not a monster.

I will never forget how easy it was when she was there with me. How she picked me up and held me when I pulled the string and the water came gushing down into the hole. She promised to make my favorite pumpkin soup for a whole week if I went to the bathroom every day instead of wetting myself. I think I was a big pain in the butt over that, but Momma never made a fuss, and soon my fear of the toilet monster passed.

Momma was a very good gardener, and the two things that she liked to do more than anything else were cooking and gardening. She often smelled like ginger and green grass, a scent that lingered in my nose long after she had put me down from an afternoon of carrying me from the garden to the house.

Whenever she cooked, she set up a chair for me to stand on to watch her make soup. She chopped ginger and pumpkin into tiny chunks for her famous pumpkin soup. Sometimes she even let me help measure out the spices and put the chunks of pumpkin into the pot. I was her official taster, and when the soup was finally ready I always got the first taste. After she ladled the soup into a serving bowl, I put my entire face into the pot to lick out every drop of the soup left there. I ended up with bits of soup on my eyelashes, cheeks, and nose, and Momma laughed until tears came to her eyes. That was some good soup. She never stopped me from licking that pot and often took my sticky hands in hers, wiping them clean and kissing them, saying, "You silly girl, there's plenty more left, you know, and you can have as much as you want." Sticking out my bowl to her, I always asked for more, and she'd fill it with the dusty orange soup. The chunks of pumpkin were so tender that they collapsed when I touched them with my spoon. The onions melted in my mouth.

During our ritual of soup making, my brothers, if they were not away at school, were often off playing with their friends, and my father was at the pottery factory. The men in our family rarely came into the kitchen when food was being cooked, except for my little brother Lance. He spent most of his time following me, crawling behind me as soon as he could and waddling once he learned how to walk. And most of the time, if he didn't have to take a nap, Momma let him stay in the kitchen with us, which meant that sometimes I had to play with him to keep him out of trouble. I watched him and made sure he was okay, and afterward Momma would tell me how much I had helped her by doing so. Knowing I was being helpful to her motivated me to be extra careful about making sure Lance stayed out of trouble when he was alone with me.

Besides Lance coming along, there was something else that changed our soup-making ritual, something I didn't understand until years after it had happened. It is attached to an early memory of my mother that goes back to when I was five years old. It is a memory that had no meaning for me until I myself was a grown-up. Now I understand that in terms of my own sense of self, it represents the confusion of my childhood.

I am standing in front of the bathroom door trying to reach the doorknob. I want to go in, but I am too short to reach and turn the knob to push the door open. So I jump up and down trying to grab the handle with my hands. My palms become sweaty from the effort. Tensie, our housekeeper, is standing behind me. She doesn't say anything; nor does she help me. She just watches me struggle to grab the knob. I hear no talking, but I know that Momma and Dad are behind that bathroom door. I have seen them go in, and all I can hear are occasional muffled sounds coming through the door. I get down on the floor and try to peek beneath the door, but the gap is too narrow and I can't see anything. The sounds coming through the door remind me of the one I make falling out of bed in my sleep and hitting the floor, a soft thump. There are no words, just that soft thumping. My parents often closed themselves in their bedroom to talk, away from us. There was never any screaming, but in my memories I have a sense of tension between them. After the locked bathroom door was opened, that tension was strongly there. They did not look at each other while we ate dinner together. Tommy and Mark were at school, so it was little Lance, Momma, my father, and me; the silence was broken only by my questions and chatter. They both answered my questions, and looking back I realize they weren't talking to each other.

That day of the locked bathroom was a day of questions unanswered. I can't describe exactly what I felt, but I knew even then that something was going very wrong. A few days later, I was in the kitchen with Momma, and she didn't fuss over me the way she usually did. I had to ask her to set up my special chair so that I could help her. "Not today, Donna," she said, and I began to whine and beg her to set up my chair so that I could watch her. She made me sit at the table. There was one pot on the stove, and the vegetables just lay on the table with the cutting board. There was no cutting or chopping like she usually did, but instead Momma stood in front of the pot stirring whatever was inside, until it boiled. I saw the steam coming off the top. That was just fine with me because I thought it meant we were going to eat soup, Momma's pumpkin soup, for which I was prepared to wait. As I waited, I watched her walk around the kitchen, but she didn't cut the vegetables. She just went to the window, paused, looked out, and then walked to the door. She finally stopped stirring the soup and took a cup of hot liquid from the pot. She didn't stop to put it in the bowl in front of me. Steam followed her as she walked past me. My eyes followed her down the hall, to the bedroom where my father was asleep. I heard him scream and then saw him run past me and out the kitchen door. I don't remember the rest. I don't remember if I cried, only that I was confused and that there was no soup for us.

Everything changed for us after that day, but nobody told me why. After that incident my father came back and then Momma was gone. We never saw her leave, and I don't even remember how much time passed. All I remember is that Momma wasn't there with us anymore. Nothing was ever explained to us because we were children, and that was the Jamaican way. Children are children, with no right to have their curiosity satisfied. At least that's how my mother and father were both raised, the real old-fashioned way. So we didn't get any explanations and had to go along with whatever was happening, without questioning anybody. We had no way of knowing at the time that my mother was working behind the scenes to make everything okay. My big brothers, Mark and Tommy, were away at boarding school, and Lance, my father, and I were left in the house on Bass Drive, with Tensie. Each day, she looked after us while my father went to work. In the evenings, I waited up for my father to come home. Some nights he brought me little chocolate mints that were soft and melted on my tongue with a taste like fresh air. Hmm, hmm, hmm, I loved eating those mints. Some nights I got Lance up to wait with me, and we'd sneak out of our bedrooms and sit on the big sofa in the dark waiting for Daddy to get home. Lance had to whisper to talk to me so that we wouldn't get caught by Tensie. Usually, Lance would fall asleep with his head on my lap. I'd rub his hair and squeeze and pat his head just the way Momma did to me when she wanted to let me know that everything was going to be okay.

Soon Daddy took Lance and me to the second house. There was no Tensie, and my mother wasn't there. "Where is Momma?" I ask my father. There was silence between us. "Daddy?" I ask again, and he says, "She went on a trip."

"Are we going to be together soon?" I ask.

No answer. "Let's go eat," he says. "Go get your things and we will go to your favorite restaurant."

"What about Momma?" I ask.

He replies, "Donna, please just do as I say!"

The following morning, Daddy left early for work. He had hired a new woman to look after us; she came that morning, fed us, and got us dressed, and then left to run an errand, she said. She didn't come back. We were alone in the house for the whole day. There was nobody to make us lunch and to take care of us. Evening comes and the lady doesn't come back, and Lance and I are hungry. There was no Daddy, no Momma, and no Tensie. The neighbors saw Lance and me playing on the veranda, but no one came to ask us if we were okay.

There was a café bar close to the house where my father often went to be with his friends. With time, I would come to understand that my father drank a lot and that it changed how he acted, but I never saw him drink in front of us. I did see him act funny at times, but he was always able to play with us, and he came home each night while we lived in the second house. I thought about the café and knew they sold beef patties there and thought we might be able to get some. I took Lance by the hand and we walked up the street to the café. The woman who owned the bar took one look at our faces and knew who our father was. "You sure are Samuel's children," she says, peering over the counter at us. "You have his eyes and his teeth," she states, proud of her discovery. "What do you want today child? Your father's not here," she says.

"Can I have some patties to take home?" I ask quietly.

She looks at me. "Everything all right over there, is it?"

"Yes," I say, remembering how Momma always said to be polite to adults. She gives me the brown paper–wrapped patties, and I hold them tightly to my chest, spots of grease from their yellow crust seeping through the paper and adding to the aroma. "My father said to put this on his bill," I tell her, and she smiles her assent to my lie. Impatient to taste their goodness, I smile back and turn to run the few blocks home, pulling Lance along behind me.

Put it on his bill did not go over very well when my father came home and found out what had happened. I explained that the new woman who was supposed to come to look after Lance and me never came back.

"Why did you go to the woman at the bar? Why not call me to tell me that you were hungry? Or that the lady didn't come?" He put me over his knee and spanked me. It hurt my feelings so bad because he had never done that to me before. I was his only daughter, and he had never spanked me ever; it was the first and only time. That very afternoon Tensie came back.

A few days later, my father came home early. He didn't have any mints for us, and he didn't look at Lance and me when we ran up to him. He just kept his head down, took us both by the hand, and led us into the house. "Where are we going?" I ask, as he pulls Lance and me along down the hall to the bedroom. He brought our cases out and placed them on the bed. "Where are we going?" I ask again. Daddy doesn't answer my questions. He keeps packing in silence, doesn't look at me, just continues to pack. "Please Donna, just help me do this," he says, and I try to put the clothes together and hand them to him. While I tried to help, Lance jumps up and down on the bed in the middle of our clothes. He is just like a toy jumping up and down on the bed, and Daddy doesn't pay attention to him. He never asks Lance to stop jumping on the bed as our clothes fill up the suitcases.

The next morning, my father carried our bags onto the veranda and told us to wait there while he got the car. I didn't ask where we were going anymore. He put us into the car and drove to the pottery factory. When we arrived, my mother was standing near the gate, and as soon as I saw her, I got out of the car and took off running toward her, yelling, "Momma, where have you been?" jumping up to hug her, with Lance right on my heels. She grabs and holds us both, pulling us tightly into her arms. "Where have you been, where are we going, what's happening?" I ask. "We're going to Grandma Edith's in the country," was all she said, gathering us up and hurriedly putting us into her car as Daddy watched. In the excitement we were put in the backseat, and I ask, "Is

Daddy coming? Who is going to take care of Daddy?" My questions were unanswered as I looked around for my father. I caught sight of him out the window. I know he heard me as the car pulled away. I looked back and watched Daddy watch us leave. He got smaller and smaller through the back window of the car. I felt sad inside, and my chest hurt. But I didn't say anything to Momma, and I didn't cry.

We finally got to Grandmother Edith's house in the country. When we arrived, Mark and Tommy were there. Momma had taken them out of boarding school and moved them there before she came to get Lance and me, she said. Momma didn't stay with us at Grandma Edith's. She did, however, come to see us nearly every day, and because I saw her so often, it didn't seem like she wasn't there living with us. My grandparents lived in a simple house and didn't have some of the things we were used to having. We didn't have Tensie anymore. And the truth is, life changed drastically living with my grandparents. They were country folk. I liked being able to walk to the store, and I couldn't at their place because they lived so far from town. And I wasn't used to walking barefoot in the banana walk. But the worst thing of all was I didn't live with my parents anymore, and even though my mother visited, she would always have to leave. She stayed most times until it got dark, eating dinner with us. When night came I hated to watch her go. I grew sad, watching her get ready to walk out the door. I felt that sadness reach inside of me to my bones.

"When will we go back home?" I asked her.

She looked away from me and finally said, taking my face with both her hands, squeezing it the way she did my head after she braided my hair, "I'm looking for a new home for us." I wanted to ask a thousand questions, like what about our old home? What about Daddy? What's happened to us? Why is this happening? Her face looked like it couldn't answer, and I didn't really know where to begin asking questions because I had too many, so I just kept quiet. But inside I knew it had something to do with the locked bathroom door and the soft sounds and the hot soup. We were not in our house together, we were at Grandma Edith's, and my father hadn't come to visit us. So much was happening, and I didn't know what to think.

There was a song that Momma and I liked to sing together, and on those first days especially, whenever she left, that song came into my head and played itself around and around. Each time, it came like an old friend, not really to comfort me, but just to be with me in my sadness. *It's crying time again, you're gonna leave me . . .*

Then one time when my mother came to visit us at Grandma Edith's, she said she was going to America to make a new life for us. "Is it far?" I asked. "Across the ocean," she said quietly. "I'm going to make a new life for us, and you will come to be with me as soon as I can send for you. Until then, I will write you and come and see you as often as I can." "When will I be with you?" is all I wanted to know. "It won't be long," she said. She hugged and kissed me and squeezed me so tight that I didn't want to let go, and then I watched her leave.

It didn't take much time after Momma left for me to start longing for the way we had lived. Longing for her presence and that of my father. I thought about how I used to play in the garden with Lance, and with my brothers when they were home from school, and about how Tensie used to give us whatever we wanted to eat. I thought about my father and the way he looked the day we left him standing in the road watching us drive out of his life. We didn't have a telephone at Grandma Edith's, so when my mother went to America she couldn't call. She wrote to us, yet letters were not like hearing her voice. I missed her all the time. I never wanted to run away, because I knew there was no way to get to her, but I thought about her most days and every night.

Shortly after my mother went to America, my grandparents built another house. They called it the top house. The original small, two-bedroom house where we stayed became known as the bottom house. The top house had three bedrooms, a modern bathroom with running water, a veranda with tile, which we had to shine and polish using coconut husk brushes until you could see your face in it.

My grandparents were basically farmers and they lived off the land, growing different kinds of crops, like coffee beans and pimentos. Farm life was very different from how we had lived with my parents. It seemed like my grandparents made us work really hard, and when we weren't in school, we were doing homework and working on the farm. In the morning, before they went to school, my brothers had to do what was called "tying the goats," which really meant taking the goats somewhere on the property to graze and tying them there. Even though I just watched, we all woke up at 6:00 A.M. and tied the goats before we left for school.

They were very quiet, private people, my grandparents. Actually, my grandmother's husband was really my step-grandfather. My mother's father died when my mom was almost nine years old. Momma said she used to call him Dada.

My grandmother Edith had two good friends, but we never saw them spend time together. It was the weirdest thing. She was like a workhorse. Every time you saw her, even just walking around the house, you knew she was going from one chore directly to another. But whatever she was doing, she was always humming a hymn, wearing men's pants, with her head tied up in a kerchief. As I got to know her better, I came to understand that she was very spiritual and really quiet. Soft spoken, but proud and firm. And she loved us, she really did love us, but it didn't seem so at the time because we were always working so hard. She told me that kids should be seen and not heard, and the way to ensure that happened was to teach us to get used to work and responsibility—that is how you raised good kids, kids able to make good lives for themselves and their own kids. She was very interested in what I needed, and not too much in what I wanted, which was different from my mother, who just wanted me to be happy. My step-grandfather used to tease us a lot, but I only realized it had been a loving teasing when we left to go to America to be with my mother, and I saw him break down and cry in the airport.

After Momma had been in America for a short time, she started flying back and forth to Jamaica to see us. Whenever she came, her visits were short, but they were like one big party. We got to ride in a car, which my grandparents didn't own, and we went to the beach. It was the best time, because those were things we never got to do with my grand-parents.

I remember her first trip back. It was raining, which loosened the gravel on the quarter-mile road that led to the top house. When her car drove up, we heard the pebbles being crushed on the driveway. We were all waiting for her. My brothers were jumping up and down on the steps and ran in tiny circles in the yard, while I sat on the steps and waited. When the car finally got there, my three brothers ran to meet it. I waited on the steps for Momma to notice me. When she got out of the car, my brothers nearly pulled her onto the ground jumping around her in their excitement, all of them talking at the same time, asking, "What did you bring for me? Is that for me?" I hung back on the steps alone, watching them. I adored her so much, but all I did was stare at her. She looked up from the boys surrounding her and saw me. She motioned with her hand for me to come to her. "Come over here and hug me," she finally said. And when I did, she took me in her arms and hugged and kissed me, all over my face and hair, and squeezed me until it was too tight in her arms. And it was only then that I felt comfortable and crazy happy because my mother was there. For the rest of the time she was with us I sat in her lap and cuddled with her whenever she sat down. I didn't care about the gifts. I was near her, sitting in her lap, beside her wherever she went. She held on to me the whole first day especially, stroking my hair and touch-ing me, to let me know that it was okay. It happened like that on each of her visits.

At that time, in the 1970s, anyone who moved from Jamaica to Amer-ica came back a big deal. All the neighbors came to see this woman who had been to America, this woman who hadn't just gone for a visit but who really lived there and worked there. To me, it felt like these neigh-bors and other grown-ups didn't know how much I wanted and needed to be with my mom, and took up her time. Or at least that's how I saw it. My grandfather killed a pig and a goat to roast. We picked grapefruit from the tree at the bottom of the steps leading to the bottom house. The neighbors brought food, and we never ate so much. When my mom wasn't there, we ate three meals a day, no snacks. We weren't deprived, but my grandparents didn't believe in snacks. We had big meals when Momma came, many of the foods that were delicacies that we didn't eat all the time, including curried goat, achee, and codfish. When she was there, the time passed too quickly, it was always too quick.

By the time Momma sent for us to come to America, we had been with my grandparents for nearly six years. She sent for Mark and Tommy first and finally Lance and me. What I didn't learn until after coming to America was that she had applied for visas for us all to come at the same time, but Grandma Edith started to cry, and my grandfather told my mom that it would be too hard on my grandmother if she took all of us at once. So he asked Momma to bring us to America two at a time.

When it was time to go to America, my grandfather had to take Lance and me to the embassy to get our papers. It was a rainy day, and he got dressed up in a suit and wore a big brown felt hat, which he called a fedora. Our neighbor, Mr. Lopez, who had a really cool car—it was a Jaguar but at the time I didn't know a Jaguar from anything else—drove us there. We left so early that we didn't have a moment to eat, and along the way, Grandfather had us stop at a tiny little restaurant for breakfast, where we had mackerel, broiled bananas, dumplings, and tea. It was the best breakfast I had ever tasted, even though Grandma Edith was a good cook. I was eating and humming, and thinking *hmm, hmm, hmm, this is so good,* and my grandfather looked at me and said, "Donna, why are you humming? It's that good, is it now?" It just felt so good to be out with my grandfather, who was usually a serious-minded man and always about business. When he sent any of us to the store to run errands, he would invariably tell us, "Don't tarry now, just go and come back," and we knew that meant not to stop and talk with our friends or to stay too long looking at the candy and cookies that we wanted to buy with the extra money he'd give us for going.

The day of our trip to the embassy started with a misty rain from the moment we left the house, and it rained the entire day. When we finally arrived at the embassy, we had to wait, but it was okay because my grandfather played games with Lance and me, something he never did at home. For the rest of the day, we waited inside with my grandfather. He left us with Mr. Lopez for a few minutes, and then we all left to go back home to my grandmother. I still don't know what we did there, but we had been gone for nearly the whole day. It had been an adventure for me and for Lance, being out with our grandfather.

A few months after the embassy trip, my mother sent us clothes and a letter to Grandma Edith telling her she was ready for us. Lance and I had been outside playing, and my grandfather came out and found us and told us that we were going to America to be with our mother. I was nearly twelve years old. The day had finally come; it was hard to believe after the long wait. The whole time we had been at my grandparents, my father had not come to see us. I don't know why, but I learned when I was ready to go to America that he had lost all those things he had worked for—the factory, the house—and now lived in a small room, all because of the drinking. I stopped asking about him after the first few weeks, because Grandma didn't want to talk about him, and no one else answered my questions.

The day we left for America, my grandmother was on the veranda with me. She had helped me pack my things. "You better behave yourself," she warned me, her reputation as a child-raiser now dependent on my behavior. "Don't think you are too big for me to beat your butt." I didn't know what to say. I was leaving her, and the house that I had grown to love. She was not an affectionate substitute parent, but she gave me what I most needed when I came to her—stability and a sure sense of safety and security.

Mr. Lopez came up the driveway and blew his horn, signaling to us that he was ready. When I said good-bye to my grandmother, I put my arms around her and held on to her crying; we cried together. I came as a stranger, but she raised me for those years and had become like a mother to me. Her last words were, "You know how we taught you to act. Just behave yourself and be a nice young lady."

Mr. Lopez, in his awesome car, took Granddaddy, Lance, and me to the airport in Kingston. Granddaddy sat in the airport and waited for our plane to be called. I could see in his face that he was sad, waiting to put us on a plane that would take us out of his life. I never saw him like that before. He was really emotional that day. When it was time to board the plane, he said, "All right Mas'r Lance, it's time for you guys to go now." I remember how he touched my brother's head and said, "Be good. You must come back to see me soon, and I want you to write all the time." My grandfather was not himself. Over the prior few weeks he had joked and teased us, but now he didn't waste any words. He hugged Lance and me both at the same time. It was a really quick hug because the lady was waving at us to come. As we walked away I could see that he had tears in his eyes. I turned back once more as the lady led Lance and me to the plane. I saw my grandfather in the distance. He waved at me, and then he was gone. Another father figure disappearing into my past.

At last, we were going to be with Mom. Finally I was going to be with her and live in America.

When we got to New York, it was snowing and freezing cold. I had never seen snow in my whole life. When we got off the plane our mother was waiting for us at the gate. She used to dress me in really goofy clothes and I had on these shoes that she had sent, like little spectator pumps with a little heel. My dress had pleats that brought the skirt down below my knees. The clothes were all brand-new, and I just felt so awkward dressed in this strange outfit with ribbons in my hair.

When she saw us, she ran and took us both in her arms. She kept saying over and over, "I'm so glad you're here, I'm so glad you're here." We stood like that for a while; she was smelling us and making us both laugh. Finally she said, "We were hoping you'd come for Christmas. Your presents are all stacked up in the closet. It's Christmas tonight." I was shy and excited and not sure how to act. I was finally with my mom after all the time that had come and gone. My mother had a coat for me and asked if I wanted to put it on, and I said no. When we went outside, the wind hit me; it was so cold that the chill just went right through my body and it was horrible, the most horrible cold I ever felt in my whole life. When she heard my squealing about the cold she made me put the coat on.

My new home was a house on Colony Street in a little town in Connecticut, and my mom had all her children in one place. My mother had remarried and my stepfather was named Norman, a man I had met and spent time with when he had come to visit us with my mom at Grandma Edith's during the last year of our stay there. He showed my mother love by loving us. He was there for us when I had problems in school, and I saw he really loved my mother; the stability he provided helped her to make and carry out her plans to give us a better life. When I got to America, she was ready to slam those plans into high gear. Things got really serious, but I wasn't ready for the abrupt change from the slow-paced island life I had just left. She was about school, about being serious, and about being good, about striving and excelling, about making things happen for yourself. I was about her showing that she loved me and was happy just to have me with her. It was kind of culture shock.

We spent time together, and my mother took me out to help her run errands, getting me used to the neighborhood, the shops, the way life was lived in America, and during that time I got to see in my mother some of the pride that came from Grandma Edith. That's the one thing Grandma Edith had taught me—take pride in what you do and how you live. And my mother, especially when she was with my brothers and me, looked and acted proud that she had those she loved around her. She seemed to be smiling constantly; each time she introduced us to someone, she said this is my daughter, and she pulled me close and held me to her, assuring me, and perhaps herself, that we were at last together. Laughing and happy to be together at last as a family was something she never got tired of saying.

My mother was one of those odd people who could be strong and affectionate at the same time. She didn't take crap from anybody. She worked hard to give us a good life. She started her own cleaning business, which grew rapidly and provided financially for our family but also kept her away from me. Even though I was now living with her, there were moments when old feelings from my past would creep up on me, until she reminded me that her absence meant that she was with me no less in her thoughts and her love. When I had problems adjusting to my new life because of my accent, and I cried because the kids picked on me, she would say, "Put out of your head what ignorant people say about you. You have the right to be here just like everyone else, to be wherever you want to be." It helped. But I knew that it also helped that Grandma Edith taught us to do so many things on the farm that we had never done before, which gave me the encouragement that I could learn to do anything if I worked at it. I saw my mom live this out in her life too. She had worked hard and sacrificed a lot to bring us to the States, and she had provided for us through the tough years. We all run into difficult times in our lives; it's how we deal with those times that determines our path in the end. Her responses to problems were planning and hard work, never despair. Once we came to our new country and new home, she was there, waiting, and she had carried us all the way.

I eventually overcame the difficulty of adjusting to life in America, and by drawing on the strength that Momma had given me, I went on to finish school, and then to college. I married and raised a daughter that I am proud of as well. It wasn't until I had my daughter that I understood what my mother felt when she had me. I understood once I became a mother that a full range of choices is not what you always have to pick from, and, as a result, you must do the best with what you have.

Along the way I encountered my own hard times, and my mother was there to encourage me and to help me pick up the pieces. She constantly pushed me to go on and to believe in myself. Through those tough years in Jamaica, after my parents split up and Momma had moved to the States, she sent letters and books and other things that we needed, and she came to visit as often as she could. She was a big letter writer and sent pictures of herself living in America. Everything she did made me feel close to her, involved in her life even though we were physically so far apart. I learned discipline from her. Not the discipline imposed on you by others, but the kind you impose on yourself, from within.

♥ *Donna Hunt is the director of client services for a medical education and communications company. She and her mother remain best friends.*